[redacted]

CD-ROM II
BACK
POCKET

P9-BZT-865

CREATING
WE

DATE DUE

FEB 8

WITH ADOBE PREMIERE

THOMAS LUEHRSEN

PEACHPIT PRESS

NOV 2 7 2002
777
LUE

Creating Web Video with Adobe Premiere

Thomas Luehrsen

PEACHPIT PRESS
1249 Eighth Street ◦ Berkeley, CA 94710
510/524-2178 ◦ 510/524-2221 (fax)

FIND US ON THE WORLD WIDE WEB AT: www.peachpit.com
To report errors, please send a note to errata@peachpit.com

Peachpit Press is a division of Pearson Education
Copyright © 2003 by Thomas Luehrsen

EDITORS ◦ Liza Weiman Hanks, Karen Reichstein
PRODUCTION COORDINATOR ◦ David Van Ness
COPYEDITOR ◦ Sally Zahner
TECHNICAL EDITOR ◦ Charles Wiltgen
COMPOSITORS ◦ Rick Gordon, Emerald Valley Graphics; Deborah Roberti, Espresso Graphics
INDEXER ◦ Emily Glossbrenner
COVER DESIGN ◦ Gee + Chung Design
COVER PRODUCTION ◦ George Mattingly Design
INTERIOR DESIGN ◦ Mimi Heft, with Maureen Forys, Happenstance Type-O-Rama
SAMPLE VIDEO FRAMES AND FOOTAGE courtesy of Cinenet (Cinema Network, Inc.)

NOTICE OF RIGHTS
All rights reserved. No part of this book may be reproduced or transmitted in any form by any means, electronic, mechanical, photocopying, recording, or otherwise, without the prior written permission of the publisher. For information on getting permission for reprints and excerpts, contact permissions@peachpit.com.

NOTICE OF LIABILITY
The information in this book is distributed on an "As Is" basis, without warranty. While every precaution has been taken in the preparation of the book, neither the author nor Peachpit Press, shall have any liability to any person or entity with respect to any loss or damage caused or alleged to be caused directly or indirectly by the instructions contained in this book or by the computer software and hardware products described in it.

TRADEMARKS
Adobe, Adobe Premiere, and Adobe GoLive are either registered trademarks or trademarks of Adobe Systems, Inc. in the United States or other countries. All other trademarks are the property of their respective owners.

Throughout this book, trademarks are used. Rather than put a trademark symbol in every occurrence of a trademarked name, we state that we are using the names in an editorial fashion only and to the benefit of the trademark owner with no intention of infringement of the trademark.

ISBN 0-201-77184-5

9 8 7 6 5 4 3 2 1

Printed and bound in the United States of America

Dedication

To Linda, Olivia, and Kate,
who provide all the inspiration and the spunk

Acknowledgments

It is truly an honor to have worked with the Peachpit Press team. Special thanks and gratitude go out everyone there, including:

Marjorie Baer, for her wisdom, diplomacy, and general good humor.

Liza Weiman Hanks, my very talented editor, for being tough, funny, and not so compromising when it comes to making chapters palatable for a general audience.

Karen Reichstein, for being the ultimate publishing professional.

Sally Zahner, for her meticulousness, and for all the pick-ups and drop-offs.

David Van Ness, for managing the production.

Victor Gavenda, for his advice and for counting megabytes accurately.

Charles Wiltgen, for his tech edits.

My sincere thanks go out to all of the following people who have made this book possible:

The intrepid students, faculty, and staff of San Francisco State University Multimedia Studies Program & San Francisco State University Cinema Department, for their support and some "beta testing" of the manuscript.

Bruce Bowman, Adobe Premiere Product Manager, and the Adobe GoLive team, including Eve Kosol.

Gina Gustafson, Keela Robison, and Greg Robbins at RealNetworks.

Amir Majidimehr, Gail McClellan, and Mark Galioto at Microsoft.

Ben Waggoner, for his energetic, ubiquitous, and free advice and support in numerous online venues.

Jesse Cortez, for taking photos.

Bill Huggins, for countless expeditions into the Windows operating system.

Christopher Lloyd, for the use of his digital still camera.

Jim Jarrard of Cinenet, T.J. Knowles of Like Dat Music, Bob Bailey of A1 Free Sound Effects, and Tom Gilleland of Beachware.

Richard Johnson at the Australian Broadcasting Corporation, Rob Tripp at iSeemedia, Stéphane Kurylak at StreamingBox.com, Christopher Neher at WRGB.com, and Brian Satchfield at Raymond James Financial.

All the gracious interviewees for the Web Video Spotlights (in order of appearance):

Daniel Robin
Lev Yilmaz
Amy Talkington
Patrick J. Kriwanek
Susie Wise & Stuart Rickey
Bob George
Logan Kelsey
Bruce Brannon & Jennifer Mapes (who helped me write Bruce's Spotlight)

Thanks also to Jeff Schader at The Skins Factory, Brian Ghidinelli at VFIVE.com, Tom Grueskin at Sputnik7.com, Brad Simon at atomfilms.shockwave.com, and Ed Swicegood and Art Lovestedt at Playstream.com.

Table of Contents

Introduction

Before the Internet existed, you had three ways to reach an audience with your video: on television, on a theater screen, or by videocassette. But it wasn't easy or inexpensive to do it, no matter which method you chose. Now, happily, you don't need deep pockets to reach a potential audience of millions worldwide. All you need is a connection to the World Wide Web, a way to digitize your video footage, and the tools and know-how to make your movies shine on the small (very small) screen. The good news: That's what this book is for.

The bad news: At this point, you'll be a pioneer, bravely creating movies that will most likely be presented over woefully inadequate network pipelines, and viewed in windows smaller than a playing card. It isn't easy to make video look good when it has to be compressed enough to get to your audience's desktop. The only way to make Web movies play smoothly right now is to make small movies. And the only way to make small movies is to eliminate as much extraneous information as possible. Compression software is smart (and the programmers who write it are even smarter), but it can't create miracles. Unless you're thinking ahead every step of the way, your movies won't look good on the Web. The choices you make in writing, shooting, lighting, recording, editing, and compressing your movie—and then integrating it into a Web site—all critically affect the final product. Think of Web video as haiku—elegant, focused, disciplined, and condensed. Think of this book as your guide to getting the most out of every element you've got to work with when every bit counts.

I know the challenges and rewards of making video for the Web. I've been working with digital desktop video since 1991 as a senior producer of CD-ROMs, videodiscs, and other video projects. In recent years, I have produced, edited, and compressed hundreds of digital video pieces for Web sites and multimedia projects. *Creating Web Video with Adobe Premiere* is an outgrowth both of classes I teach at San Francisco State University and of my fascination with new media in general.

What You'll Learn About Web Video

In this book, you'll learn the nuts and bolts of creating and publishing your own Web movies using Adobe Premiere video editing software. You'll also learn about the state of the art of Web video through profiles of leading producers in the field and close-up looks at current Web video work. And by the time you've finished this book, you'll know the basic technical and aesthetic steps of creating effective video presentations specifically for the Web, from original concept to Web-ready video clip.

Along the way, one dominant theme will recur: As a video producer your greatest constraint is the Internet's *bandwidth*—in other words, the physical capacity of the Internet to transmit your video files. No matter how good your video, if you can't send it over the Web efficiently, it won't look good to—and might not even be viewable by—anyone else. Throughout this book, you'll learn essential tips and techniques to work around this constraint.

You'll notice a minor theme as well: It's worth taking a moment to stand in your audience's shoes before you even pick up your camera. Web video offers such a different viewing experience than traditional film and television that without some thoughtful consideration of what your audience will see and how they'll see it, you're likely to end up with a good movie that's unsuitable for presentation on the Web, even if it's technically possible to present it that way.

Think about it. Your typical viewer is hunched over a computer screen about two to three feet in front of their nose. They're waiting for a few seconds while the movie downloads to their computer or streams over the Web. Most likely, they're viewing your video by themselves, rather than sharing the experience, as they would if they were watching a movie in a theater or television with friends. Whatever Web video is (and as a pioneer you'll play a part in determining what it becomes), it's different than traditional video.

Obviously, I wouldn't have written this book if there weren't more to Web video than its limitations. Web video also offers great advantages. Because it plays over the Web, your video is immediately available to millions of people all over the world—at least in theory. Because Web video is such an intimate, individual experience, your viewers are more likely to pay close attention to it than they might the typical television show. Because the Web is an interactive medium, you can get immediate and personalized feedback from your audience. Because it's playing on a computer monitor rather than a television monitor, you have far more colors to play with. And finally, most computers now have the same digital audio playback quality as audio compact discs (CDs), which is far superior to the audio available on most televisions.

Who Should Read This Book?

Students who take my Web video class come for a variety of reasons, and with differing skills and experiences. Some are just exploring new territory, others have already carved out video careers and need to immerse themselves in the digital realm, and still others are Web mavens who need to learn the basics of video production and editing. I imagine that readers of this book will come with different talents, experiences, and questions as well. *Creating Web Video with Adobe Premiere* caters to anyone interested in making movies for the Web, regardless of previous experience in either realm. It is designed so you can find out what you need to know quickly, without having to wade through topics you're already familiar with. This book is for you if you fall into any of the following three groups:

Web Developers Who Want to Get into Video

If you're in this category, you know something about how to put a Web site together (meaning you know your way around hard drives, graphics file formats, pixels, and HTML), but you may not know anything about digital video or how to produce it for the Web. Whether you're a Webmaster for a company who wants to learn how to add video clips to your site, or a Web developer driven by the pure love of motion pictures, this book will get you up to speed before you can say "MiniDV cam."

Video Producers Who Want to Get on the Web

If you're in this category, you know something about creating a video (cameras, lights, screenplays, key grips), but you may not know anything about the Web or how to produce a Web site. Whether you're an independent filmmaker just back from the Sundance Film Festival or a producer in a corporate communications department dreaming of becoming the next Fellini, this book will tell you what you need to know to get your movies on the Web.

And Everybody Else

If you're in this category, you have a personal computer, a connection to the Internet, a copy of Adobe Premiere, and an idea for a movie that you want to show on the Web. You might not know anything about how video works or very much about the Web. You might not have a camera or know a microphone cable from a telegram. Don't worry. This book will show you what you need to know, using how-to examples designed to walk you through the process step by step.

Some of the Web-specific chapters will be common knowledge for experienced Web aficionados, and some of the video topics will be old news for video producers. I've tried to make it clear at the beginning of each section which topics are covered, so that you can find just what you're looking for. After all, the Web's not the only thing out there that's bandwidth-constrained, is it?

How to Use This Book

You can use this book as a how-to guide, and go through the process of creating Web video from beginning to end. Or, if you're already familiar with certain steps in the process, such as shooting video for the Web, but want to learn more about others, say editing with Adobe Premiere, you can use this book as a reference guide and skip to the specific chapters that interest you. Along the way, the Web Video Spotlights are there to engage and inspire you with inside stories from masters of the form. If they make you put the book down to go up on the Web to watch, even better.

- **Windows Only/Macintosh Only:** The main tools that I discuss in this book, Adobe Premiere and its accompanying plug-in software, are *cross-platform*; that is, they work with both Windows and Macintosh operating systems. Similarly, this book attempts to be *platform agnostic*. In any given task, things should usually work the same way on both the Mac and Windows operating systems; but from time to time they don't. In those cases, I make sure to point out the differences.

The first three chapters in this book tell you everything you'll need to know both to watch Web video and to produce the raw footage you'll need to make your own. In Chapter 1, "Watching Web Video," you'll learn about the basic hardware and software necessary to watch Web movies, and I'll walk you through the installation of all three of the major media players, so that you'll be able to watch virtually any movie playing on the Web today. In Chapter 2, "Shooting Smart," you'll get the insider's guide to buying a video camera and learn my favorite shooting techniques so you can use your camera to produce the best possible footage from the get-go. Chapter 3, "Sounding Good," covers all the audio essentials to ensure that you record what you want, the way you want it. You'll learn why good audio is even more important, sometimes, than good video—and an essential part of any Web videographer's bag of tricks.

The next three chapters walk you through the process of capturing, editing, and compressing your Web movie. Chapter 4, "Capturing Capably," shows you how to do the essential first step in digital moviemaking—getting raw footage from your camera onto your hard disk. In Chapter 5, "Editing Effectively," you'll learn how to create and edit a movie from beginning to end using Premiere. You'll also get the insider's tour of Premiere's best editing features for Web moviemakers—and warnings about which features to avoid. In Chapter 6, "The Big Squeeze," you take your Premiere movie and compress it to a shadow of its former self.

Of course, once you've made and compressed your Web movie, you'll want to publish it and get it out to the millions worldwide (or at least to your family). Chapter 7, "Hard Disk Delivery" tells you everything you need to know to publish your movie as a high-quality progressive downloading file. Chapter 8, "Streaming Your Way," describes how to publish your movie for delivery from a true streaming server. Don't worry if this sounds somewhat geekish right now; by the time you've worked your way through the first six chapters, you'll know exactly what I'm talking about—and you'll even be able to bandy around terms like *codec* and *RTSP* at dinner parties.

What's on the CD

The instructional files provided with this book are designed to give you all you need to edit, compress, and upload digital movies and integrate them into Web sites. The CD provides video and audio clips for you to use with the projects in this book, as well as sample audio files, music clips, sound effects, HTML files, Adobe Premiere and Adobe GoLive project files, and tryout versions of Adobe Premiere 6.0 and GoLive 6.0.

While this book is written primarily for Premiere 6.5 users, at the time of this writing, there is no tryout version of Adobe Premiere 6.5 available. While the majority of the projects in this book are appropriate for *both* versions of Premiere, the Titles section in Chapter 5 describes many features specific to Premiere 6.5. If you're using the tryout version of Premiere 6.0 provided on this book's CD, this book gives you alternate suggestions where appropriate.

A Guide to Those Icons

Keep an eye out for the following visual cues to help you along as you read:

TIP ▸ *These shortcuts and other bits of information will help you make better video. And some are just fun facts.*

This symbol appears wherever there's a reference to example files, video clips, or software included on the CD-ROM that accompanies this book. Remember to copy the corresponding files to your hard disk and then *eject* the CD-ROM, particularly for the chapters that focus on Adobe Premiere. If you don't, Premiere may attempt to play back, or link to, the files on the CD-ROM, which will slow down your system. If you don't have room on your hard drive to copy the whole CD-ROM, you can use the folders one at a time. Then, when you finish that section of the book, you can delete those folders to make room for more.

WARNING ▸ This symbol means Important! I use it to get you to pay attention to one of my cardinal rules and/or to keep you from doing something really stupid.

Web Video Spotlights are profiles of, and interviews with, Web video pioneers.

And now, without further ado, let's get on with the fun stuff. In this next chapter, you'll learn everything you need to know to start *watching* Web video. After all, if you want to start building your own project, you must first learn how to use the tools of the trade.

CHAPTER ONE

Watching Web Video

You're ready: Camera in hand, ideas galore, actors in the wings. The Web's waiting and you're off to shoot. But wait. Don't do it. Hang on, kick back, and survey the territory first. Watch some Web video before you make it. You'll shoot, write, and edit smarter if you're thoroughly immersed in what's out there right now. You might even enjoy yourself. And you'll discover something that's truly motivating: Movies that have been produced specifically for the Web *always* look better than movies that have been recycled from other sources.

Getting Ready to Watch

You'll need more than popcorn for your Web watching adventure, of course. Since you're reading this book to learn how to produce Web video, chances are you already have a computer, a connection to the Internet, and a Web browser. But although that basic system might be fine for reading and writing email, your video-viewing experience will be much better (and by that I mean the movies will play more quickly and more smoothly) if your computer is powered by at least a Pentium or PowerPC microprocessor, and your connection to the Internet is the fastest one that you can afford.

Making the Connections

These days you have three choices for video-ready Web connections. You can dial-in to the Web using a 56Kbps modem (slower modems just weren't built with movies in mind); you can get a broadband connection by subscribing to a Digital Subscriber Line (DSL) service or a cable-modem service; or you can install a dedicated line just for transmitting computer data.

Your modem works by turning digital signals (ones and zeros) into analog signals (8,000 tones per second), and vice versa. That's what makes it possible for your digital computer and your analog telephone to work together. A 56Kbps modem theoretically transmits data at 56 kilobits (or 56,000 bits) per second. (Due to a side effect of FCC regulation, it's actually 53 Kbps in the U.S. and 56 Kbps everywhere else.) With a 56Kbps modem you can expect to wait while movies download to your computer, and at typical modem data rates, creating Web video that doesn't appear jerky, jumpy, and pixelated is challenging, to say the least.

If you're serious about watching Web video, don't bother with a dial-up connection. Get a broadband connection, which uses existing telephone lines (in the case of DSL) or television cables (for cable modems) to send and receive data many times faster than any dial-up connection can. Call me a Web snob, but I can't imagine life without broadband even for simple Web browsing and email. Once you've tried it, you won't go back, no matter what the price. A complicated Web page that takes minutes to download over a dial-up connection will download in seconds over a broadband connection, and movies that pause and jerk will play smoothly and download quickly. The majority of viewers watching from home will have dial-up connections, so you'll want to be sure to test your movie on a dial-up connection.

Cable modems work differently than the analog modem in your computer. They're boxes that send and receive data by using the lines that bring cable TV into your home. You pay for the service with a flat-rate monthly fee, no matter how much you use it. It's a lot faster than a dial-up connection, but it's not available everywhere. You have to check with your local cable provider to see if cable modem service is an option. And even if you can get one, you have to share that television cable with all the folks in your neighborhood, so if lots of them are using cable modems too, things can bog down.

Your other option for a home-based broadband connection is a DSL connection. These lines use existing phone lines to send and receive digital data. Because the computer data is sent over different frequencies on the line, you can still make voice calls simultaneously. Some DSL services allow you to use DSL over a single phone line; other services require you to install a separate line. As with cable modem service, you pay a monthly fee no matter how much you use the system. DSL services are offered by local phone companies, and also by Internet Service Providers (ISPs, like Earthlink or Verio) who procure the lines from the phone companies and then offer services to residential customers.

DSL connections are less susceptible to bandwidth hogs than cable networks, but the speed of your digital connection depends on how close your home or office is to your phone company's central office. If you go to `www.dslreports.com` and enter your zip code, you can find out how close you are to the nearest DSL central office and whether there are DSL services available in your area. If you're too far away, either you won't be able get the service at all or you'll have to wait for the phone company in your area to install new phone lines or convert some of the circuitry in your connection to their lines. This can take anywhere from a few days to a few months. If it turns out that DSL service isn't available to you yet, that's the price you pay for being on the cutting edge—a sizeable percentage of the households in America can't get DSL service.

Along with your service, you'll need to get a DSL modem (usually available from your DSL provider) and its accompanying software. If you're a Mac user, make sure to double check that the DSL modem and software are Mac-compatible before you sign up.

Another, pricier option for connecting to the Internet is a T1 or T3 line. These dedicated lines offer speeds several times faster than DSL lines or cable modems. However, these lines cost hundreds or even thousands of dollars per month—which is why they're used primarily by businesses.

Firewalls

They sound like something a contractor would be worrying about, but firewalls exist in the digital world, too. A firewall is software or hardware (or a combination of both) that sits between your computer and the rest of the universe. You can configure it to let in only the data that you want in and to keep hackers out so that they don't wreak havoc. Firewalls unfortunately can also prevent you from watching Web video—not because movies are inherently harmful but because of the way some video is transmitted over the Web. It comes to you over ports—which you can think of as Internet "channels"—that are different from the most common ports used to receive Web pages, send and receive e-mail, and so on.

Firewalls are common in the corporate world. Now, they're becoming increasingly common at home as well, due to the growth of broadband connections, which are always on and therefore present a virtual open door to intruders.

If you've tried to watch video on your computer, and seen only an empty movie window with nothing playing, chances are the movie hit a firewall. If you're at work, you can try to convince your company network administrator to reconfigure the firewall (since, of course, those videos you want to watch are work-related!). But otherwise, you're out of luck. If you're at home, on the other hand, you can simply disconnect your firewall (temporarily).

Beefing Up Your Browser

Your browser, of course, is the software you use to access the Web, and you're most likely using either Netscape Navigator or Microsoft's Internet Explorer. (I won't hazard a guess as to how many of you are using one or the other, that's for the courts.) Way back in the 1990s, browsers changed the world of the Internet from a text-based place populated mostly by pencil-pushing nerds to the World Wide Web that we know and love. Browsers do one main thing: They find and display Web pages that are composed of HTML code and their associated graphics and text files. To play sound, animation, and movies, your browser needs a brain transplant. You've got to get it a *media player*, which is software that works with your browser to play and display video and audio files.

Updating Your Browser

You can get the most current version of your browser at:

- Netscape (`http://home.netscape.com/download`)
- Internet Explorer (`http://www.microsoft.com/windows/ie/default.htm`)

If you're using a DSL or cable modem service, the browser installation software is customized to work with the specialized hardware those services require. If you're using either kind of service, check with your ISP for the correct version of the browser software and check regularly for updates.

Media players have three parts: Software that enables your computer's operating system to support the format, a browser plug-in that uses this new OS software to support the format in your Web browser, and a standalone player application for any playback outside of your browser.

Right now, RealNetworks, Apple Computer, and Microsoft are each trying to make their media player software the standard format for watching video and listening to audio on the Web (and on any future derivations of the Web, such as interactive TV). What each company would like to do is to control the future standard for all consumer digital video, the way VHS is now the standard for consumer analog video playback (although DVD is certainly in the process of de-throning it).

If you've got a relatively current computer, it probably has QuickTime (if you're using a Mac) or Windows Media Player (if you're using a PC) already installed as part of your system software. But since no one has won the standards battle yet, you'll have to install all three to be able to watch any movie on the Web. And as a Web producer, you'll need all three to test your movies thoroughly so that your viewers will be able to watch them no matter which media player they're using.

Even though you need all three to be Web video-ready, they're not exactly alike. Each has its advantages. In my opinion, and that of many other Web video professionals, QuickTime offers the best cross-platform video delivery and makes it easiest to publish your movies on Web sites. RealNetworks' RealOne Player offers the best in streaming technology, and is the most robust player, in my experience. (Streaming video allows movies to play on your computer without having to be downloaded to your hard drive first.) Microsoft's Windows Media Player isn't my favorite—historically, it has been quite buggy on the Macintosh for one thing—but you can't ignore it: It's installed on more computers than either QuickTime or RealOne Player.

TIP ▸ *Your computer's Web video playback performance will vary depending on the version of your operating system, the type of media player software you're running, the type (and version) of your Web browser, and the way that all of these programs work in combination. You'll have to experiment to see what combination works best for you.*

Installing the Media Players

Here's how to install each of the media players you'll need to watch the latest and greatest Web movies. Even if you already have one or two of them, make sure that you have the most current version of all three before you proceed, because media players change constantly to keep up with new developments in compression and Web video delivery.

Installing QuickTime

Apple Computer's QuickTime is important for several reasons: Since 1991 it has been the most viable and robust *authoring* (creation) technology for video on personal computers, as well as an excellent media *player* technology. For these reasons, many of the sample clips in the exercises on the CD-ROM are in QuickTime format (**Figure 1.1**).

FIGURE 1.1
The QuickTime icon.

While QuickTime comes preinstalled on all Macs, both PC and Macintosh users can also download QuickTime from the site below. You can also upgrade to QuickTime Pro and get updates at this site.

1. Go to `www.apple.com/quicktime/download`.

2. Fill in the online registration form, choose your operating system, and click Download QuickTime. A small installer file will download to your computer.

3. Click the Open button or double-click the downloaded file to start the actual installation process.

TIP ▸ *The QuickTime download may take up to an hour on slower connections!*

4. When the QuickTime software has finished installing, restart your computer. You should now be able to play QuickTime movies, both online and offline.

5. Test the QuickTime Player by playing one of the movies at **`www.apple.com/quicktime/qtv`** or elsewhere on the Apple site (**Figure 1.2**).

6. Each time the QuickTime Player starts up, you will be asked if you want to upgrade to QuickTime Pro. If you say yes, you will be connected to the Apple Web site, where you can buy a copy for $29.99 and download it. (Or you can call Apple and buy it over the phone.) If you don't want to bother with QuickTime Pro right now, just click the Later button. Unfortunately, you'll keep getting the upgrade query.

FIGURE 1.2
A movie playing in the QuickTime Player window.

Cinenet

TIP ▸ *If QuickTime doesn't seem to be working, check with the QuickTime help site at* **`www.info.apple.com/usen/quicktime`**.

Installing RealOne Player

RealNetworks pioneered Web streaming technology in the mid-1990s and claims that it offers the most popular video player software on the Web today. It certainly offers the best streaming technology, though QuickTime and Windows Media Player are working hard to offer their own alternatives to it. Its free player is called RealOne Player if you're using it in Windows and Mac OS X (**Figure 1.3**), and is called RealPlayer if you're using it in Mac OS 9. To install it:

Figure 1.3
The RealOne Player icon as it appears in Mac OS X (left) and in Windows (right).

1. Go to `www.real.com/`.

2. If you're using Windows, look for the link to the free RealOne Player. It's a text link, about halfway down the page, that reads: "Free RealOne Player." Clicking that link takes you to a Web page advertising the deluxe $19.99 version, known as RealOne Player Plus. Ignore that for now. Click the link for the free version on the right; it reads: "Download the Free RealOne Player Only."

3. In Mac OS X, you should see a pop-up window advertising RealOne Player for OS X. In Mac OS 9, look for the tiny text link called "RealPlayer 8 Basic." Click the appropriate link to download the player.

4. Fill out the form to register as a member (it's free). A series of prompts will step you through the rest of the download process.

5. When you've finished downloading, an Install Wizard will step you through the installation process. Proceed through the setup screens as prompted.

6. Once you have the player installed, test it by playing one of the movies or channels at `www.real.com` (**Figure 1.4**).

TIP ▸ *The RealOne Player installer (both Windows and Mac) has two extras that readers can pay for: 1) a one-time fee of $19.95 for a souped up version of the player; and 2) $9.95 for exclusive RealOne Player content.*

FIGURE 1.4
The RealOne Player playing on a Mac (left) and on a PC (right).

TIP ▸ *If the RealOne Player doesn't seem to be working, check with the RealOne Player help site at* `http://service.real.com/rpoptions.html`.

Installing Microsoft Windows Media Player

If you're running a recent version of Windows, you have Windows Media Player installed as part of the operating system (**Figure 1.5**). If you're not, or you're using a Macintosh, you can download and install it:

FIGURE 1.5
The Windows Media Player icon.

1. Go to: `www.microsoft.com/windows/windowsmedia/en/download/default.asp`.
2. Choose which version of the player you want to download and click Download Now.
3. Run the installer file. The installation process is largely automatic.
4. Once installation is complete, test your Windows Media Player by playing one of the movies or channels at `http://windowsmedia.com/mg/home.asp` (**Figure 1.6**).

FIGURE 1.6
The Windows Media Player in action.

TIP ▸ *If Windows Media Player doesn't seem to be working, check with the Windows Media support site at* `www.microsoft.com/windows/windowsmedia/support.asp`.

Movies are available for playback with all three media players on the companion CD-ROM.

Paying More for Deluxe Versions of the Media Players

Although the basic media player software is free, when you run RealOne Player or QuickTime, you're confronted with the issue of whether to spend more for deluxe versions of the software.

In the case of RealOne Player, you are invited to buy the Real Player Plus (RealOne Player Plus for Windows) with offers of better video and audio quality and advanced picture and audio controls for $19.95, a one-time charge. If there is specific content that you are willing to pay for, then paying more for the RealOne Player might be worth it, but to my eyes the video quality is the same as it is with the free version. And for $9.95 per month, the RealOne SuperPass is a "premiere network of the Web's best programming" that includes exclusive online content such as CNN, the NBA and Major League Baseball.

QuickTime is free. However, Apple will try to sell you a $29.99 application called QuickTime Pro every time you start up QuickTime. This is basically the media player software with additional features. QuickTime Pro is a very handy tool when you are creating Web video. You don't have to buy it now—you can always upgrade later. While the Pro version won't improve playback performance, it does offer an extensive toolset for editing and authoring video files. Apple also offers QuickTime 6 users the ability to play back MPEG-2 content via the QuickTime 6 MPEG-2 Playback Component add-on for $19.99. See Peachpit's Visual QuickStart Guide *QuickTime 6 for Macintosh and Windows* for more details about QuickTime Pro.

Movie Controllers

Even though all three media players do essentially the same thing, they all have different looking movie control buttons. Here's a map to the territory:

Figure 1.7
The three media players display their control buttons somewhat differently, but all do the same thing.

QuickTime Player

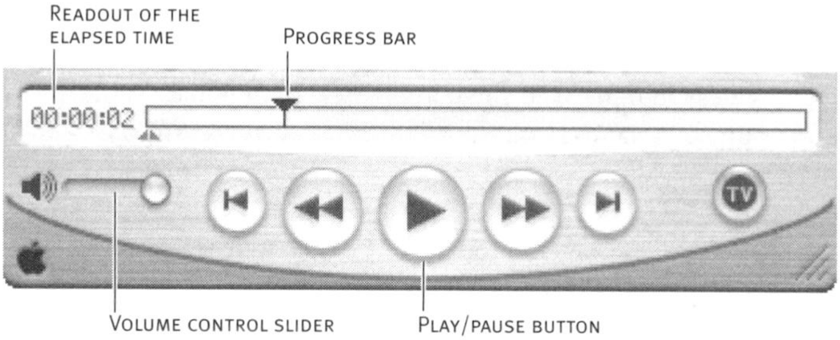

RealPlayer (Mac OS 9)

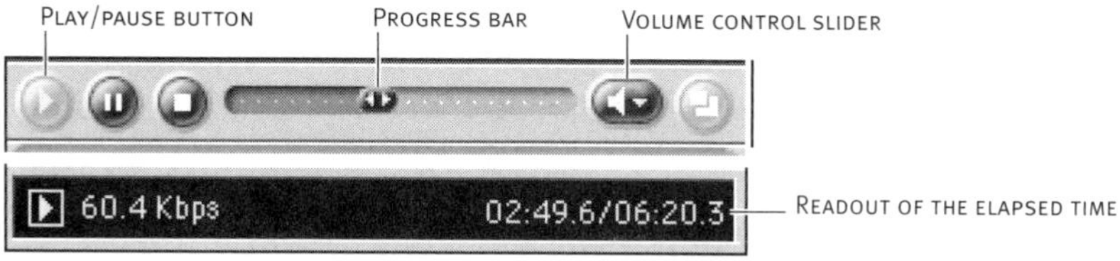

RealOne Player

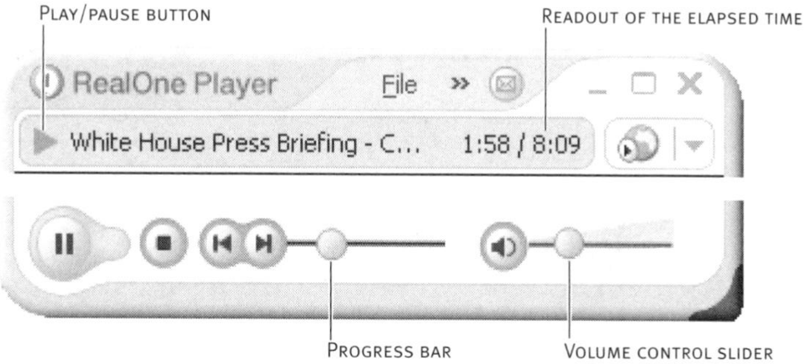

Windows Media Player

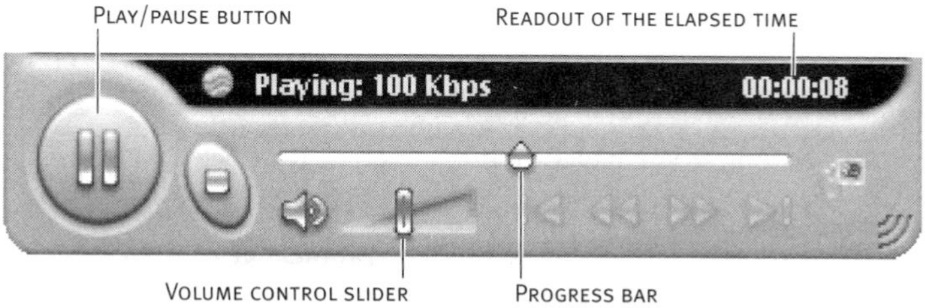

Special Delivery

You're almost there. You have a fast connection to the Internet, you've got all three media players installed, the popcorn's ready, and the phone's off the hook. Just one more thing—take a moment and learn a bit about *how* the movies you're about to watch are coming to your desktop. When you're watching Web video, it doesn't really matter how it gets to you, as long as it plays once it gets there. But when you're making Web video it's critical to understand the delivery system, because different delivery routes require you to make different choices when you're compressing and publishing your final editions.

Delivery method is a topic we'll return to in more detail later in this book. But here's the big picture: Web video comes to you via an *on-demand* system or via a live *Webcast*. On-demand video is the Internet equivalent of going to a video store to rent a movie. You simply navigate your browser to a Web site and click to watch the movie whenever you feel like it. Live Web video, in contrast, is just like live television; you navigate your browser to a Web site and click to tune in to the program as it is happening. **Figure 1.8** shows a kind of family tree of Web video.

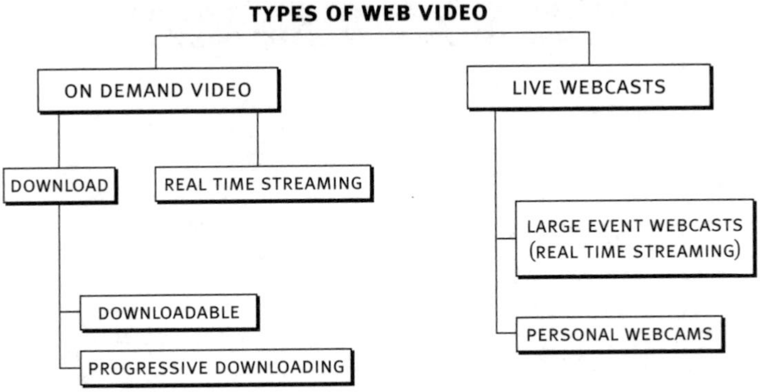

Figure 1.8
Web video comes to your desktop in several different ways and each one requires you to make different choices when you're shooting and editing your movie.

For all but the few Web video producers who work for professional live broadcasting companies, the most important branch in the tree is the one on the left: where on-demand video forks into *downloading* and *streaming* offshoots. Think of each branch as related but different—like taking a bath versus taking a shower. Downloading is like taking a bath: You open the tap and wait for the water to "download" into the tub. When you turn off the tap, the water remains in the tub. You can use the water as long as you like until it is "deleted" from the tub. Downloaded movies are copied to your hard disk. Downloadable files are stored on a regular Web server, along with HTML files and associated graphics files. Of course, while the tub is filling up, you're stuck impatiently waiting, wrapped up in your towel. Well, the software wizards have solved that one—now downloading movies can use *progressive downloading technology*: part of the movie is downloading to your hard disk while another part is playing on your desktop, so you don't have to wait so long to start watching.

A streaming file is like a shower: You turn it on, and after it warms up a little bit, you're ready to go. When you turn the water off, that's the end of the experience. Streaming movies do not involve the hard disk in your computer. Streaming movies play live over the Web: They are delivered from a special server (called a streaming server) directly to your computer screen as you watch it, that's why its called *real-time* streaming.

So which one should you use for your movie? It depends on how long your movie is going to be, and who the audience is. But here are some guidelines: Real-time streaming is best for video programs that are over five minutes long; progressive downloading works better for short videos that need to be of extremely high quality. Real-time streaming is more complicated to set up and requires special streaming server software or the purchase of streaming media services from your Web hosting service; progressive downloading requires only that you embed your movie into an HTML page and publish that page to your site. Depending on the Internet traffic at the moment you view a streaming video, there will be fluctuations in the video and audio quality as you watch; when you watch a progressive downloading movie, the movie will always play back in the same way, though users of slow modems will have to wait longer to watch the movie because it will take longer for the movie to download to their computers. If you want to do live Webcasting, real-time streaming video is your only option. And if you want to create a pay-per-view system or make sure that your communications are secure, you also want to use the real-time streaming video method, since progressive downloading movies create a movie file on your hard drive that can be repeatedly watched offline and passed on to others.

Live Webcasting, the other branch of the family tree, uses real-time streaming video. *Webcasting* means any live camera connected to the Web. (I would include in that definition a nearly live connection, as in "within a minute or so.") Large-event Webcasts are usually expensive undertakings that involve a significant investment in personnel and equipment. Small-event Webcasts (really small ones) like broadcasts of the inside of your hamster's cage, your house, or your kid's classroom can be accomplished with inexpensive Web cams that automatically take pictures then upload them to a Web site. But neither version of live Webcasting requires the kind of production, editing, compression, and publishing that I'm focusing on here. That's a whole other book.

World Wide Video

Finally! Class is over! Now go out and watch. Here are some examples of Web video in each of the Web video family tree categories and some film festival sites, just for fun. Check them out and see for yourself what's out there.

Where to Watch

ON-DEMAND WEB VIDEO

Streaming Video: MSNBC.com

`www.msnbc.com`

MSBNC.com includes free clips from a variety of recent stories on the NBC television network. (Click on "TV News.") MSBNC also has live Webcasts (such as breaking news and live and taped NASA activities). For live coverage, go to `http://www.msnbc.com/m/lv`.

PROGRESSIVE DOWNLOADING VIDEO

Movie Trailers at apple.com

`www.apple.com/trailers/`

For my money, apple.com consistently has the best-looking Web video, period. Most are in the form of progressive downloading movie trailers and offer a choice of high-, medium-, or low-resolution clips; choose one appropriate for your connection speed and computer.

LIVE WEB VIDEO

Webcasts: Live Television News from Around the World

`http://broadcast-live.com`

This site is a very extensive collection of live (and some on-demand) television and radio broadcasts from around the world, organized by language, country of origin, and subject.

Just for Fun

These sites are all film festival/entertainment sites. They generally share some combination of the following features:

Channels—The movies on these sites are typically sorted into various channels according to their content. Categories from the various sites include: Action, Animation, Arts, Celebrity, Comedy, Documentary, Drama, Erotica, Extreme, Gay & Lesbian, Music, Sci Fi, Thriller, Travel, and World.

Submissions—In early days of Web video (1999), sites like these would accept almost any video you sent them. Nowadays, they are more choosy. They have programming committees that pre-screen your movie. If they like what they see, they'll show it (and compress it) for free. In some cases, you can pay a fee (e.g. $100 per year) to show your movie on the site anyway.

Viewer Reviews—In most cases, viewers get a chance to rate the movies and add their reviews and opinions on the page where the movie is displayed. This often results in lively discussions and debates.

AtomShockwave

`http://atomfilms.shockwave.com/af/home/`

More than a million visitors check out this site each month. It was founded in late 1998, which makes it the oldest site in this category. Atom has traditionally signed exclusive distribution deals with the filmmakers, so you generally won't see these movies on other sites. (The deals also often include other markets, such as TV and other non-theatrical venues.) The sister site, Shockwave.com, (`http://www.shockwave.com/sw/home/`) features vector-based Flash animations—not the subject of this book, but a lot of fun to watch.

IFILM.com

`http://www.ifilm.com/`

IFILM bills itself as an "online film portal with over 80,000 films." Its content tends to include a lot of showbiz information and is often oriented toward motion picture industry professionals.

ReelMind.com

`http://www.ReelMind.com/`

ReelMind is a free self-promotion site. It allows you to post your films, animation and text from your own personal page. (You're allowed up to a maximum of 35 minutes of film, animation and/or music.)

continued ›

Just for Fun > *continued*

The New Venue

`http://www.newvenue.com/lobby/index.html`

The New Venue is a small but potent showcase of short films that usually includes a interview with the filmmaker.

Hypnotic

`http://www.Nibblebox.com/index.asp`

Hypnotic works a lot like Atom Films: distribution deals are signed for the Web and other markets. This site is allied with Universal Picture movie studio, so it often includes larger, more commercial movie productions.

WEB VIDEO SPOTLIGHT

Neighborhood films.com

Neighborhoodfilms.com is a documentary film project that grew out of Daniel Robin's series "The Valet Chronicles," about a particular street corner in the San Francisco neighborhood of North Beach. He uses the Web to tell stories that give viewers an intimate look at the neighborhood where he worked as a parking valet, and the people who live there. Recently, he began accepting submissions of documentary work from other neighborhoods around the world, as well. You'll find the site at `www.neighborhoodfilms.com` (**Figure 1.9**). You'll need either a DSL or cable modem connection to see what's there.

The idea behind the site is to show life in a neighborhood as it happens. Daniel doesn't write and direct from a script—he just uses his camera to capture the rhythms and personalities he sees. Then he reviews what he's got and finds the beginnings of the story he wants to tell. After that, he goes back to the neighborhood and starts looking for pieces that will embellish the story he's already gotten on tape. Daniel thinks the Web is perfect for this, for "showing slices of life that the have the integrity of truth, or at least a personal truth revealed through a compassionate eye."

He keeps each story three to four minutes long because he thinks that's about the extent of people's current attention span on the Internet. More than anything, he believes, the Internet is perfect for telling personal stories because ultimately that's what people really care about.

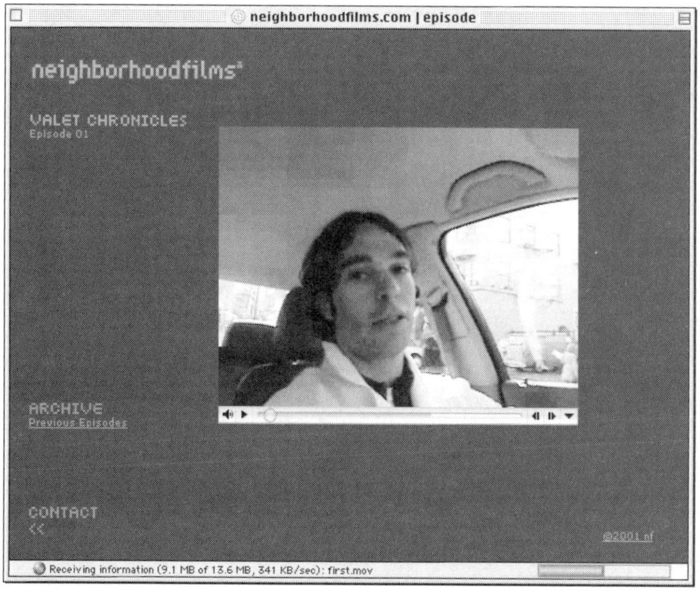

FIGURE 1.9

At `Neighborhoodfilms.com` you'll see short, intense stories about neighborhoods and the people who inhabit them.

"I like to think of my work as an extension of how email changed personal communication: The Web begs people to create new ways of communicating; and neighborhood films, through video, is just one way."

Soon after he began posting his films, he started getting thousands of hits from all over the world. His advice to Web video makers? "Think about the environment in relation to how you approach your content—make your movie for the Web from the beginning; don't try and tell a traditional story there," he says. "Set your movie to begin playing immediately when the player opens so that people will spend time watching your movie, rather than figuring out how to get it to play. And before you post a movie, show it to somebody you trust. Once the movie is out on the Web there's no taking it back."

CHAPTER TWO

Shooting Smart

Good-looking Web movies are not made by magic. In fact, the process is rather like a fairy tale in reverse: You turn princes into frogs or gold into straw. If you're doing it right, you start with something really good, then transform it into a shadow of its former self. Here's what every Web wizard knows: The better your video looks before it's compressed, the better it will look *after* compression. It all starts with the camera you use. If you're buying a camera now, you should buy the best one that you can afford. If you've already got a camera, you need to learn how to use it to shoot scenes that will look their best on the Web—you can skip right to the "Shooting for the Web" section at the end of this chapter for tips and techniques.

Choosing a Camera

Buying a camera today comes down to one key decision: digital or analog? The answer is digital—if you can afford it. Today's digital video cameras produce better pictures than the cameras television professionals used less than a decade ago. If you've watched a movie on VHS and then watched it on a DVD you already know what I mean.

Here's another way to measure the difference: Consumer-level digital video cameras capture with enough detail that you can see up to 500 individual vertical lines—500 lines of resolution—before they start blurring together. With VHS, you can only discern about 250 vertical lines before they start blurring together! That's close to *twice* the resolution of analog VHS cameras. Not only that, but digital cameras record CD-quality audio, allow you to make endless copies of your movies without any loss in quality, make it incredibly easy to transfer your video directly into your computer, and are smaller and lighter than their predecessors. But if you've already got an analog camera, or don't want to spend the extra money that digital video cameras cost, don't despair. You can make Web video, too. You'll just need to convert, or *digitize*, your footage into digital video before you can edit and compress it—tasks that capture cards and stand-alone devices are designed to do (see Chapter 4, "Capturing Capably").

How much do video camcorders cost? I'm shooting at a moving target here (no pun intended), but here's the overview. If you're strapped for cash, or Web video is just a sideline venture, you can still buy a perfectly serviceable analog camcorder for $300 to $ 1000. Consumer-level digital video camcorders are generally priced between $400 and $3000 and are good enough for almost all Web video projects. For $3000 to $20,000, you can buy a digital video camcorder that offers better picture quality and more flexibility, but I'd recommend renting, not buying, these.

Once you've decided to go digital, you'll soon discover another set of decisions you need to make. There's an alphabet soup of digital video formats out there to make sense of, different tape cartridges to sort out, and a features list that can make your head swim.

Consumer Digital Cameras

Take a walk through any camera store, and you'll mostly see MiniDV format cameras for sale (**Figure 2.1**). These small, easy-to-use cameras are aimed at video consumers, though many professionals also use them because they're much better than high-end analog cameras and cost so much less. These cameras record up to 80 minutes of video on MiniDV cassettes, which are smaller than a pack of cigarettes (**Figure 2.2**). You might also see DV cameras for sale, which are bigger than the MiniDV cameras because they use a larger tape cassette, which records up to 210 minutes and is close to twice the size of the MiniDV cassettes. But both these cameras are classified as DV cameras, which really means three things: 1) They use the DV *data format*, which dictates how video is compressed as it is shot; 2) they use a DV *tape format*, which is a method of recording digital video to tape; and 3) and they use a DV *cassette* (mini or not). The DV format is the most versatile, powerful, and affordable digital format around, and I recommend MiniDV or DV cameras for most hobbyists and many professionals.

Figure 2.1
MiniDV camcorders offer lightweight versatility, ease of use, and excellent value. (This is a Canon GL-1.)

Figure 2.2
MiniDV cassettes, shown here on top of a standard DV cassette and a VHS cassette, are the smallest videotape format available.

A digital video camera isn't much good if you can't connect it to your computer and transfer your footage at high-speed. Luckily, the engineers who developed the DV format realized this. All DV cameras have FireWire ports (also called 1394 or iLink by some manufacturers) that make it simple to plug your camera into your computer. With a FireWire connection (**Figure 2.3**), you can transfer your video files from your camera as easily as you move folders and files around on your hard drive. Even better, FireWire connections allow you to control your digital video camera from your digital editing software, making video capture a snap. If you have a recent Macintosh, you're in luck, because FireWire connectors are built right in. Some PCs come equipped with FireWire cards already installed, but most will require you to purchase and install an inexpensive FireWire card separately.

TIP ▸ *Even though DV cameras come with a FireWire port, most don't include a FireWire cable, so make sure you buy one while you're out shopping.*

FIGURE 2.3
This FireWire cable lets you transfer digital data at lightning-fast speeds. One plug connects to your camera and the other to your computer.

One derivative of the DV format that you'll also see at the store is Digital8, which is at the low-end of the DV price range. Digital8 cameras record in the DV data format, but they do so onto Hi8 cassettes, which cost less than MiniDV cassettes and can be easier to find. (Hi8 cameras are consumer analog cameras, but they record relatively high-resolution analog video.) Digital8 cameras and decks can also play back Hi8 cassettes that were recorded by analog Hi8 cameras. That's handy because you can use the camera to digitize your existing tape collection by plugging it into your computer's FireWire port and then playing back your old tapes. If you're strapped for cash but want to take advantage of FireWire data transfer, Digital8 is a good way to go.

A Camera that Compresses Video for the Web

Just as this book goes to press, there is a very new development on the Web video horizon. The GY-DV300U 1⁄3" 3-CCD DV STREAMCORDER is a 1⁄3-inch 3-CCD Mini-DV camera that comes equipped to connect to the Internet so you can distribute video from the camera in real time over the Web. An adapter attaches to the bottom of the camcorder with a connection for a PCMCIA card, which, in turn, connects (either wired or wireless) to PC. The camcorder comes with "StreamProducer" streaming server software, so that you can then stream the video (in Windows Media format) live from the camera on a Web page that can viewer can access. Up to four GY-DV300Us can be connected to the PC. The resulting movies stream at 12-15 frames per second, with a frame size of 352 x 288 pixels and a data rate of about 410 kilobits per second.

FIGURE 2.4
The new GY-DV300U seems to be the ultimate Web video device: a high-quality DV camera that can stream video directly to the Web.

Analog Cameras

There's no question that using a DV camera is easier and more efficient for creating Web video than an analog camera. DV cameras capture far better pictures and make it much easier to transfer them into your computer. In a perfect world you'd use nothing else. But if you're on a limited budget, analog cameras still offer an affordable way to get started, though you also have to factor in the cost of video capture hardware, as I'll discuss in chapter 4. Here are the different types of analog formats you can choose from.

Composite Video/VHS ($300 to $1000)

If you have a camera at home that you've had for awhile, this is most likely what you've got. It offers images at a maximum of 240 lines of horizontal resolution, which isn't very good these days, but it is what most of us are used to video looking like. While VHS is still the most common playback format, it is practically useless for any serious video production, because making copies (an essential step in editing analog video) markedly degrades its quality.

S-Video and Hi8 ($600 to $1000)

Both S-Video and Hi8 (**Figure 2.5**) format camcorders (two high-resolution formats developed by two different companies) offer much higher fidelity and higher resolution than the VHS format. Instead of 240 lines of resolution, S-Video and Hi8 offer close to 400 lines of horizontal resolution, which isn't as good as DV's 500 lines but is a noticeable improvement over standard VHS picture quality.

FIGURE 2.5
Hi8 camcorders capture higher resolution video than VHS camcorders and record to smaller videocassettes.

Analog Component ($12,000 to $50,000)

Sony's BetacamSP, an analog component camera, captures the best picture of all of the analog cameras (its resolution is the same as that of a DV camera) and costs the most. If you're using a Betacam for a Web video, it's probably because your corporate communications department or TV station already owns the gear and won't invest in new digital equipment yet. However, the Betacam format offers a certain advantage: Because the Betacam captures more color information than all but the top-end digital cameras, which cost even more, it's a good choice for projects that require *chroma keying*—an electronic effect in which an image blocks out portions of a background and appears to be layered on top of it, like the weather report on your local TV news.

Cameras for Professionals

If you're planning to release your movie both over the Web and on broadcast television, then you should consider renting top-end digital video equipment. These camera formats (such as Sony's DVCam for $4500 to $20,000 and Panasonic's DVCPro50, which runs from a whopping $10,000 to $30,000) tend to be bigger and bulkier than their consumer DV counterparts but they offer better electronic circuitry, better (and interchangeable) lenses, and sturdier construction, and they can capture more color information, which means clearer, sharper pictures (**Figures 2.6** and **2.7**). These high-end cameras both use a wider *data track* (the physical area of the tape being used for recording) and a mechanically faster tape speed. This combination results in more information being recorded to the videotape and less chance of electronic noise or glitches on the tape. They also offer more precise controls and adjustments of camera functions like *aperture* (exposure), shutter speed, and audio levels. All of these features matter for the high standards of a sophisticated videographer and for certain Web video-shooting techniques (such as shallow depth of field) described in the "Shooting for the Web" section later in this chapter.

Figure 2.6
High-end digital video cameras (such as this Sony DSR-500WSL1) use a wider data track and faster tape speed to record with less video noise than lower-end digital cameras.

Figure 2.7
High-end digital video cameras like this Panasonic AJ-PD900WA Camcorder also offer better color fidelity than lower-end digital cameras.

Figuring Out Features

No shopping expedition would be complete without a bewildering array of features that are hard to decipher and even harder to evaluate. Just remember to keep yourself focused on what you're going to do with the camera. There's no sense in buying features you're not going to use.

If you're mainly interested in capturing the world as it happens, you don't need most of the bells and whistles out there. All of today's cameras offer sophisticated automatic controls and adjustable zoom lenses that will be just fine for you. It's like buying a still camera: For some people, the all-automatic ones are just the ticket; but for those who want to take pictures in very dark or very light environments, who want to fool around with unusual focus effects, or who want to use extreme close-ups or long-distance shots, one of those automatic models just wouldn't do the trick. So it goes with video cameras. If you're going to do specialized filming in dark or light environments or you need flexibility in focusing and exposure, you're going to need manual adjustments and interchangeable lenses—and you can expect to pay more for the privilege.

CCDs: More Is Better and Bigger Is Better

Digital cameras don't record images on film. Instead, they use light-sensitive chips to measure the color, shade, and intensity of the light that comes through the camera's lens. These *charge-coupled devices*, or CCDs, are your camera's eyes, so it makes sense that the more of them a camera has, the better that camera can see the world around it and the more information it can capture. CCDs are measured in pixels (and range from 300,000 to 1 million pixels per CCD), but you'll usually hear cameras described as either *one-chip* or *three-chip* cameras, which refers to the number of CCDs the camera uses to convert images into electronic signals. (There are a few *two-chip* cameras out there, but they're not in the mainstream.)

One-chip cameras use one CCD to gather all of the brightness and color information coming into the camera, while three-chip cameras use prisms to split incoming light into separate red, green, and blue components, with a CCD dedicated to each color. Color reproduction and image detail are much better on three-chip cameras—but you'll pay a higher price, usually about three times higher, than for the one-chip cameras. These cameras are also larger than their one-chip brethren, in part because the extra CCDs consume a lot more power. Unless you're working at the highest end of Web video and want to mix your digital footage with footage from other video formats, or you want to do broadcast TV quality work or transfer your work to film, one-chip cameras are good enough.

You can't get a camera with more than three CCDs, but you can buy a camera with larger CCDs, in both one- and three-chip models. Low-end cameras have ¼-inch or ⅓-inch CCDs, but high-end cameras have ⅔-inch CCDs. Because CCDs are the eyes of the camera, the bigger chips are able to capture color more accurately and with a finer range of detail.

Flexible Focus: Choosing Lenses

Most MiniDV and Hi8 cameras come with a zoom lens that's permanently attached. This is just fine for most users who want to shoot on the run and not worry about special techniques that rely on changing the length of the lens (such as extremely long-distance or close-up shots).

With cameras that cost $4000 or more, you'll get the option of interchangeable, detachable lenses, which let you take off and put on new lenses for special shots. Interchangeable lenses almost always have better *optics*, which means that they use better materials to capture and focus the light coming into the camera. They also come in a greater range of focal lengths, which is a measure of the distance from a camcorder's lens to a focused image. Wide-angle lenses have short focal lengths; telephoto lenses have long focal lengths; zoom lenses vary their focal lengths. It's worth it to invest in these lenses if your work requires shots that you just can't capture with a built-in lens; but be aware that you can spend as much, or more, on a good lens as you can on the camcorder itself.

To test a lens's quality, zoom out to its widest angle. You can figure this out by looking at the lens itself, where you'll see a range of numbers, such as 6.5–72mm. The lower the number (for example, 6.5), the wider the lens. After you zoom out to its maximum angle look for distortion around the edges, which will look like fuzzy curved lines where there should be sharp, straight lines. Obviously, distortion isn't good, so look for lenses that keep this to a minimum. Also test the manual focus and aperture settings, if available, and make sure that the controls are easy to get at and to understand.

TIP ▸ *You'll see cameras advertised with digital zoom features. This isn't the same thing as having a genuine optical zoom lens, which works by actually changing the size of an object in the camera's view by moving a glass lens. Instead, digital zoom works by using the camera's internal computer to magnify the pictures you're taking at the expense of its resolution. You might use it now and then, but it is no substitute for the real thing.*

Web-Only Video: Frame Mode

If you're shooting video exclusively for the Web and don't ever plan to play your video from tape, check to see if your camera offers progressive-scan features, sometimes called *frame mode*. Frame mode allows you to shoot your video in the same way that a computer, rather than a television, displays it, saving you an extra step in preparing your video clips for the Web. Don't use this feature if you think you might ever want to transfer your video to tape, though, because it reduces clarity, particularly in high-motion action scenes.

Controls: Auto or Manual?

Less-expensive video cameras come with automated everything: autofocus, auto-exposure, auto–white balance, autoshutter, and so on. The more you spend on a camera, the more you can manually adjust these types of settings. On most consumer cameras, manual controls like these are often hidden in a labyrinth of text-based menus. Generally speaking, as you pay more for a camera, you get dedicated knobs and controls that are easier to adjust. While such manual controls offer you extra control, they also make it necessary to make more decisions the settings you use, which can be annoying if all you want to do is capture your kid's birthday party or capture documentary footage at a fast-paced event. In contrast, an all-automatic camera just won't do if you're shooting a commercial for a brand of chocolate syrup and you need to have complete control over the exposure of, and focus on, the syrup as it is being poured over vanilla ice cream. If you want to fine-tune your shot—for instance, keeping the chocolate in focus while the rest of the picture fades off in a blur—look for a camera that's easy to adjust.

Color: In the Eyes of the Beholder

Is color reproduction a critical part of your Web movie? Pay close attention to the white balance features of any camera you're considering. Better cameras offer a manual white balance setting, which gives you better control over the final color reproduction in your footage.

In general, outdoor light is slightly bluer than pure white is, while indoor light, which is usually lit by bulbs, is more reddish. Suppose you're holding a sheet of black and white newspaper in your hands. When we humans encounter this newspaper indoors, our eyeballs send a message to our brains: "Incoming: reddish newspaper!" But our brains are smart enough to overrule the data coming from the eyeballs, and the data gets registered as "black and white newspaper, indoors." In a sense, our brains have built-in white balance.

Video cameras aren't smart enough to do that last step. They need to be *told* what the color of the ambient light is; hence, the little buttons that have either a sunshine or a light bulb icon on them on inexpensive cameras. These buttons automatically set the white balance by using an arbitrary average setting. More expensive cameras have a manual white balance setting, which allows you to set the balance while pointing the camera at an actual object that you know is white, like a white shirt, in the light that you'll be shooting in.

How It Feels

Of course, any camera also has to measure up as a tool you wouldn't mind carrying around all day long. I consider these kinds of features to be subjective, since we all differ in what kind of look and feel works for us. Make sure that the camera isn't too big, or too heavy, or even too small, for you to work with. Consider the battery life it offers—is it sufficient for the way you plan to shoot your movie? Does the viewfinder show you the shot in black and white or in color, and which do you prefer? (Pros generally prefer black-and-white viewfinders because they have a sharper image.) Do you view what you're shooting by looking at one of those little LCD screens that swivel out from the camera's body? These are becoming increasingly common, but they use more battery power than an eyepiece. There's no right answer to any of these questions, but you need to consider them in finding a camera that will be a joy to use, rather than a pain in the neck.

Professional Cameras Are Less Noisy

Today's camcorders are electronic and mechanical marvels; each of these cameras packs an amazing amount of technology into a very small space. One effect of this miniaturization, unfortunately, is *video noise*. With all of these tiny electronic components in such proximity, some electrons may end up where they aren't wanted, resulting in almost-imperceptible, random imperfections in the video image. Professional-level cameras, like the DVCam and DVCPro50, have shielded electronic circuitry and, thus, less video noise.

Shooting for the Web

Web video is tricky. You've got to be smart about how you use your camera. Wide-angle shots aren't going to play well in a small movie window. Hand-held camera technique is just going to result in a blurry mess by the time compression software finishes with it. Quick takes and many fast cuts aren't going to look good either, and for the same reason—the more your images change from frame to frame, the harder it will be to compress your movie without losing essential details. The best way to shoot movies that look good after they're squeezed to Web size is to keep your camera stationary and avoid a lot of movement in the frame and excessive detail. Here's how:

Keep the Lens as Still as Possible

When you're shooting for the Web, think simple camera work; in fact, think *no* camera work. The single most important thing you can do to ensure high-quality Web video is to keep the camera lens as still as possible, to avoid creating a lot of movement from frame to frame. Ideally, this means putting the camera on a tripod and tightening all of those levers on the tripod so that the camera is firmly fixed in place. I'm talking static...immobile...petrified! If you don't have a tripod, put the camera on a table or chair, or on the floor. Frame the shot, push the record button, and then just leave the camera alone. This is, of course, the ideal situation; reality usually demands something else. Maintaining a stationary camera may mean that you have to get creative about how to choreograph your subject's movement, but its worth it.

Suppress any urge to hold the camera by hand. Excessive camera movement will result in a blurry mess. The best example in recent memory of camera work not suitable for Web video is *The Blair Witch Project*, a horror movie in which no two frames in the whole movie are stationary! If you want to see something really scary, try and compress that!

Avoid Movement in the Frame

The second most important factor when shooting Web video is to avoid movement *within* the frame. Even if your camera is firmly locked onto a rock-solid tripod, you've got to worry about who you're shooting. Say you're shooting a movie featuring your six-year-old daughter. The worst-case scenario for Web video would be to have her moving a lot (for example, dancing) in front of the camera. The ideal scenario would be to have her sitting still (good luck). On second thought, maybe you should just try shooting someone older, or film her when she's asleep.

If you can't bring the action to a standstill, then at least try to slow it down. Think talking heads. *Book Notes*, a cable TV series, is a good showcase for Web video. (Check out the show's Web site, which features clips of the show's guests: `www.booktv.org`.) The *Book Notes* subjects (usually authors) are practically motionless, except for their moving lips as they speak. An added bonus for Web video is the flat black background used for the *Book Notes* set (see "Hide That Detailed Background," below).

It's true that if you surf the Web you'll find movies with lots of movement in them. The ones that look good have other things working for them, such as high-resolution source footage that was captured and compressed skillfully. Reducing the amount of movement in your movie isn't a guarantee that it will look good on the Web, but it's a good start.

If You Must Move, Use a Tripod

Hey—I saw that! You did a camera move didn't you? I knew you wouldn't be able to resist moving the camera! If you have to move the camera (to pan to the top of a skyscraper in the middle of a city skyline, or to follow a football game from the stands, for example), use a high-quality tripod, one that has really solid legs and moves smoothly and stops quickly when you tilt the head. This ensures two things: smooth movement and the option of movement in only one dimension (either panning left and right, or tilting up and down) at a time, which helps the compression software tremendously. But no fast whip pans or tilts allowed. Zooming is particularly difficult for compression software to handle. So avoid zooms, too! Keep it nice and slow.

Hide That Detailed Background

Ideally, compression software wants to work with flat planes of color, and with very little detail. A flat, smooth gray wall is a better background than a bumpy gray wall, or a gray wallpaper pattern. Compression software can't distinguish the relative importance of the little details in the wallpaper and the facial gestures of your lead actress. The wallpaper may be static, but if *anything* (including your video frame or the lighting) changes even slightly, the compression software will have to spend a part of your movie's precious bandwidth on the wallpaper instead of the actual star of your show. A better idea: Find a less-detailed background.

Early in my digital video career, I helped produce a CD-ROM featuring interviews with luminaries in the multimedia industry. One interview took place outdoors in a parklike setting. In the background, tree branches with green leaves were waving in the wind. The compression software devoted almost all of the bits in that movie to the details of those tree branches, leaving a gray, blurry smudge where the face of the corporate CEO should have been. If the cameraman had been thinking "video compression" instead of "interesting shot," he could have used the bright blue (very flat) sky as a background instead, with much better results (**Figures 2.8** and **2.9**).

FIGURE 2.8
Avoid detailed backgrounds, such as this foliage. The compression software will have to spend a part of your movie's precious bits on the background foliage instead of the actual star of your show.

FIGURE 2.9
Flat, solid-colored backgrounds, such as this gray wall, will always compress better than detailed backgrounds.

Use a Shallow Depth of Field

Another way the cameraman could have removed detail from that background would have been to maintain a shallow *focus* (depth of field). He could have done this by moving the camera physically closer to his subject, zooming in on his subject, and using a wider aperture (this controls the amount of light that falls onto the camera's CCDs). Doing these things would have kept the CEO in focus, while making the background more indistinct (**Figure 2.10**). He would have needed to have a camera that offered manual controls over the aperture and focus to do this, though. An all-automatic camera would have adjusted both to keep the scene as a whole as sharp as possible, which wouldn't have let him focus on the CEO at the expense of the background.

Figure 2.10
Use a shallow depth of field to take the background out of focus. This reduces the amount of detail in your shot significantly, and thereby makes it easier to compress.

WARNING ▸ Important! Never point your video camera lens (or even its viewfinder) into the sun. Serious damage to the camera's CCDs (and your eyes) may result!

TIP ▸ *Your on-camera talent (interviewees, actors) should not wear stripes, plaids, or checked patterns, as all of these complex graphics are difficult to compress. Use a wardrobe with solid colors, or very simple patterns, and medium tones.*

Shoot as Close Up as Possible

If TV is a close-up medium, then the Web is a *really* close-up medium. Since Web video has such a small image, shoot close-ups! Panoramic vistas of the Serengeti Plain or the Grand Canyon just won't cut it in a 160-by-120-pixel window (**Figures 2.11** and **2.12**). Don't forget to leave room for subtitles and credits in the lower third of the frame, if necessary. Titles and graphics should be at least one-fourth the size of the frame in height. Anything smaller may be difficult to read. And remember: Avoid significant detail or activity in the background!

Figure 2.11
Bad idea: extremely wide angle shots like this do not work in Web movies. When this movie is compressed for a 56k modem, you'll hardly see the girl in the frame.

Figure 2.12
Better idea: Tighter shots work better on the Web.

Keep High-Contrast Conditions to a Minimum

In general, the standard practice for shooting any kind of video (including television) is to avoid high-contrast scenes—meaning scenes with both extremely bright and extremely dark areas (**Figures 2.13** and **2.14**). That's because video's *exposure latitude* (its range from the brightest values to the darkest values) is very limited compared to that of, say, 35mm film. Web video exacerbates this problem. For example, a scene in a dark room that has a window opening onto bright sunshine would be difficult to shoot well because you would have to either set the exposure for the room interior (which means the window would be overexposed) or set the exposure for the window (leaving the interior underexposed). Trying to expose for both the room interior and the exterior view out the window would be futile for all forms of Web video.

Linda Baron

FIGURE 2.13
Avoid very high contrast scenes like this: most video cameras just can't handle this extreme range from light to dark.

Linda Baron

FIGURE 2.14
Better idea: choose a camera angle or change the lighting so that the scene has more mid-range (gray-level) brightness values.

Go for Long Takes

When there is a significant change, such as a cut, in your movie, compression software must insert a *keyframe* in the compressed video sequence. A keyframe is a frame that contains the complete video image and is the basis for the following sequence of related frames (the subsequent frames in the sequence contain only those parts of the picture that have changed). Frequent keyframes increase the *data rate* needs of a Web movie. The data rate is the amount of information (for example, kilobits) per second used to represent a movie. For Web video, it's better to shoot longer shots and thereby require fewer cuts. However, if the choice is between a wide, horizontal pan and a simple cut to the next shot, the cut will use less bandwidth.

Use Proper Lighting Techniques for Web Video

The scope of this book allows me to just scratch the surface of what there is to say about the craft of motion picture lighting. The difference between traditional movie lighting techniques and Web video lighting techniques revolves around the issue of controlling the amount of detail in the image.

Hard lights tend to result in lots of detail, which, as you know by now, is a bad idea. Instead, use soft lights for even and muted lighting when you're shooting indoors. I try to bounce or diffuse the light on my shoots. Shoot early or late in the day, wait for cloudy days, find a place that is already shady, or use light colored fabric above your subject to diffuse the light.

Compared to film, all forms of video are limited in terms of the number of colors they display. Many Web video codecs don't work too well with bright, saturated colors, especially primary red. These colors tend to smear a bit both on TV screens and in Web video. It is especially important to avoid saturated colors in lettering or titles. Particularly avoid bright red and yellow hues. Blues, greens, muted reds, or any combination of the three, work the best.

Know Your Audience's Limitations

To do an efficient job shooting Web video you need to have a sense of how most people are going to be watching it. If you can be certain that your viewers will be corporate users with high-speed data lines, you can get a bit fancy with cuts and pans. Because they'll have the fastest possible connection to the Internet, you won't have to compress your movie as drastically just to get it to their desktops. But if you're shooting a wedding, and the bride and groom want to broadcast their vows on a personal Web page, you can assume that most viewers will be watching your work on a slow dial-up connection. You'll have to keep things simple, because you're going to have to use maximum compression to get that movie to play smoothly—even if it's a fairytale marriage.

Shooting smart matters a lot. But it's not the whole story. In the next chapter, you'll learn why Hollywood veterans say, "Audio is half the picture." In fact, in Web video, audio is *more* than half the picture.

WEB VIDEO SPOTLIGHT

IngredientX.com

Ingredient X Entertainment is the work of Lev Yilmaz. The site was started by Lev in mid 1999, primarily as a showcase for his eight years of work as an independent video producer. Ingredient X's site is found at **www.ingredientx.com/index.htm** (**Figure 2.15**), and its critically acclaimed Web-based animation series "Tales of Mere Existence" is featured at **www.atomfilms.com**.

Lev Yilmaz wanted to show his backlog of video work to the public and found the solution in Web video. As he puts it, "Before that, showing my work usually involved borrowing TVs from friends and lugging them to coffee shops on open mic nights. It was all very frustrating." Today IngredientX.com includes a rich mix of animation, puppetry, and performance art, all delivered 24/7 on the Web.

As kids, the two brothers made numerous films that were parodies of American life and spoofs of infomercials, used car salesmen, and so on. Lev continued with his filmmaking in art school, and both brothers have worked professionally for clients and multimedia companies. Lev bemoans the fact the large mass media empires (film/TV/news media) have tried to co-opt the Web (including Web video) into their system. As Lev puts it, "What I hope people do more than anything else is to use this as an *alternative* to the mass media and not another branch of it. You can

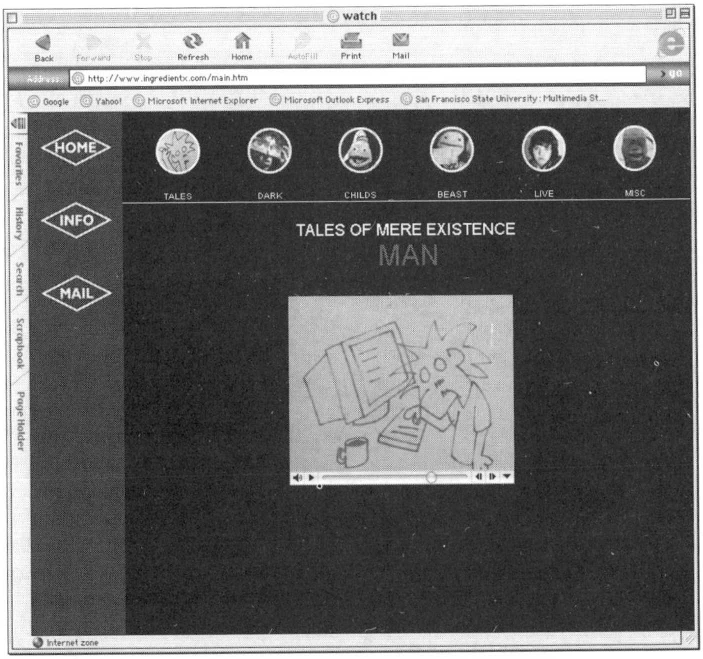

FIGURE 2.15
At IngredientX you can see funny, quirky films that you wouldn't see anywhere else.

use it to express opinions, either personal or political, that may not be so popular in the mainstream press. Individual people can still be incredibly powerful when they have the guts to say something they care about."

The Yilmaz brothers purposely keep the movies on Ingredient X short for a small file size because they know their audience: "Our audience is on the young side and they probably only have (56k) modem connections. When everybody has broadband, the playing field will unquestionably change, but I don't think anybody could really tell you how at this point."

The movies are decidedly low-tech in their presentation. For example, the "Tales of Mere Existence" series has a unique animation style that involves shooting a backlit screen with the video camera while the characters are being drawn onto the opposite side of the screen by hand.

They use QuickTime as their media player format "because it's so damn simple, and pretty much anyone can use it regardless of their connection speed. People also can save the movies on their hard drives if they want, which I think is cool, although it's probably a horror show for anybody who wants to implement an all-American pay-per-view sort of system for this stuff."

Here are some more tips from Lev for Web video makers:

- **Don't be afraid to make mistakes**

  You have to make some bad videos because you have to see what doesn't work for you in order to figure out what does. If you're just starting out, try making a video really quickly before you have time to doubt yourself, like in an afternoon. That's a great exercise for the more experienced as well when you get stuck on what to make.

- **Take influences from everywhere**

  It's good to see what other people are doing in Web video, but don't look at that as the rule book. Read stories. Read the newspaper. Look at paintings and photos. Listen to music. If you see or hear something you like, apply it to your work.

- **Don't get hung up on effects and technology**

  This is probably the most common hurdle I see for new media makers. So many get hell bent on learning software and special effects that they neglect the storytelling, and the piece suffers horribly.

CHAPTER THREE

Sounding Good

Pssst—want to hear a secret? Movie pros know that a great sound track can make even the best movie look better. Audiences tune into sound—that's why they rate the visuals higher on movies that have better-sounding sound tracks. So movie producers and directors spend a lot of time and money creating high-quality sound tracks, and have done so ever since the introduction of sound to motion pictures in the 1920s. On the Web, good audio matters just as much as it does on film and TV, if not more. It's one of the best tools in your movie maker toolkit, because you can record and play back CD-quality audio. And that can make all the difference when your highly compressed video has to play back at a slow frame rate in a tiny window.

Making Sense of Microphones

Recording good sound means paying attention to a few basic rules on the set. It also means making the best use of your equipment and using the right equipment for the right conditions on your set or on location. Your camcorder probably has a built-in microphone, but that's not your only option. You can also buy an external microphone that's tailored for recording specific kinds of sound and can vastly improve the quality of what you capture. Basic external microphones start at around $30 and range as high as $200; better-quality microphones will start at $50 and top out at around $400.

More expensive microphones are more sensitive to sound and can capture the whole range of frequencies the human ear is capable of; less expensive mics can cover only part of that range. More expensive microphones also have less *self-noise*—noise that is introduced in the audio signal itself—in part because they have better cabling and cabling connectors. Do you need to spend the extra money on a high-end microphone? If your job depends on the quality of your Web video, the answer is yes. If you are shooting your kid's birthday party, the answer is probably not. Microphones come in a wide variety of shapes, styles, and sizes, but making sense of what's out there and understanding what you need really boils down to understanding how you plan to use one.

TIP ▸ *You'll see microphones described as either* condenser *or* dynamic *microphones.This is a reference to how they capture sound. Condenser mics are generally small and are extremely sensitive to quiet sounds, which results in a higher-quality recording. Dynamic microphones are less expensive, are practically indestructible, can record extremely loud sounds, and don't require a power supply. Use dynamic mics when you're recording in harsh conditions—such as bad weather, where there are loud sounds, or where your gear is in for some rough treatment. Otherwise, condenser mics are a better choice.*

Shooting on a Budget: Built-In Microphones

Built-in (on-camera) microphones make for a convenient, all-in-one package, but they aren't ideal for recording sound. Built-in microphones are usually *omnidirectional*, which means that they pick up sound in every direction. The bad news for on-camera mics is that they invariably pick up the camera noise. Omnidirectional mics are good when you want to capture the atmosphere and ambience of a place, because they'll pick up whatever's in the camera's frame. Otherwise, to minimize recording unwanted sounds (like the sound of your breathing or other unwanted sounds on the set), get your camera as close to the sound source you're recording as possible. Also, try to make what you are recording louder than anything else on the set. If you're recording someone speaking, for example, ask them to speak up.

TIP ▸ *No matter what kind of microphone you're using, make sure you're recording what you think you're recording (and not picking up annoying buzzes, hums, or other noises) by plugging a set of headphones into the output jack on your camcorder and listening in. You'll hear what the camera's recording.*

Scenes with Actors

Imagine that you're making a movie with dramatized scenes and you have total control of the recording situation and location. To get the best possible sound, you should use a short *shotgun* condenser microphone. Shotgun microphones are sensitive to sounds in front of and in back of the microphone. You can use one to focus on the actors' voices and exclude unwanted noise (**Figure 3.1**). But you'll need the help of a *boom operator* (a person who holds the microphone). The best way to use a shotgun microphone is to attach it to the end of a *boom pole* and point it down at the actors from just above the camera frame. This will capture the most natural and intimate recording of human voices if you do it right.

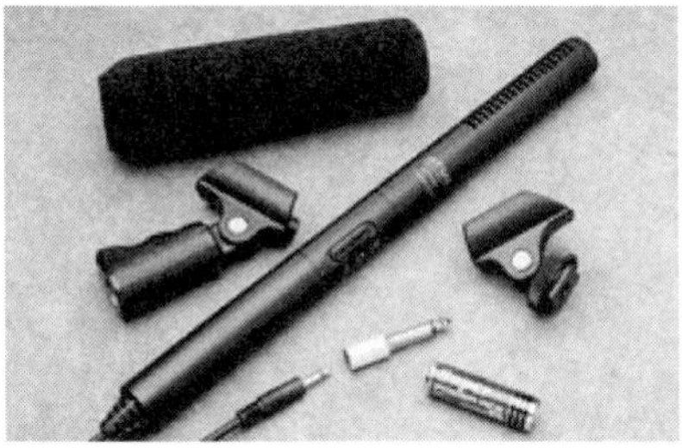

FIGURE 3.1
The ATR55 Condenser Shotgun Microphone ($75) is a good beginner's shotgun mic. It has two range settings: Normal for close- to medium-distance recording, and Tele for long-distance pickup.

The "Man on the Street" Interview

You are reporting news from the streets and sidewalks of a major city. You're questioning passersby about the latest news. You should probably use a handheld dynamic microphone, also known as a *voice* or *PA* (public address) mic (**Figure 3.2**). This type of mic requires no setup—just make sure you've got one that's compatible with your camcorder (see "Connecting to Your Camera," later in this chapter), and plug it into the microphone jack. And it usually comes with a rugged construction and a *cardioid* pickup pattern, which means that it is most sensitive to noise in a heart-shaped pattern in front of the mic (**Figure 3.3**). This pickup pattern reduces unwanted noise from the street traffic and from the reporter who's holding the mic. This is the fastest and easiest way to use an external microphone. One other bonus: These mics are relatively inexpensive.

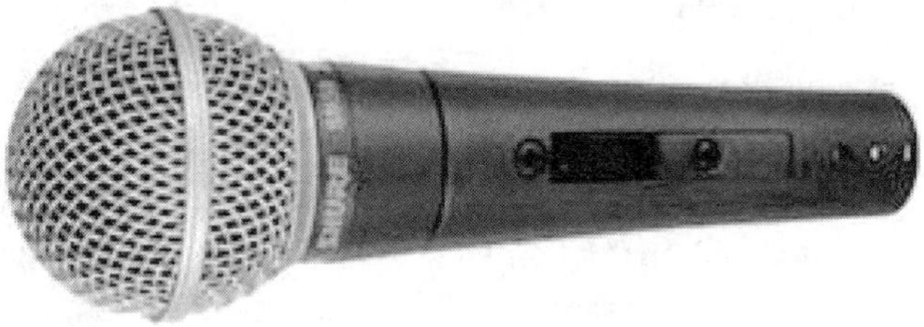

Figure 3.2 Handheld dynamic microphones, like this Shure SM58 Dynamic Microphone ($110 to $120), make it easy to get out and do on-the-street interviews.

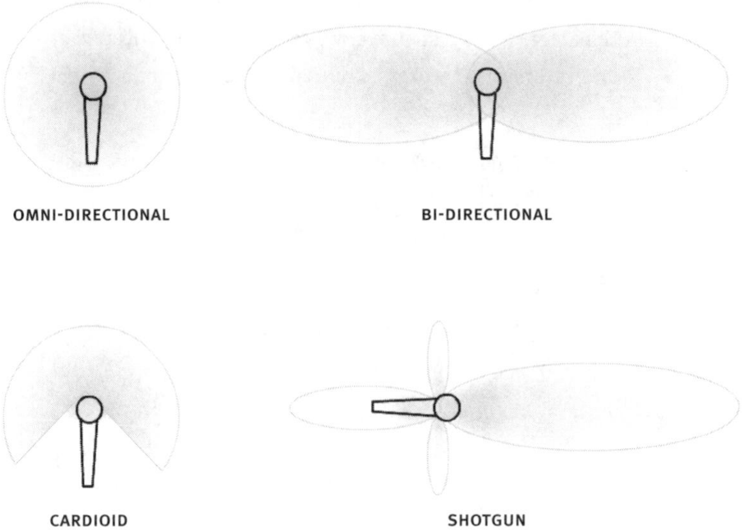

Figure 3.3 Microphones have pickup patterns that make them sensitive to sounds coming from specific directions. Matching the pickup pattern to what you need to record is one key to capturing good sound.

Recording at Concerts

If you are asked to shoot any kind of concert, you normally want to connect a cable from the sound engineer's mixing board to the line-in jack (not the mic jack) of your camera so that you can record the cleanest possible sound. But if you do have to mic the musicians, the type of mic you use will depend on the music and recording conditions. If it's a really loud and raucous rock concert, you'll want the rugged and indestructible reliability of a handheld dynamic microphone like the one mentioned above, at least for the vocals and those musicians who have a tendency to break equipment. Make sure it has a cardioid pattern to capture just the musicians and not handling noise or the amplified sounds from the PA system. If it's a relatively quiet acoustical music setting, such as the recording of a solo cellist, you should use a condenser microphone, because it can record more accurately when the music is quiet (**Figure 3.4**). Condenser mics are more fragile than their dynamic brethren, so you have to handle them carefully.

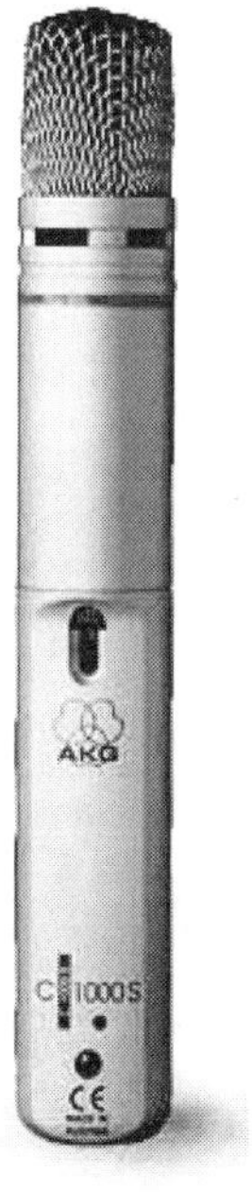

FIGURE 3.4
Condenser microphones, like this AKG C1000S ($150 to $180), work well when you're trying to capture quiet sounds.

The Talking Head Interview

You're shooting an hour-long interview of someone in her home. It will be a *talking head* interview; she is seated in a chair, and only her head and shoulders are visible. This is a job for an omnidirectional *lavaliere* mic (**Figures 3.5** and **3.6**). Lavaliere mics are tiny and inconspicuous. They can easily be pinned to the interviewee's lapel, very close to her mouth, and still be relatively unnoticeable. If the same interview were shot outdoors, you would probably want to use a more directional microphone, like a hand-held shotgun mic, to avoid unwanted background noises.

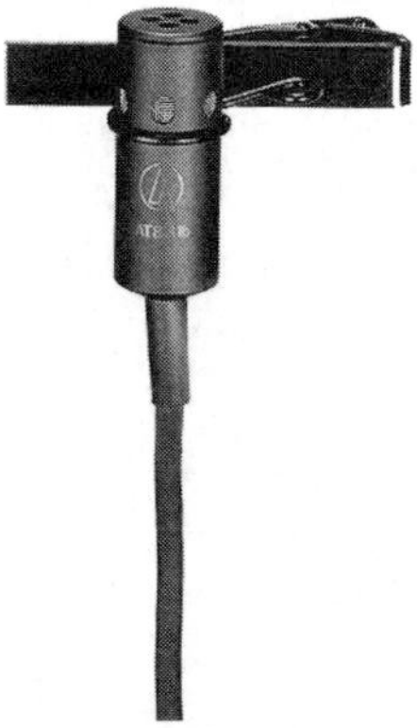

Figure 3.5
Lavaliere microphones, like this Audio-Technica AT831R Lavaliere Condenser Microphone ($150 to $190), work well when you're doing interviews or other recording where you want the mic to be inconspicuous.

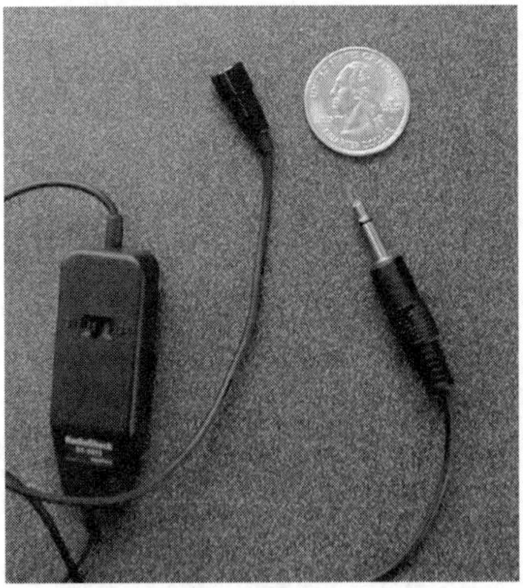

Figure 3.6
The Radio Shack Optimus Ultra-Miniature Tie-Clip Microphone is an omnidirectional lavaliere microphone similar to the built-in mics on many low-end video cameras. A good choice for beginners, it will improve your sound tremendously for very little expense ($24.99, battery included).

TIP ▸ *A microphone's range depends on the power of the recording device you're using. If you crank up the record level on your camera, you'll pick up more sound on your set—but you'll also pick up more unwanted noise.*

Connecting to Your Camera

If your Web video project requires an external microphone, you've got one more technical hurdle to tackle before you can start recording. You've got to connect it to your camcorder. The first thing you should do is to check the microphone input jack on your camera to see what kind of connector it requires. All consumer-level camcorders (those costing $4000 or less) use unbalanced ⅛-inch mini-stereo connectors (**Figure 3.7**). Professional-level camcorders (such as the Sony Betacam, and the DVCam and DVCPro50 format cameras) use a three-pronged XLR connector, also known as a balanced connector (**Figure 3.8**). Whether a cable is balanced or unbalanced is a result of the number of wires inside the cable that carry the audio signal. As you might expect, unbalanced connectors go together with unbalanced cables; balanced cables use balanced connectors. What really matters is making sure that your camcorder and your microphone use the same kind of cables and connectors so that you can connect them together.

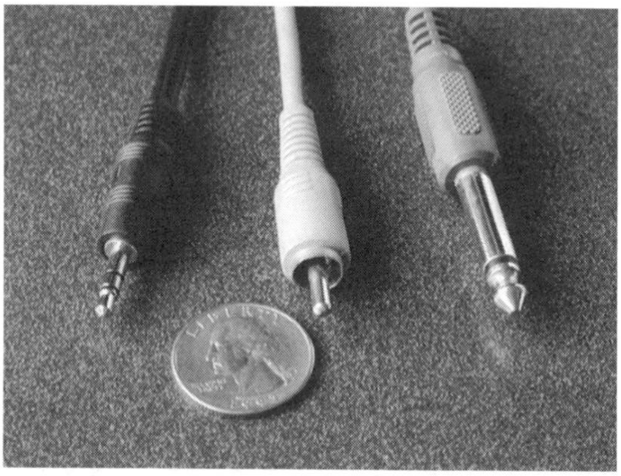

Figure 3.7
Unbalanced cables come with different kinds of connectors: (l. to r.) ⅛-inch mini, RAC, and ¼-inch phono plugs.

Figure 3.8
If you're shooting with a professional-level camcorder, you'll need this three-pronged XLR (balanced) connector.

If you've got a consumer-level camera, such as a MiniDV camera, and you're using a low-end microphone, such as the ATR55 Condenser Shotgun Microphone or the Radio Shack Optimus Ultra-Miniature Tie-Clip Microphone, you can just plug the microphone into your camera and head out to shoot. Low-end microphones, which usually sell for about $100 or less, usually use ⅛-inch mini-stereo connectors, just like the consumer-level camcorders.

TIP ▸ *In addition to a microphone input jack, most cameras will also have a line-in jack. Be careful not to confuse the two! Line-in jacks connect your camera to devices that provide their own amplification, such as a portable CD player. As a rule of thumb, if the device you're connecting plugs into the wall and has a volume knob attached, or requires batteries, you should use the line-in jack, not the microphone jack.*

Things get more complicated, though, if you buy a higher-end microphone and want to use it with a consumer-level camera. Say you have a MiniDV camera and want to use an AKG C1000C Condenser Microphone, or any of the other microphones mentioned above that cost more than $100. You've got a problem. The camera has an unbalanced ⅛-inch mini-stereo jack and your microphone comes with a balanced, three-pronged XLR connector. To get the microphone connected to the camera, you're going to need an adapter. The best ones for this job are the Studio 1 XLR-PRO and the BeachTek DXA-4 Dual XLR Adapter ($150 to $200). Both are small metal boxes that attach to your camera, taking the signal from the microphone and converting it to the appropriate signal for your camera's microphone input (**Figure 3.9**). These adapters are available from any professional video equipment retailer; they also work well with digital audio tape (DAT) recorders (see below).

FIGURE 3.9
An audio adapter lets you use professional-quality mics with consumer-quality video and audio equipment.

WARNING ▸ Important! Those of you who don't like to read manuals and who insist on plugging your microphone into all apparently compatible input jacks should turn down the volume on all devices before you begin plugging things in, or you'll get some unpleasantly loud surprises!

TIP ▸ *No matter what kind of devices you're connecting, think about* strain relief *when connecting any electronic equipment. Just plugging in a connector and letting it dangle from the camera's microphone jack will, at best, wear out the jack; at worst, cause the jack to break inside the device, requiring expensive repair. Instead, use a rubber band or gaffer's tape to secure or bind the excess cable so that its full weight is not on the jack. Or, consider using short extension cables or right-angled plugs instead of just straight ones to lessen the strain on the cables* (**Figure 3.10**).

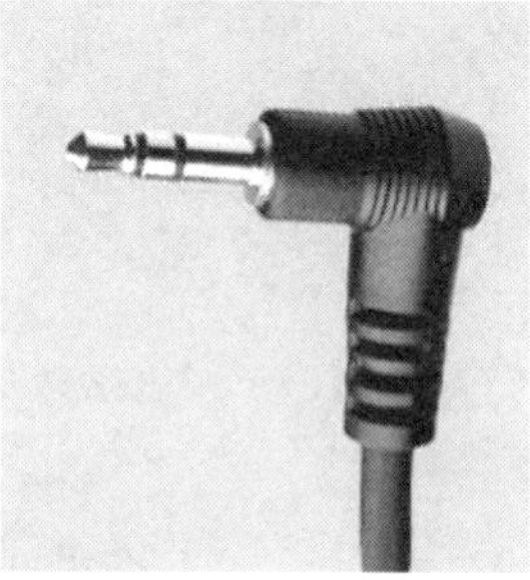

Figure 3.10
A right-angled miniplug takes some of the burden off the jack.

Recording Audio Separately

Sometimes it makes sense to record audio separately: Maybe the audio recording circuit on your camera isn't working or your microphone cable is too short to reach the sound source. Or let's say you want to record a continuous audio track of your son's one-hour piano recital and then edit it later with a variety of shots that you shoot at the event. This way, you can make a high-quality, continuous audio recording while you shoot (turning your camera on and off, and pointing it in various directions to get the best shots). In this case, you will need *other* audio recording devices. Portable options include digital audio tape (DAT) recorders, analog audiocassette recorders, and MiniDV recorders. One such recorder is the Sony TCD-D100 Portable DAT Walkman Field Recorder ($675). It offers high-quality recording in a small package.

If you're using external audio recording devices, you will need to *slate*—or synchronize—the camera and the audio recorder. The classic example of this is the black and white clapper board familiar to all movie fans: Someone says, "Scene 2, take 5!" and slams the clapper shut. This leaves a visual and audible reference point that the editor can later use to sync the video and audio together (**Figure 3.11**). You don't have to use a clapper board; hitting any two objects together (such as clapping your hands) so that the camera can clearly see and the microphone can clearly hear will also do the trick.

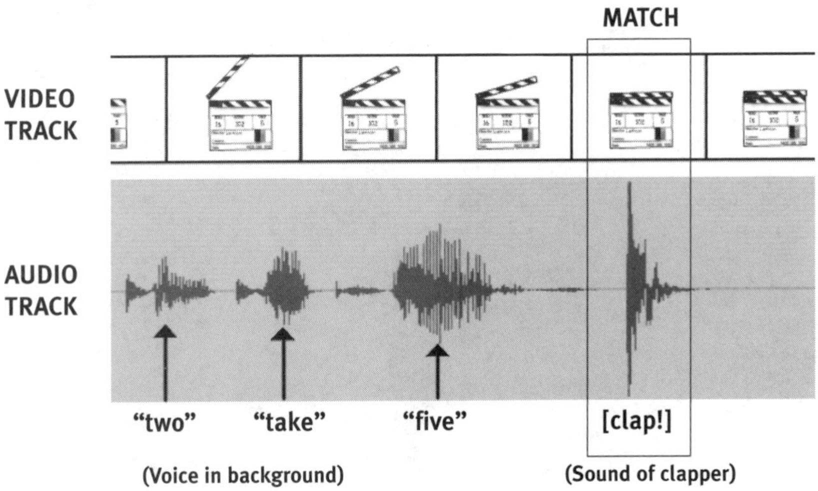

FIGURE 3.11 The clapper board technique leaves matching visual and audible reference points in the video and audio tracks, respectively. This allows for easy syncing in an editing program.

In any case, *in addition* to using your separate recording device, it is a good idea also to record audio using your on-camera microphone if you can. (Yes, that built-in microphone *is* good for something.) Since the on-camera audio track will already be synchronized with the video, you can use it as a *guide track* (reference track) to sync the video from the camera with the audio from the tape recorder in a timeline-based digital editor like Premiere (**Figure 3.12**). A second benefit of using both recording methods is that you'll have a backup recording in case something goes wrong. Even though it would probably be a lower-quality audio recording than what you could capture with an external device, some kind of backup is better than nothing.

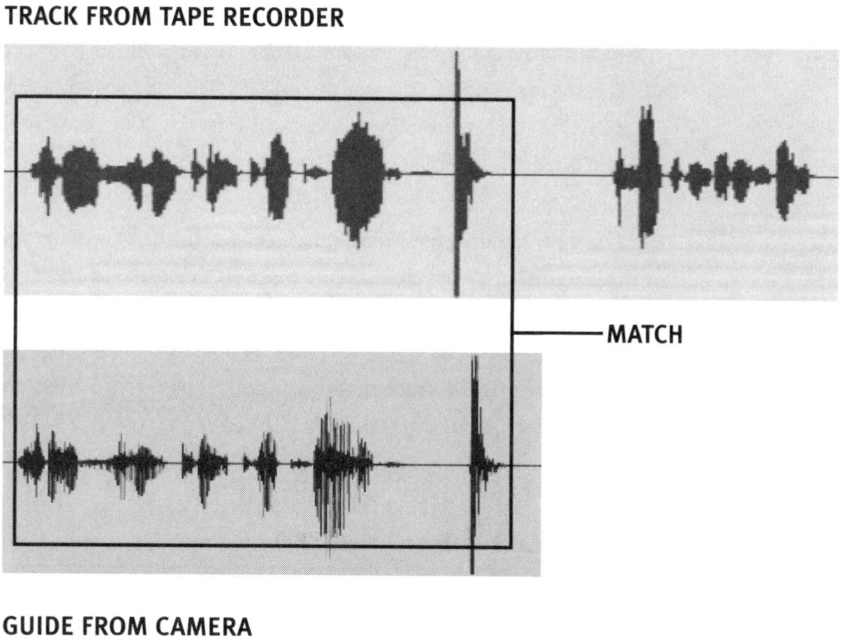

Figure 3.12
If you're recording sound on a separate tape recorder, it's still a good idea to record on-camera sound as well. You can use the on-camera audio as a guide track to sync up the audio and video.

If you're using multiple microphones on your shoot—for example, if you're shooting a panel discussion in which each panelist is mic'ed separately, or you want more control over the audio signal, you need a *mixer*, which goes between the microphone and the recording device. It lets you combine the separate signals coming in from two or more microphones into one audio channel and monitor the volume level of each incoming signal.

Tips for Recording Good Audio

Recording high-quality audio for the Web is generally no different than recording high-quality audio for film, TV, radio, music CDs, or any other format. But there are a few tips to keep in mind when recording audio exclusively for the Web.

Select the Highest Sample Rate Possible

Even consumer-level digital video cameras can record audio at CD-quality levels. Some cameras allow you to select the number of times per second the voltage in the microphone signal is sampled, known as the *sample rate*. The higher the sample rate of a sound file, the smoother that sound's playback quality. These cameras also allow you to select the *sample depth*, which dictates how many bits the computer will use to describe each sample it takes. Be sure to record at the highest sample rate and sample depth possible. The bigger and the more frequent the samples you feed to the compression software, the better your Web movies will sound.

TIP ▸ *If you're recording to an analog video camera or to an analog tape deck, you'll have to rely on the hardware capture card that you'll be using to digitize your audio track (more on this in Chapter 4, "Capturing Capably"). While you'll end up with a digital audio file to edit this way, you'll get better Web audio files if you record digitally from the start (either with a camcorder or with a digital audio recorder), because digital audio files have better dynamic range and less noise.*

Keep the Sound Simple

While computers are capable of CD-quality audio, people still sometimes attach cheap loudspeakers to their computers, and their computers are often located in noisy rooms. If your Web movie has an elaborate, multilayered sound track (with several layers of dialogue, music, and narration), people may well miss most of it.

TIP ▸ *Unless it's isolated on a very specific frequency, it's difficult to remove noise from a sound track that has dialogue. That's why it's a good idea to record the cleanest audio possible while you're shooting.*

Getting Audio Without a Microphone

As with video footage, there is a way is to get audio from somebody else instead of creating it yourself. Stock music and sound effects libraries offer sound tracks that you can use.

So that you have some files to work with, I have included stock music and stock sound effects on the CD-ROM that comes with this book.

Get That Microphone Closer!

Get the microphone as close as possible to the person or thing you're recording. Ideally, you would have an experienced boom operator who would hold a shotgun microphone at the sound source, just above or just below the edge of the camera frame. The second choice would be a good-quality, body-mounted lavaliere microphone with a short pickup radius (which would reject unwanted sounds off in the distance). Unfortunately, lavaliere microphones usually pick up more noise than directional microphones.

Keep It Quiet

Your goal when recording audio is to reduce noise, both *ambient noise* and *electronic noise*. Ambient noise is all the unwanted sound that occurs on the location or set where you're shooting. Electronic noise is generated either in your recording device or in any equipment connected to it through a cable.

Audio compression software doesn't know the difference between unwanted noise and the sounds you actually want to include in your Web movie. If you give the compression software a noisy signal, it will waste precious bits of the data rate on the noise. Here's a better idea: Record the cleanest (noise-free) audio possible.

When working in an uncontrolled location with a lot of ambient noise, you can do things to minimize the noise:

- Put sound blankets (furniture pads or any sound-absorbing material) on walls and floors to deaden echoes.
- Put sound blankets on windows to minimize traffic noise from the street.
- Turn off the air conditioner or any other noisy appliance.
- Avoid rooms with reflective, noisy surfaces (like stone tile floors). Find a room with wall-to-wall carpeting instead.
- Wait for that plane or bus to pass by before rolling.
- If you're shooting outside, make sure to use a *wind screen*—a foam sock that you pull over the microphone so that it doesn't record wind noise.
- If at all possible, record *voice-over narration* (narration that's not on camera) in a studio, after the shoot is over. This gives you much more control over the sound environment.

Go Manual!

Turn off the automatic volume control on your camera. Most cameras have a fully automatic mode (designated with the capital letter *A*) and a manual mode (designated with the capital letter *M*). Manually adjust the levels while listening to your sound source with headphones. Good headphones will seal your ears so you hear only what is actually being recorded. Good video cameras will have *volume unit (VU) meters* that indicate the volume level of the signal (either with a needle or an LED readout) while it is being recorded to tape. This gives you some visual feedback while you're adjusting the volume level as the sound source loudness is changing. Put simply, you want to adjust the volume level so that there is activity in the *middle* of the meter, with only infrequent movement into "the red"—or the upper—portion of the meter. Too little movement in the meter will result in a low, noisy recording; too much movement into the red will result in distorted sound and, in the case of digital cameras and recorders, digital noise. If you are not sure about the meter levels, then just use your headphones as your guide.

Reduce Electronic Hum and Noise

The low-voltage signal in an unbalanced microphone cable can easily pick up noise and hum from nearby electronic devices. Keep audio cables away from power cables, or at least cross them at right angles. This minimizes the amount of contact between the cables. You also might get a hum if your camera is plugged into the same power circuit as other audio and video equipment. If this is the case, try a different outlet or use batteries. If the camera is connected electronically to anything plugged into an electrical outlet, disconnect it.

Using Separate Microphones for Separate Tracks

High-end cameras (the ones costing over $4000) have more than one audio input and will record audio separately, on different *tracks* on the tape. This means that you can plant multiple microphones in different parts of the shot (for example, one microphone per person, in a panel discussion). Then you can *mix* (adjust the relative levels) of various tracks later when you're editing. On professional shoots, use at least two microphones if possible: one lavaliere and one handheld directional microphone. This allows for more options later in editing to mix in just the right amount of room tone.

TIP ▸ *Before you leave a particular location or camera setup, it's always a good idea to record the sound of the room. This will often be useful later in editing, to smooth over transitions and scene changes in your program. Ask the crew or anyone else present to just be quiet for a moment while you record the sound of the seemingly "silent" space.*

Sidebar: What Sound Looks Like

You will often hear the words "frequency" and "pitch" used interchangeably. For the purposes of this book, we will make the following distinction: "frequency" is the physical measurement; "pitch" is how high or low the vibration sounds to our ears.

Besides the speed (frequency) of the vibration, the other defining feature of a sound is how strong the vibration is. The stronger the vibration, the louder it sounds to us. Physicists and sound geeks use the term "amplitude" to describe this. So, just for the record, *amplitude* is the physical measurement of the strength of the vibration. (And "loudness" or "volume" is how the strength of the vibration is perceived by us humans.)

Over time, waveforms create complex patterns. You will see these complex shapes when you edit sound tracks in Premiere. **Figure 3.13**, for example, from Premiere, shows a recording of a human voice. If you look closely, you can also see individual waves.

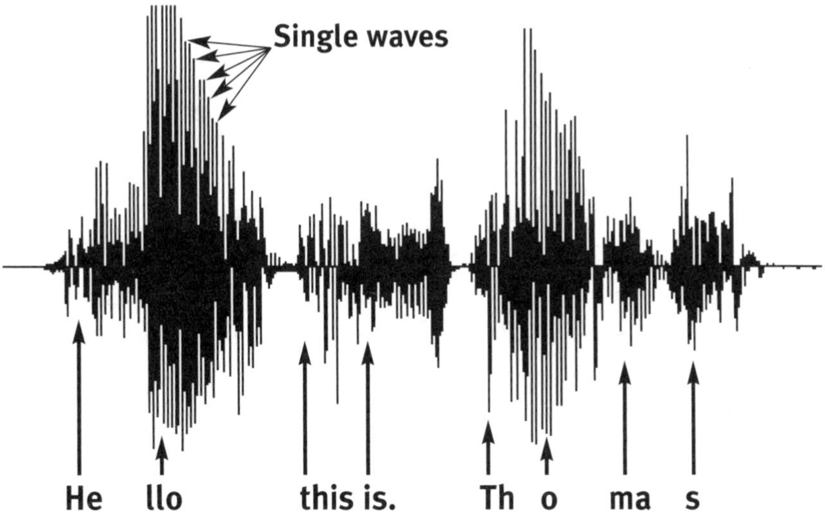

Figure 3.13
This snapshot from Premiere shows a recording of human voice as it looks in waveform.

WEB VIDEO SPOTLIGHT

ON24

ON24 (**www.on24.com**) provides Web video of live events and on-demand Web video of previously recorded events, as well as fully produced and edited corporate Web video presentations (**Figure 3.14**).

In 1999, Patrick J. Kriwanek was the head of the motion picture program at the Academy of Art College in San Francisco and had produced numerous music videos and corporate projects. "One day, several former students approached me to join them at their new dot-com startup company," he recalls. "The startup turned out to be ON24."

Kriwanek describes the first step in ON24's production process. Before the producers start on a project, they discuss the customer's Web video needs in a preproduction meeting. As Kriwanek explains, "We have a checklist similar to what a pilot of a 747 airliner goes through before takeoff. By the time we're done with that list, we know everything that we need to produce the program."

For a live Webcast, an ON24 production team travels to the location of the event to shoot it with Betacam cameras. They use a transmission system from Polycom (**www.polycom.com**) to encode a TV-quality video stream and send it over an ISDN line (a high-speed phone/data line) to the ON24 office in San Francisco. (A second Polycom unit is required to decode the high-quality stream at the San Francisco end.) That signal is then compressed into RealNetworks' RealOne Player and Windows Media Player video streams and sent out to PCs everywhere

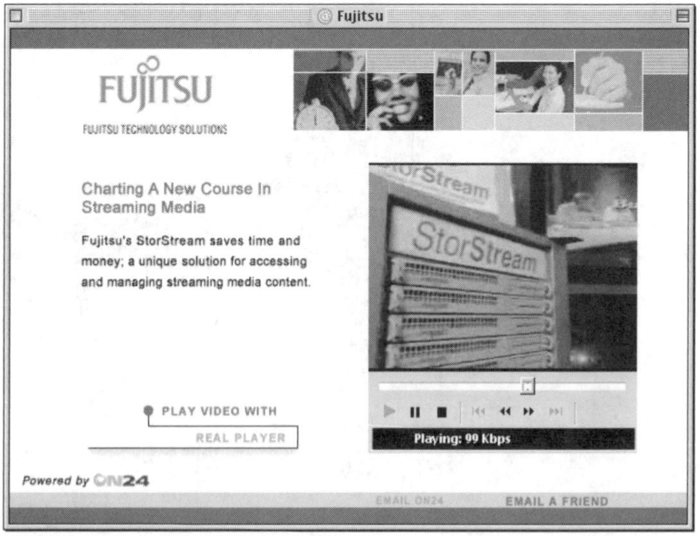

FIGURE 3.14
ON24.com specializes in producing live and on-demand Web video presentations for corporate clients, such as this one for Fujitsu.

from streaming video servers at the ON24 server farm in Sunnyvale, California. If it's a big production, with thousands of Web viewers, ON24 may hire a company like Akamai Technologies (**www.akamai.com**), which maintains a worldwide network of thousands of servers to speed delivery for large streaming media and e-commerce sites.

Kriwanek points out that streaming through corporate firewalls is an ongoing problem: "IT [information technology] people hate streaming coming through the firewall because it takes a completely different skill set to manage it, make it work, balance it—and everyone hates *them* when it doesn't work."

ON24's staff of 50 producers and engineers delivers a major live event almost every day. The professional services team integrates the streaming video into a Web page. Often the Web page includes related graphics and information, such as a PowerPoint presentation, alongside the streaming video. So far, ON24's media player of choice has been either Windows Media Player or RealOne Player—or both. Kriwanek says, "98% of our business and medical clients use one of these two players."

As for tips to budding Web video makers, Kriwanek says: "Don't let the jerky picture fool you; Web video is the most thermonuclear thing since the atomic bomb. It won't be long before the technology is here to make good-looking Web video the prevalent form of media communications."

CHAPTER FOUR

Capturing Capably

Your Web movies are going to be digital movies. No matter what kind of camcorder you're using, the best-shot video in the world isn't going to do you any good unless you can get it off of videotape and onto your hard drive. That process is called *video capture*. Before DV devices were available, this step could be a real adventure. You had to buy a digitizer card, which meant adding extra hardware to your PC or Macintosh; and that card had to be compatible with your existing hardware and software. These cards weren't always plug and play, and the whole process wasn't for the faint of heart. (Of course, this route is still an option if you're using older equipment.) But these days the DV format and FireWire connections make it virtually painless to transfer DV video from camcorder to computer—but doing it efficiently and effectively still requires some patience and practice.

Equipping Your System for Capture

Capturing video is a routine matter—assuming you shot your movie with a DV camera. In that case, the transfer is really just like copying files from one disk to another. If you shot your video with an analog camcorder, you need to digitize it first and then transfer it to your hard drive. Capture cards (also called *digitizer cards*) use their own circuitry to convert the analog video into digital format and send the finished product to your computer.

Before the video reaches your hard drive, however, it must be compressed, since raw video files are too big for most of today's personal computers to process. If you were to use uncompressed video, it would require about 30 MB of storage for every second of video, and your computer would have to process 30 MB of data per second to play it back. Most desktop computers are more comfortable crunching through video at about one-tenth that rate. DV cameras compress the video while they record it; analog capture cards compress the video when they digitize it. But either way, the compression process inevitably degrades video quality. That's why it's so important to shoot the best video possible from the outset.

Choosing Your Gear

No matter what kind of camcorder or video deck you use for your Web video project, you need to connect it to your computer. So the first issue to address is whether your video is in analog or digital format. Let's start with the simplest solution: DV. If you're using a relatively recent Macintosh, you're already set up for DV transfer: Your computer comes with a built-in FireWire port (**Figure 4.1**). If you're using a PC, however, you'll need to add a FireWire port by installing a FireWire PCI card—that is, unless your system came with one already installed. Once you have a FireWire port on your computer, all you need to do is connect the camera with a FireWire cable (also known as an IEEE 1394 or iLink cable). After that, capturing video is as easy as copying files from one hard disk to another (more on this later). If you're using a Mac that was built before 1995, you'll need to install a FireWire card.

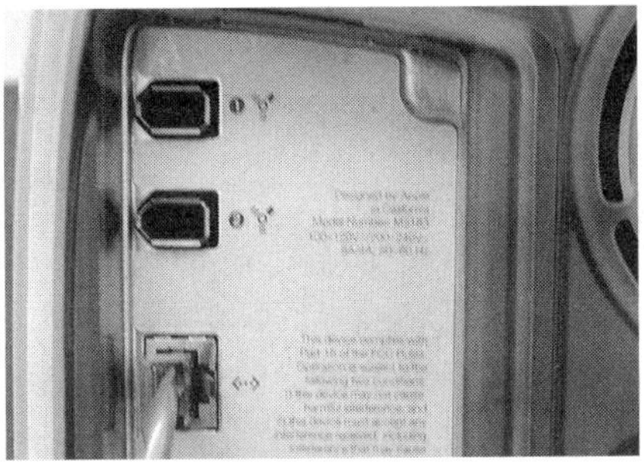

FIGURE 4.1
The two 6-pin FireWire ports on a Macintosh G4 are located on the back, just above the Ethernet port.

Capturing DV: FireWire Cards

The first place to check to find FireWire PCI Cards is Adobe's Web site (`www.adobe.com/products/premiere/hdwr.html`), since it can show you which DV capture cards have been certified for use with Adobe Premiere. There are a lot of them—I last counted 48. But they break down into three main categories, which I call: Basic DV, Basic DV Plus Software, and The Full Nine Yards.

Basic DV

If you have the editing software and all you need is an actual FireWire port, you can get a bare-bones model (with two or three ports) that works on both PC and Macintosh systems. The OrangeLink FireWire 1394 PCI card sells for around $60 (**Figure 4.2**). It's an affordable way to get your computer wired for DV.

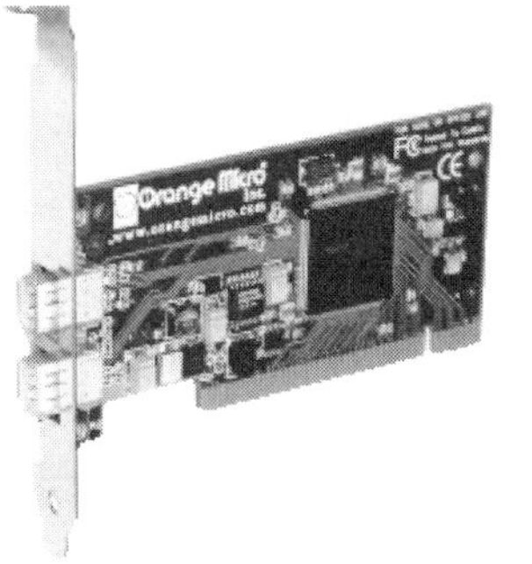

FIGURE 4.2
The OrangeLink FireWire card is an affordable way to get a Mac or PC wired to accept DV.

Basic DV Plus Software

If you also need video editing software, the PYRO PlatinumDV Bundle (around $260) is a good deal. It's a three-port FireWire 1394 PCI card, similar to the OrangeLink card, but it also comes bundled with Premiere and Adobe Photoshop LE—plus a bucket-load of other useful software.

The Whole Nine Yards

If you want to move up a step from just getting yourself FireWire-enabled, you can buy a digitizer card than accepts both DV and analog video. This is a great way to go if you're shooting digital video at the moment but have archival analog footage that you can't live without. The Windows-only Pinnacle DV500 PLUS PCI card (around $600) is one of the least expensive cards that can capture both analog video and DV (**Figure 4.3**). It comes with a *breakout box*, which allows input and output of DV, as well as composite (VHS) video and S-Video It also has extra horsepower to speed up the rendering of certain types of visual effects and comes with Premiere, Adobe Photoshop LE, and a bunch of other useful stuff.

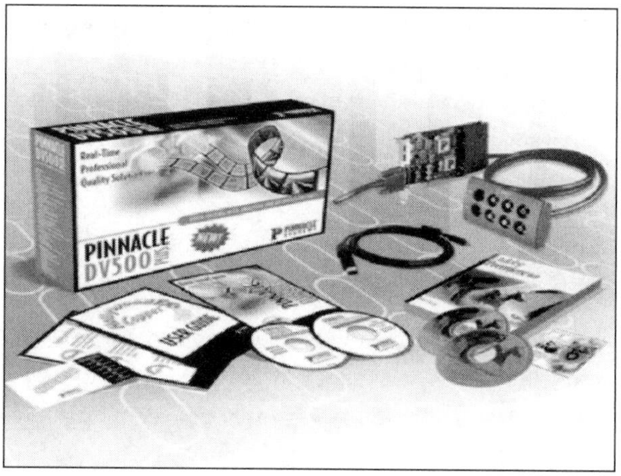

FIGURE 4.3
The Pinnacle DV500 PLUS system includes a breakout box for both DV and analog input and output, as well as a copy of Premiere and lots more software.

If you are using an analog camcorder (either VHS, S-Video, or Betacam), you can choose from one of the following options:

- a video capture card
- an analog-to-digital converter
- an analog-to-FireWire (DV) converter
- an analog-to-USB converter

Capturing Analog Video: Digitizing Cards

The first option is a digitizer card that plugs into an expansion slot on your computer, whether it's a PC or Macintosh. This card converts your video into digital form and compresses it so that your computer can handle the data. These products typically have two parts: a PCI card, which you install in your computer; and a *breakout box* containing the inputs and outputs for VHS, S-Video, and Betacam video sources (**Figure 4.4**).

FIGURE 4.4
The breakout box for the Pinnacle Systems TARGA 3000 analog digitizer card has inputs and outputs for VHS, S-Video, and Betacam video sources.

These analog digitizers tend to cost much more than the FireWire solutions available to DV users. They're also harder to install and operate. But there are two advantages to analog digitizers. First, the compression scheme used by most of these cards captures more color information than the DV format. If you want to produce blue-screen or green-screen chroma key shots meant for compositing with other layers of video (a common technique used on TV weather reports), capturing more color is an important feature. Second, a digitizer card offers more flexibility than FireWire capture does because the data rate on digitizers is adjustable. That means you can choose to either turn down the data rate to save on hard drive space or turn up the data rate to maintain the highest quality image (assuming you've got the room to store a larger file). And some analog digitizers also allow you to select an image size that's anywhere from 160 by 120 pixels up to a full screen.

TIP ▸ *Some analog capture cards allow you to export your video clips in MPEG-2, the format you'll need to work in if you want to create interactive DVDs. These cards also usually have features like real-time transitions and effects.*

TIP ▸ *Premiere version 6.5 and later includes software-based MPEG-2 encoding (Windows only).*

Converting to Digital Before You Transfer

Here's another way to capture analog footage: Convert it to digital and *then* capture it. If your DV camera or deck has analog inputs, typically either composite or S-Video, you can simply connect your analog source (for example, a VHS VCR) to the inputs and press Record on your DV camera or deck. This will make a DV copy that you can then transfer to your computer via a FireWire connection. In case your camera or deck doesn't do this, you might want to buy or rent a converter box that does the same thing. Converter boxes come in two categories: analog-to-

FireWire (DV) converters and professional analog-to-digital converters. The pro boxes can usually convert to and from all types of analog and digital video. They range in price from $1,600 to $8,000. It can save you the cost of buying a capture card or an expensive DV camcorder or deck with the same capabilities. The less expensive boxes (covered here) all require a FireWire input on your computer.

A popular box in this category is the Canopus ADVC-100, with a street price of about $350 (**Figure 4.5**). It converts either a composite or S-Video signal to DV or vice versa. Although you'll get your video into DV format, you won't have all the features you'd get with tape that was shot in DV format originally, such as time-code and full FireWire device control (see "Device Control and Timecode" later in this chapter.)

FIGURE 4.5
The Canopus ADVC-100 converts analog video to DV format digital video and vice versa.

Another, less expensive, product in this same media-converter category is the Dazzle Hollywood DV-Bridge, with a street price of $200 (**Figure 4.6**). It does the same thing the Canopus box does except it comes in a more vertical chassis, designed to sit on your desktop.

FIGURE 4.6
The less expensive Dazzle Hollywood DV-Bridge converter box has a vertical chassis designed to sit on your desktop.

The Formac Studio DV/TV converter (street price about $380) breaks new ground in the converter box category by including a built-in TV and radio tuner that automatically searches for and identifies 125 TV channels and radio stations (**Figure 4.7**). That means you can use it to easily capture TV broadcasts at DV quality. (Without proper permission, however, this violates the copyright owner of the broadcast.)

Figure 4.7
The Formac Studio DV/TV is a converter box that lets you capture TV broadcasts in addition to other analog source video.

Unlocking Video Copy Protection

Let's say you have a little project in which you want to intercut scenes from a recent feature film with scenes from your son's seventh birthday party. You go to the video store and rent a DVD; you hook up the video from the DVD player to the video input of your DV camcorder or converter box. As you start to record, you get a warning message saying that this video is copyrighted material and that you're prevented from making a copy. This is Macrovision at work: The movie industry's copy-protection technology is present on most DV devices. Enter Miglia Technology's Director's Cut 'Take 2', with a street price of $350 (**Figure 4.8**). This is a DV converter box that does not have any Macrovision protection, so you can use it to copy any commercially available DVD or videocassette. (Of course, just because you can, doesn't mean that you should. With a few exceptions, if you're using content that was created by someone else, you need to get a license, in writing, to use it legally.) The Director's Cut also has some professional features like a quarter-inch jack, volume adjustment for headphones, and an extra S-Video–out port for monitoring the video signal being sent to the VCR on a TV.

Figure 4.8
Miglia Technology's Director's Cut 'Take 2' is a DV converter box with professional features.

The Analog-to-USB Option

Although the frame size will be smaller than the other capture options, there is a very inexpensive device called the USBG-V1 from USB Gear (street price is around $60) (**Figure 4.9**). This small converter cable plugs into the USB port of your computer and converts in only one direction—from composite or S-video to digital. This type of USB converter is a good choice for live streaming from a camera because it doesn't compress the signal as much as DV converters do.

Figure 4.9
The very inexpensive USBG-V1 converter comes with its own Windows and Macintosh software.

Other Hardware You Might Need

Once you get your video onto your hard drive the fun starts—you get to edit and publish your movie for the world to see. Here are a few other pieces of hardware that make the process easier and more convenient.

Making It Easier

First, treat yourself to a lot of *RAM* (random access memory). It isn't expensive, it is easy to install, and with it, your computer can do a lot more. You'll be able to have more software open at once and your software will work more efficiently. Second, a device-controllable *video deck*, such as a MiniDV deck, is a good thing to have. You can use it as a video source (in addition to your camcorder) and you can use it to create videotapes of your edited movies. And if you do a lot of video editing, you'll also need to have a *video monitor or a television* attached to your video deck or camcorder, so that you can see your movies playing back at their full frame size and frame rate when you play them back from tape. If you playback your movies on the computer exclusively, you're only going to see them playing back in Premiere's small windows (usually 320 x 240 pixels) at a low resolution. What you're seeing is a proxy for the real thing. Depending on the horsepower of your computer's processor, the image on the computer screen will have a reduced frame rate and resolution.

Finding the Right Hard Drive

Digital video takes up lots of hard drive space. To store 5 minutes of DV video, you'll need about 1 GB of storage. To store 1 hour of DV video, you'd need about 13 GB of space. If you're shooting a dramatized movie with actors, the rule of thumb is that you will shoot four times as much footage as you'll end up using in your final program. By that measure, if you are making an hour-long program, you'll need 52 GB (4 times 13 GB) of storage to edit it. And documentaries have a much higher shooting ratio, typically 10:1. So a 1-hour documentary would require 130 GB to be properly edited.

You don't just need lots of storage space; you also need drives that can transfer at least 5 MB of data per second—which is fast, but doesn't require you to buy the fastest drives around. If you're going shopping for storage specifically for DV files, look for a drive with any of these three acronyms on the box: IDE, ATA, or UltraDMA, which all refer to the same hard drive standard (IDE/ATA). For DV editing, I recommend a 7200 RPM (not 5400 RPM) model. And if you are buying an external FireWire hard drive, make sure it has the Oxford 911 bridge chip for improved performance. If the price is too good to be true, then it is probably missing one of these two features.

TIP ▸ *For DV and DVCam footage, IDE/ATA drives are generally sufficient, but high-speed analog digitizer capture cards and codecs may require SCSI hard drives (a different hard drive standard), which are faster but much more expensive.*

Finally, you want to start with drives that are completely empty, if possible. Heavily used hard drives become fragmented over time as information is deleted and rewritten on the drive's surface. In addition to causing wear and tear on your hard drive, fragmented video files play back poorly, causing skips and interruptions in your movie.

There are three ways to defragment a hard drive so that it will be ready for video capture. The first is to empty the disk completely and then initialize it before capturing to it. That means backing up the data on the drive and either deleting files or erasing the entire disk. That way, as a new file is captured, it will write a contiguous (nonfragmented) file. The second is to copy the fragmented files to a separate disk. Delete or erase the originals. Then copy all the files back to the now empty original disk. The computer will rewrite the files as contiguous files. And last, you can use a software utility, such as Norton Speed Disk, that rewrites the fragmented files on your hard disk as contiguous files.

TIP ▸ *Mac OS 9 users: Make sure to turn off unnecessary system extensions before you begin to capture video; that will free up your computer's processing power for the task at hand.*

Capture While You Shoot?

Are you sick and tired of the tedium of capturing many hours of footage into the computer? There are new devices that can eliminate the capturing stage of DV video production (or, at least, let you capture while you shoot). These boxes can record directly from your digital camcorder via IEEE-1394 (FireWire, i.Link) to hard disk without the need for a computer. The clips are stored as standard DV files. When you are ready to edit, your clips are immediately available to your editing system (such as Adobe Premiere). This method offers some obvious advantages: it can save you hours of capturing time since the clips are immediately on a hard disk, and a backup tape copy can be recorded in the camera at the same time. This eliminates a lot of wear and tear on the tape and capturing camcorder or deck. In addition, these devices free you from the length of one video cassette per shot.

The Sony DSR-DU1 (**Figure 4.10**) can record up to three hours of DV or DVCAM video. With an adaptor, the unit can attach directly to the backs of many professional Sony camcorders. It also offers loop recording, minimizing the chances of missing a shot.

The FireStore device (**Figure 4.11**) can connect up to 8 external FireWire hard disks. (Since a single 40 GB FireWire drive can store approximately 3 hours of DV video, you could, in theory, shoot a single shot that lasted almost 24 hours! Good for shooting Guinness Book of World Records record-breaking attempts, such as "most skips on a skipping rope in 24 hours.")

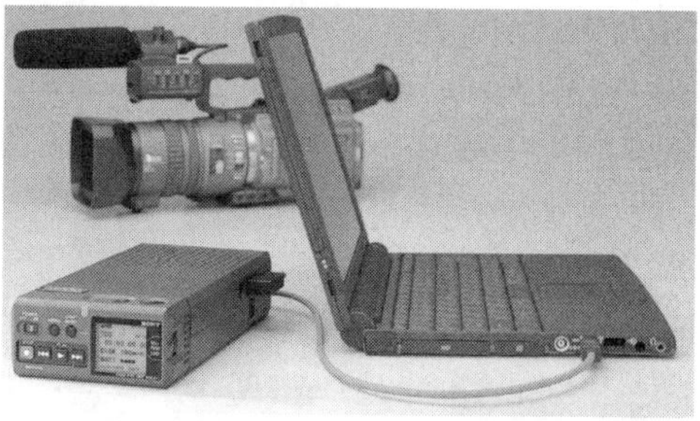

Figure 4.10
The Sony DSR-DU1 can add versatility to your production process.

Figure 4.11
The FireStore device captures your footage to external hard disks while you shoot it.

Capturing Video with Premiere

Now that you're got the right gear, you're ready to capture your video into Premiere. Here's a guided tour of the capture process using a DV video source. If you're using an analog video source and a digitizer card, the process will be similar, though some of the settings will, of course, be different. Why focus on DV? Two reasons. First, it's a standard, so it gives us a common baseline for our discussion. And second, it should be quite clear to you by now that DV is far simpler to use as a video source than video from older analog equipment, and it offers fantastic quality. That means that you can focus on making the capture process efficient and effective, rather than wasting your time trying to get it to work at all.

Installing Premiere

If you don't already have Adobe Premiere 6.5, you can install the free 30-day tryout version of Premiere 6.0 that is included with this book's CD-ROM. (As mentioned earlier, at the time of this writing, there is no tryout version of Premiere 6.5 available.)

1. Insert this book's CD into your computer's CD-ROM drive.
2. Double-click the Install Premiere 6.0 Tryout icon.
3. Click Install to install the Easy Install, which includes Adobe Premiere 6.0, Cleaner 5 Web Export, and Real Media Export Plug-ins. In Windows, this option will also install QuickTime 4.0.
4. When prompted, click OK to confirm that you would like the Cleaner and Real Media export files installed. (Windows users: When prompted, click OK to confirm the installation of the Windows Media export files and QuickTime 4.0.)
5. If you are installing Premiere on a Macintosh computer that doesn't have QuickTime (or if you are running Windows and would like to upgrade to QuickTime 5.0), you should download it from Apple's Web site (`www.apple.com/quicktime`). See "Installing the Media Players" in Chapter 1 for instructions on how to install QuickTime.

When you launch Premiere, you will be asked to choose between two types of *workspaces*, or window settings. Click the "Select A/B Editing" button to load Premiere's Load Project Settings window. This is where you can adjust Premiere to work with specific types of video and audio. (To reach this window once Premiere is already open, choose File > New Project.)

TIP ▸ *If you get an error message telling you that you don't have enough memory to open Premiere, buy yourself some more RAM. If you're doing any sort of video editing, you'll waste too much time trying to come up with workarounds for a RAM-starved machine.*

Whenever you open Premiere without opening a specific Premiere project file, you are presented with Premiere's Load Project Settings window (**Figure 4.12**). This is Premiere's way of saying, "I need to know what kind of video and audio you're feeding me and what kind of video and audio output you would like to create."

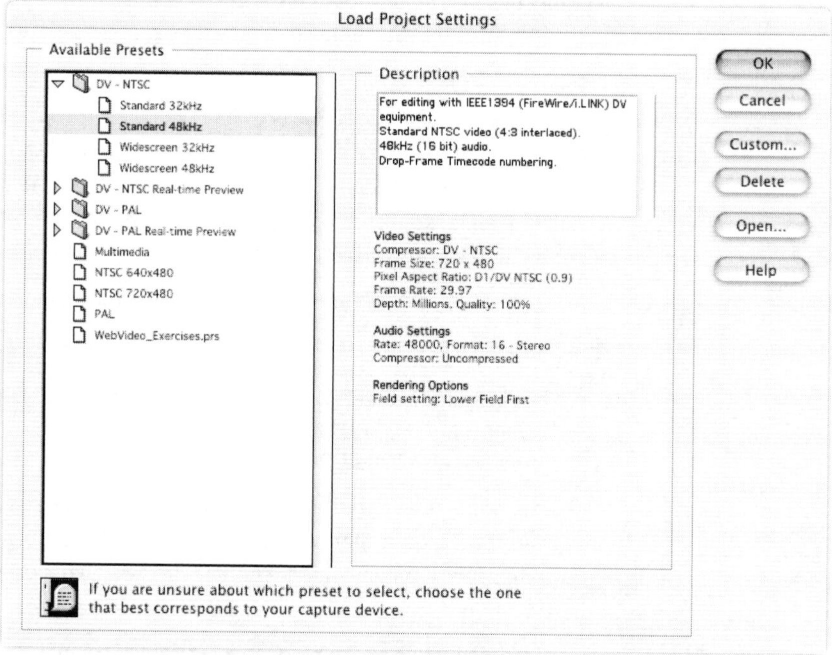

FIGURE 4.12
Premiere's Load Project Settings window allows you to set your audio and video capture settings.

On the left side of the screen is a list of Available Presets. These are different settings Adobe has created for popular combinations of video formats and capture cards. The DV-NTSC settings at the top of the list are specifically for DV equipment with FireWire connections. If you're using a different capture device, look at the documentation that came with your hardware for guidance as to your card's specific settings and options.

1. Select the DV-NTSC Standard 48kHz setting if you are in a country that uses the NTSC television standard. (NTSC countries include the USA, Canada and Japan.) Select the DV-PAL Standard 48kHz setting if you are in a country that uses the PAL television standard. This tells Premiere that you have a DV camera or deck attached via a FireWire cable, and that your desired output is DV footage via the same FireWire cable.

2. Click OK to open Premiere's three main windows: the Project window, the Monitor window, and the Timeline window. These are your workspaces when editing in Premiere; we'll explore them in detail in Chapter 5.

3. Choose Preferences > Scratch Disks and Device Control from the Edit menu to open the Scratch Disks and Device Control panel of the Preferences dialog box (**Figure 4.13**).

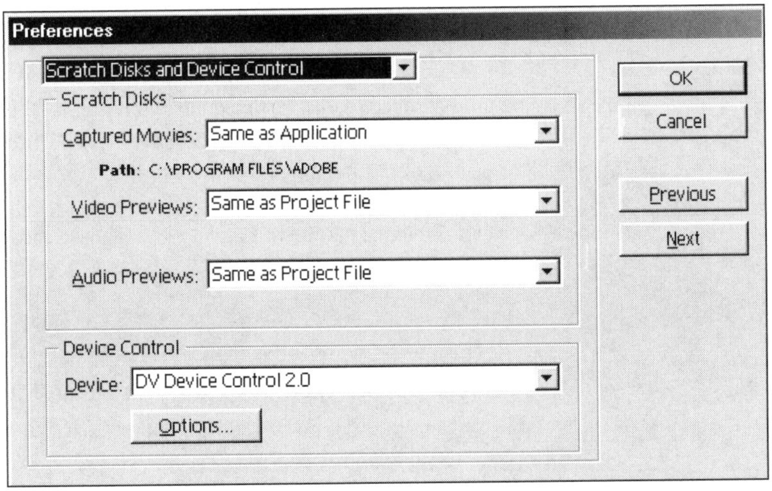

FIGURE 4.13
Premiere's Scratch Disks and Device Control panel allows you to select the hard drive that Premiere will use to save your captured files.

4. From the Captured Movies pop-up menu, choose the hard disk that you'll be using for capturing and editing.

Device Control and Timecode

Device control refers to controlling a video deck from within Premiere, or any other editing software, when capturing clips. *Timecode* is a system of using unique numbers to identify each frame of video, expressed in hours, minutes, seconds, and frames.

Using device control has the following advantages:

- You can control the tape deck and view its source video directly from Premiere instead of switching between Premiere and manual tape controls.
- You can use the Movie Capture window or Batch Capture window to create a batch list of *In Points* (starting timecode) and *Out Points* (ending timecode) for each clip, and then record all clips in the list automatically.
- You can capture the timecode that exists on the tape so that Premiere uses it during editing. (Not only does this help you locate shots on your source tapes, but it's also a necessary step for creating edit decision lists (EDLs) for moving your project to a different type of video editing system, or to an automated tape-to-tape editing session at a professional post-production facility.)

DV equipment has timecode and device control built in as a standard feature. To use device control with other types of capture cards, you'll need a frame-accurate tape deck or camcorder that supports external device control, a cable that connects the deck to your computer, a Premiere-compatible plug-in that lets you control the tape deck directly from Premiere, and a source videotape recorded with timecode.

5. Click the Options buttons under the Device pop-up menu to open the DV Device Control Options window (**Figure 4.14**). If the Options button is not available, either your DV device is not connected to your computer or you didn't choose the DV preset as described in Step 1.

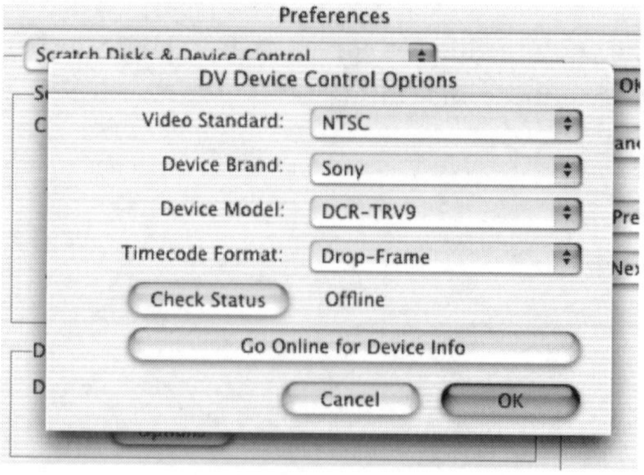

FIGURE 4.14 Premiere's DV Device Control Options window allows you to select the right settings to ensure that device control works properly.

6. Using the pop-up menus in the Device Control Options dialog box, choose the appropriate video standard, device brand, device model, and timecode format for your deck or camcorder. NTSC is the video standard used in North America; most consumer DV equipment records in Drop-Frame timecode mode.

7. Close this window and close the Preferences window.

8. Choose Capture > Movie Capture from the File menu. This opens the Movie Capture window, which contains a video screen on the left and two tabbed panes on the right: the Logging tab and the Settings tab (**Figure 4.15**). A row of playback control buttons will appear underneath the video screen to provide device control. If your settings are right, your connections are proper, and your camera is playing a tape, you will see the live video signal from your video source playing in this Movie Capture window.

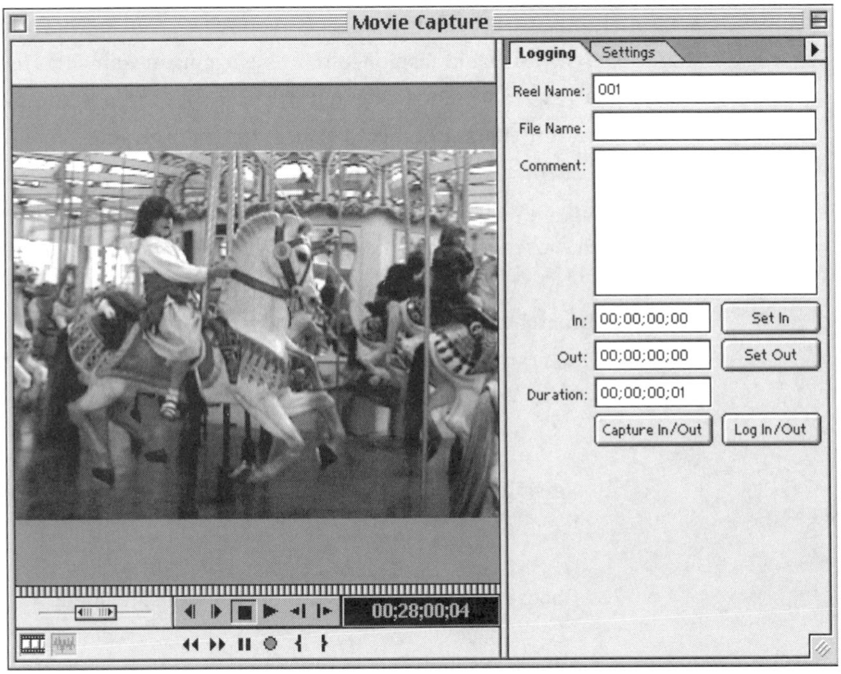

FIGURE 4.15
Premiere's Movie Capture window lets you control the capture process.

9. Click the Settings tab to confirm or change the DV setting preset that you chose in Step 1, as well as both the capture location and the device control settings you chose in Steps 4 and 6.

10. Use the playback control buttons underneath the video screen to locate a part of the tape you'd like to capture.

11. Select a specific section of the tape to capture using the Set In and Set Out buttons in the Logging tab. Then click Capture In/Out to have Premiere automatically start recording to the hard disk you've chosen as a scratch disk.

TIP ▸ *If you do not have Device Control, press Play on your source video camcorder or deck. Click the red Capture button once. Premiere will start recording to the hard disk you've chosen.*

Logging and Batch Capturing

Premiere, like most desktop video editing systems, has sophisticated features for keeping track of all of the footage you're using for a given project. This usually starts with an old-fashioned process: logging in your shots by looking at everything you've got and annotating it. If you have a lot of footage to capture, *logging* (the process of making of record of all of the shots on your camera tapes) becomes a critical first step in editing your program. It forces you to make decisions about what you will leave in and what you will take out. Premiere lets you to annotate each shot thoroughly, including its timecode and any comments, labels, or rating you'd like to add. Then you can select which shots you want Premiere to automatically batch capture. For logging and batch capturing to work, Premiere requires frame-accurate timecode and device control. You get both with DV.

Logging

1. Rewind your source tape to the beginning, or to wherever you want to start logging it.

2. Choose Capture > Movie Capture from the File menu.

3. Fill out the information in the first three fields of the Logging tab on the right side of the Movie Capture window.

   REEL NAME: This is a unique name or number for each source tape. When you batch capture, or when you need to recapture a particular shot, you will have to know which *reel* (tape) it came from. Premiere will ask you to "Insert Reel

#01," for example. Premiere is kind of dumb this way: One tape looks like any other tape to Premiere. That's why proper tape naming and labeling is so important. (See the "Timecode and Labeling" tip below.)

File Name: Find a naming system that works for you stick with it. In general, you want to use short root names, and then add extra info in the remaining space. When logging consumer DV footage that starts with hour 00 (See the "Timecode and Labeling" tip below), I like to include the reel number at the beginning of every filename. For example, in the filename "DE02MUS_WA01," DE02 means "demo reel #2," MUS means "museum shot" and WA1 means "wide angle shot # 1."

Comment: This handy field of information will stay with this log entry (and with the corresponding captured clip) no matter how you use it in Premiere. I like to use this field to rate shots as I see them for the first time after shooting. (First impressions are always the most accurate.) For example, I will rate clips on a scale from 1 to 10, with 10 being best. Later, in Premiere's Project window, I just click the top of the Comment column to sort by my 'rating' number. (Be sure to use two-digit numbers (such as 01, 02, or 03 so that they sort properly.)

4. Find the beginning of the first shot you want to log using the playback control buttons, and click the Set In button to mark it.

5. Find the end of the first shot you want to log using the playback control buttons, and then click the Set Out button.

6. Click the Log In/Out button. Premiere will ask you for a File Name and a Log Comment. If you have already filled in this information, just click OK to confirm it. Premiere automatically opens a new Batch Capture window. This is a text file; it's a table that includes the Reel Name, In Point, Out Point, Duration, File Name, Comments, and Capture Settings for each shot that you log.

7. Repeat Steps 4 through 6 until you have logged the whole tape. Notice that Premiere automatically increments the names of clip to be captured. For example, once you log a clip labeled "DE02MUS_WA08," Premiere assumes the next clip is to be labeled "DE02MUS_WA09." Be sure to choose File > Save to save and back up this Batch Capture Log; it is now a valuable database of the shots on your camera tape(s).

Batch Capturing

The beauty of logging tapes in Premiere is that once you've done it, you can use the Batch Capture logs you've created to automatically capture just the clips that you need for your current project.

1. Open the Batch Capture log you created in the last steps.

2. On the left side of the Batch Capture log, click the field just to the left of the Reel Name of the first clip you would like to capture so that a black diamond appears next to it. The black diamond indicates that this is a clip you would like to capture. Repeat this process for every clip in the list you want to capture (**Figure 4.16**). An empty spot means the clip will be ignored. A check mark means the clip has been captured.

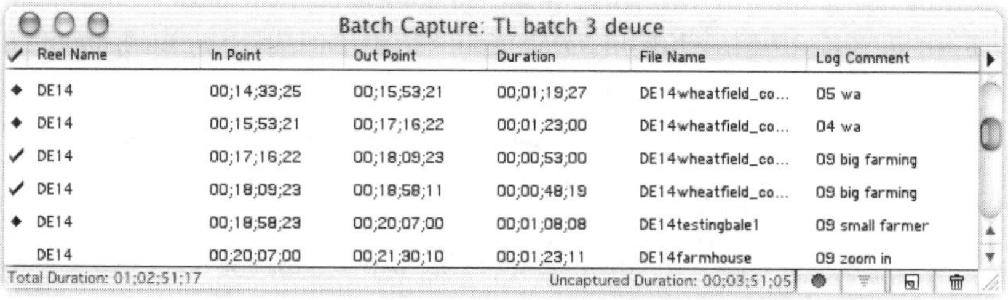
Batch Capture: TL batch 3 deuce
Reel Name | In Point | Out Point | Duration | File Name | Log Comment
DE14 | 00;14;33;25 | 00;15;53;21 | 00;01;19;27 | DE14wheatfield_co... | 05 wa
DE14 | 00;15;53;21 | 00;17;16;22 | 00;01;23;00 | DE14wheatfield_co... | 04 wa
DE14 | 00;17;16;22 | 00;18;09;23 | 00;00;53;00 | DE14wheatfield_co... | 09 big farming
DE14 | 00;18;09;23 | 00;18;58;11 | 00;00;48;19 | DE14wheatfield_co... | 09 big farming
DE14 | 00;18;58;23 | 00;20;07;00 | 00;01;08;08 | DE14testingbale1 | 09 small farmer
DE14 | 00;20;07;00 | 00;21;30;10 | 00;01;23;11 | DE14farmhouse | 09 zoom in
Total Duration: 01;02;51;17
Uncaptured Duration: 00;03;51;05

FIGURE 4.16
Batch lists are text logs of the shots on your videotape. They allow you to automatically capture any shots you select, as indicated by the black diamonds along the left-hand side of the list.

3. Click the red capture button at the bottom of the Batch Capture window. Premiere asks you to insert the proper source reel (tape) into your deck or camcorder. Insert the proper tape and click OK. Premiere will wind the tape to the appropriate spot and capture for every shot marked with a black diamond. When it is finished, it puts a check mark next to the names of the captured clips and asks for the next tape.

4. Continue inserting the proper tapes and clicking OK until all of the desired shots have been captured.

TIP ▸ *Professional video cameras allow you to set a different timecode hour number for each tape—that way you can tell them apart while editing. (You'll know instantly which tape a shot came from by looking at its timecode.) Consumer-level DV cameras always write timecode starting with hour zero. This means that the first two digits of the timecode on every tape recorded with a consumer DV camera starts out with 00. So, to tell them apart, it's a very good idea to label each tape immediately with a unique name and then follow that system when you name captured clips from that tape. And make sure you label the actual videocassette (not just the box) because cassettes can get lost or separated from their boxes.*

TIP ▸ *Another bonus of using timecode and device control is that (if your hardware allows it) you can easily recapture footage at different resolutions. For example, you first capture your whole batch list at a low resolution (320 by 240, 15 frames per second) and edit your whole program with those small files, saving a lot of hard drive space and time (not waiting for rendering). Then, when all of your edit decisions are final, throw out the low-res files and recapture only the clips you're actually using in your program at the full-screen, full-motion resolution for final output.*

Troubleshooting Capture Problems

- **No video, no audio:** If you don't see any video in the Movie Capture window or hear any audio in your captured movies, make sure you've entered in the proper capture settings and that the cables are attached correctly.

- **Dropped frames:** Most video editing/capturing software (including Premiere) has a preference setting that alerts you when a frame is dropped. This means that some data was lost during capture. Likely culprits are a slow processor and/or slow or a fragmented hard disk. (Make sure you have the proper scratch disk selected.) If the problem persists on a Mac, try allocating more RAM to Premiere. (Sorry, but Windows doesn't allow this.)

- **Video looks fuzzy and jerky on the computer screen:** There's nothing actually wrong with your movie. Because older or slower desktop computers don't have the processing power to fully decompress digital video, if you are using a DV/FireWire setting, the image you see on the computer screen is just a proxy for the real image, which is meant to be shown on a TV screen from a videotape. That's why it looks so bad. To see the full quality of a DV signal, connect a TV or video monitor to the composite or S-Video outputs of the DV deck or camcorder.

- **Premiere doesn't capture the first 60 seconds of footage:** The mechanics of today's video camcorders make the first 60 seconds and last 60 seconds of a videotape cassette susceptible to stretching. When this happens, it makes it difficult for a camcorder or video deck to play back the image and the timecode on that portion of the tape. Solution? Try capturing manually: Play the tape, then push Premiere's red record button. And next time, don't use the first 60 seconds or last 60 seconds of tape for any important shot.

TIP ▸ *Don't use videocassettes over 60 minutes in length—manufacturers make them physically thinner so that they can fit more tape into the same size cassette. Because they're thinner, longer tapes are more likely to stretch.*

- **Logging tapes and batch capturing is boring and time consuming.** If you're logging thousands of very short shots, this process can get tedious, and yes, it can wear out the delicate mechanics of your camcorder. Better idea: Buy a lot more hard disk space and capture the footage in larger time chunks. Then use Premiere's marking feature described in the next chapter to label the short shots and sections.

- **What's with the file size limitations?:** For those of you running older applications or system software, be warned: If you capture 10 minutes or more of DV footage (3.6 MB per second), you'll quickly bump up against file size limitations imposed by parts of some operating systems (such as Windows and the Mac OS) and media player formats (such as QuickTime or Video for Windows)—usually a maximum of 2 GB. The bottom line: Most modern video editing software and media players have workarounds for this problem. They link together 2 GB files in the background to ensure that long video files will play back seamlessly. For more on the subject, go to: `http://www.adobe.com:80/support/techdocs/100d2.htm`.

Fixing a "Missing Time Code" Error

One of the most common error messages you're likely to get while doing a batch capture with Premiere is the Missing Time Code error. Premiere is telling you that there are breaks in the timecode of your source videotape.

Normally, timecode gets recorded to the DV videotape in a sequential manner, using the hours:minutes:seconds:frames system (**Figure 4.17**). For example, "00:45:30:15" indicates that the current frame is 45 minutes and 30 seconds, and 15 frames from the start of the tape. This way, each frame gets a unique frame number.

Sometimes, though, this timecode isn't continuous, which triggers Premiere's Missing Time Code notification and causes your batch capture process to fail. Here's how that scenario usually goes: You're shooting your movie. You just got a great shot, and before moving on to shooting the next scene, you decide to play back the last take just to make sure you got what you need. So you set your DV camera to VTR mode and rewind the tape. Then you play the tape and watch the scene. The tape plays past the last recorded frame and into an unrecorded (virgin) section of the tape. Then you stop the camera. When you restart the camera in Record mode, the camera (because it's in a virgin section of the tape) starts recording timecode from 00:00:00:00 again. This creates a break in the continuous timecode numbering (**Figure 4.18**). When Premiere hits that blank spot on the tape, it will stop and give you an error message. Or it might find duplicate timecode numbers on the tape and get confused. Either way, batch capture won't work.

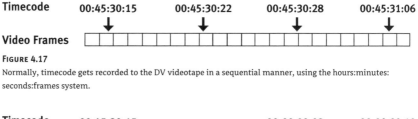

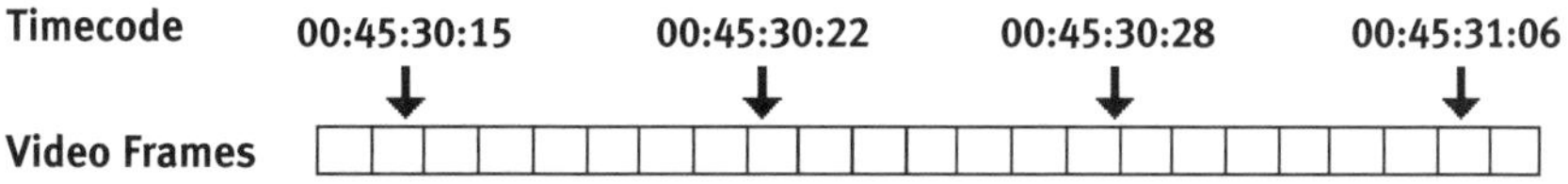

Figure 4.17

Normally, timecode gets recorded to the DV videotape in a sequential manner, using the hours:minutes: seconds:frames system.

Figure 4.18

If you play the tape past the last recorded frame and then start recording again, you will create a blank (unrecorded) spot.

continued ›

Fixing a "Missing Time Code" Error › *continued*

Here are three ways to avoid this problem:

Solution 1: After you shoot a scene, count to five before you stop the camera. This gives you a 5-second landing pad when you stop the camera after playing back the last shot. It ensures that there are plenty of frames recorded with timecode for the camera to detect when you start shooting again with the same tape. (This is what your camera does automatically when you keep it in Record mode: When you press Record, the camera backs up the tape one frame and starts recording using the timecode from the last recorded frame, plus one frame.)

Solution 2: Unpack your brand-new DV tape, insert it in the camera, and press Record (in either VTR mode or camera mode with the lens cap on). Go to lunch. An hour or so later, the whole tape will be time-coded from end to end and will be ready to use. Rewind the tape and use it as you would a new tape. Your camera will not re-record DV timecode if it is already present on the tape. There will be no time-code gaps, and batch capturing will work every time.

Solution 3: To fix a tape with multiple timecode breaks on it already, copy the tape to a second DV tape using the FireWire cable. This will write a new set of continuous timecode to the new copy, but it won't fix any visual gaps left by shooting gaps on the original tape (**Figure 4.19**). This solution requires two DV devices (either a deck or a camera), one being a source device and the other a record device.

Figure 4.19

When you make a copy of the tape to a second DV tape using the FireWire cable, a new set of continuous time-code will be included on the new copy, making it possible to use Premiere's batch capture feature.

WEB VIDEO SPOTLIGHT

The New Arrival

Amy Talkington's film *The New Arrival* is the world's first immersive movie (**http://atomfilms.shockwave.com/af/content/atom_809**). An immersive movie lets you navigate through a scene from any angle. While the movie is playing, you can pan left and right, zoom in and out, and choose where you want to look. Take some time right now and go watch it (**Figure 4.20**). This Web Video Spotlight will make a lot more sense if you do. (If you keep getting a message telling you to install RealPlayer, even though you already have, try to update your RealPlayer with the BeHere plug-in by opening up RealPlayer, going to View > Preferences, and clicking on Upgrade.)

Until March 2000, Amy Talkington was a traditional filmmaker with little interest in new media and the Web. Then, AtomFilms approached her to make a film using a new technology: BeHere's 360-degree camera. She jumped at the opportunity, and *The New Arrival*, the world's first 360-degree dramatized film, was born. As Talkington puts it, "This technology really explodes everything about traditional filmmaking, which is based on editing linear stories with a specific frame."

When you make a movie like this, you have to anticipate every direction the audience may choose to view from. The BeHere camera has a special circular lens with a built-in mirror (like those on some department store security cameras) that records a doughnut-like circular image. "Interactive movies like this are really a medium distinct from traditional film or video," says Talkington. "It's like the difference between painting and sculpture: A sculptor has to anticipate that his audience may view his

FIGURE 4.20 Amy Talkington's film *The New Arrival* is the world's first *immersive* movie, one that lets you view the action from any angle.

work from any angle. In making this movie, we did very careful choreography with the actors, so that no matter where the audience chose to look, there would be something interesting to see."

Talkington says, "One thing that will emerge from this language of immersive movie making is the idea that there is no one way to watch a movie...it invites repeated viewings. I hope that new Web video producers will watch *The New Arrival* and be inspired to try out this new interactive medium."

You can learn more about the making of the film at:

`www.cantinapictures.net`

and

`www.amytalkington.com`.

CHAPTER FIVE

Editing Effectively

Desktop digital editing offers you an incredible array of features producing exciting video. Avoid most of them. When you're editing for the Web, simplicity is truly a virtue. To make sure that your movie's going to be viewable over the Web, avoid too many cuts, fancy transitions, or dancing titles. Focus your attention and creativity on using the phenomenal tools at your fingertips to serve the old-fashioned virtues of telling a good story well. In this chapter—only a brief introduction to Adobe Premiere—you'll learn how to set up a project, edit clips, create a layered soundtrack, and add titles. You are going to learn these skills by creating a 30-second Web commercial using clips from the accompanying CD. By the time you're done, you'll have a movie that's ready to compress and optimize for the Web—your tasks in the next chapter.

Getting Ready to Edit

Before you can make your movie, you need to set yourself up to work productively. That means making sure that Premiere's installed, that you know the basics of editing (and I mean the absolute basics), and that you've got the big picture in mind—or rather, the small picture. By that I mean that you need an overall sense of how best to use Premiere to create movies that are going to look good on the Web.

We'll get to the step-by-step instructions in a moment, but the following editing tips will help you make your movies look as good as possible on the Web:

- Avoid Elaborate Transitions

  Transitions like *cross-dissolves* (in which every pixel in the frame changes with every frame of video for the duration of the transition) are the worst visual effect for Web video because they require so much compression muscle (although we use them in this chapter for learning purposes and because they're what our movie needs). Try to use hard cuts and simple wipes instead wherever possible.

See for yourself. In the Examples folder on the CD, you'll find a movie called escape_cuts_only.mov that has no transitions, just cuts. When you follow the compression exercises in Chapter 6, you can use this movie instead of escape.mov to see the difference that transitions (or lack thereof) can make to post-compression quality.

- Avoid Frequent Cuts Between Scenes

  The more frequent the changes between shots in your movie, the larger the file size and data rate of the movie will be. That means that your movie will have to be compressed more drastically to play over the Web, which will degrade its quality that much further.

In the Examples folder on the CD, you'll find two movies, both compressed for the Web: no_cuts.mov (with one long shot) and frequent_cuts.mov (with many cuts).

- Know That Shots with Fine Detail Will Change

  Don't worry about that dandruff on your interview subject's shoulder—in most Web movies, the image will be so compressed that no one will see it anyway.

Also in the Examples folder, you'll find two movies with different degrees of detail: flat.mov (with a simple background) and details.mov (constantly moving background).

- Look for Shots with Simple, Static Backgrounds

  Choose the take that has a plain, solid-colored background over the take with the ornate wallpaper or the trees swaying in the wind.

- Ignore Title-Safe and Action-Safe Areas

  On television sets, the outside edges of the image are always cut off a bit, so video professionals created *title-safe* and *action-safe* areas to make sure that nothing important in the image was cut off. Web video shows every pixel in the frame, so you can run your images all the way to the edge.

Look in the Examples folder to view titling.mov, a movie that shows titles running to the edge of the frame, as well as those confined within the safe zones.

- When It Comes to Image Size, the Web Is Not TV

  Until now, television images have always been composed in a rectangle that is slightly wider than it is tall. Web video can be any size and shape. Be creative (**Figure 5.1**).

FIGURE 5.1 Think outside the box: Here's an example of a nontraditional-size movie that you could only make for the Web. (Image courtesy of Team Banzai Media Group.)

In the Examples folder on the CD, you'll find two movies of varying sizes: wide.mov (which is short and wide) and tall.mov (which is—you guessed it—tall and skinny).

TIP ▸ *There are two ways to make tall or wide movies in Premiere: (1) You can distort (squeeze or stretch) your movie: Go to Project > Project Settings > Video, make sure the 4:3 Aspect box is unchecked, and type in any dimensions you like for your movie; or (2) you can use cropping to create wide or tall movies without distorting them (see the section of Chapter 6 called "Export Movie Settings: Special Processing").*

Installing the CD files

Before you begin editing, you need to do two things. First, you'll need to make sure you have Adobe Premiere installed (If you haven't done this yet, see the Chapter 4 sidebar, "Installing Premiere"). Second, you'll need to copy the video clips, audio clips, and a settings file from this book's CD to your hard drive so that you'll have some material to work with.

Here's how to install the footage on the accompanying CD:

1. Insert this book's CD into your computer's CD-ROM drive.
2. Copy the Chapter5_Editing folder on the CD to your computer's hard drive.
3. Eject the CD from the computer. (This prevents Premiere from attempting to play back, or link to, the files on the CD.)
4. In the Chapter 5_Editing folder that you just copied to your hard drive, locate the WebVideo_Exercises preset file, located inside the Premiere_Presest folder.
5. Copy the WebVideo_Exercises preset file to the Settings folder (**Figure 5.2**) inside the Adobe Premiere folder on your hard disk.

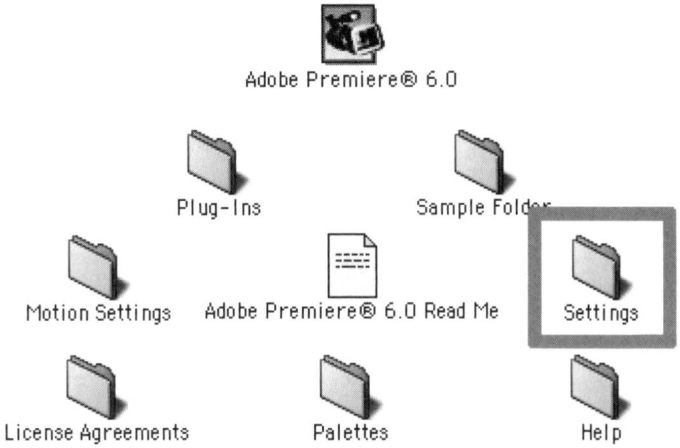

Figure 5.2
You'll find Premiere's Settings folder located in the same folder or directory as the Premiere application or .exe file.

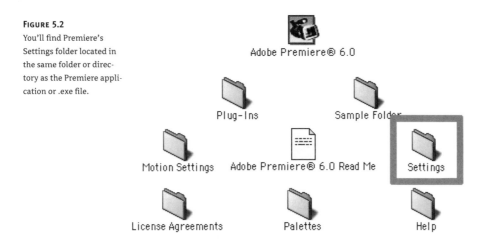

Getting Started in Premiere

Make sure you've installed the WebVideo_Exercises preset file to the Adobe Premiere folder on your hard disk, as described above.

1. Double-click the Premiere icon to open Premiere, or launch it from the Start menu in Windows.

2. In Premiere's Load Project Settings window, click the WebVideo_Exercises preset in the list of Available Presets on the left side, then click OK. (If you don't see the WebVideo preset on the list, it's because you didn't copy it from the CD to the Settings folder inside the Adobe Premiere folder.) Once you select the preset, Premiere's Project, Monitor, and Timeline windows will open.

TIP ▸ *If you want to use footage that you recently captured instead of what's on the CD, you must use the same project settings that you used when you were capturing that footage. For example, if you captured video using the "DV-NTSC Standard 48kHz" setting, choose that same preset setting from the list on the left and then import your footage.*

Premiere's Three Windows

The Project, Monitor, and Timeline windows are where you'll spend all of your time in Premiere. The Project window is where you collect all of the files and clips you'll use in your movie. The Monitor window is where you actually view your movie in progress. And the Timeline is where you arrange your movie clips in the proper sequence. You'll be working in all three windows simultaneously as you work through the exercises below.

TIP ▸ *Any time you adjust the size, position, and arrangement of Premiere's windows to better suit your working style, you can save the arrangement by using the Window > Workspace > Save Workspace command. This will "memorize" your current arrangement. Then just select Window > Workspace to restore your saved layout arrangement whenever you need it.*

The Project Window: Organizing Your Source Materials

Premiere's Project window stores and organizes all of the media clips and files that you import for use in your video program. If a given media file (video, audio, still image, or title) is going to be in your final movie, it has to be in the Project window first. In the following step, you'll import the files you'll need to make the 30-second commercial in the second part of this chapter.

Importing Source Clips

1. With the Project window as the active window, and Bin 1 selected, choose File > Import > Folder (**Figure 5.3**).

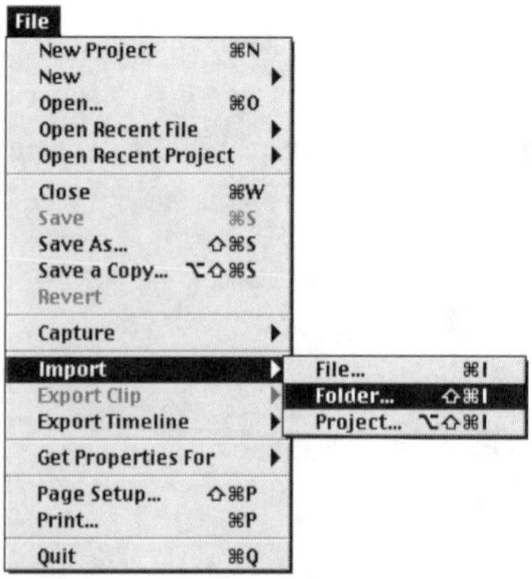

FIGURE 5.3
Importing a folder of clips: The File>Import Menu allows you to import single files, a folder of files, and even an entire Premiere project.

2. In the Choose a Folder dialog window, navigate to the Chapter5_Editing folder, open the Escape_Practice_Files folder, select the "calif" folder, and then click the Choose button to import it. Do this for each folder in the Escape_Practice_Files folder except the Projects folder, which contains only project files and no source media. This creates a bin in the Project window corresponding to every folder in the Chapter5_Editing folder. Double-clicking on a bin brings up a list of the contents of that bin in the right pane of the Project window.

Like folders in the Windows and Macintosh operating systems, Premiere's *bins* allow you to organize the media files that you import into your project. You can drag and drop clips from one bin to another and create sub-bins to create a hierarchical filing system. The icon buttons at the bottom of the Project window let you view the contents of the Project window in a variety of ways, including the List view (**Figure 5.4**), which shows a text listing of the files; the Thumbnail view (**Figure 5.5**), which displays thumbnail-size frames of your clips with comments; and the Icon view (**Figure 5.6**), which also displays the duration of each clip.

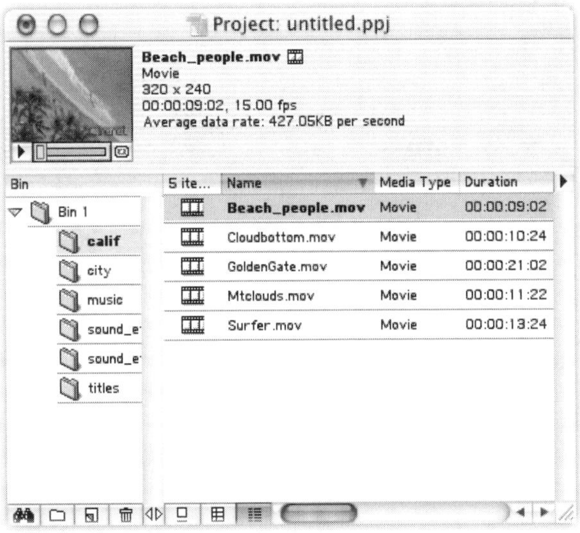

FIGURE 5.4
Premiere's Project window, shown here in List view, is where you organize all the media files that will be in your movie.

FIGURE 5.5
The Thumbnail view allows you to attach comments to each clip.

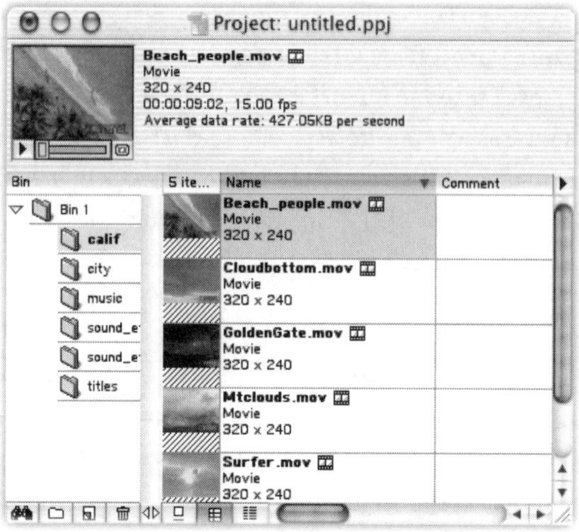

FIGURE 5.6
The Icon view displays a poster frame of each clip and shows each clip's duration.

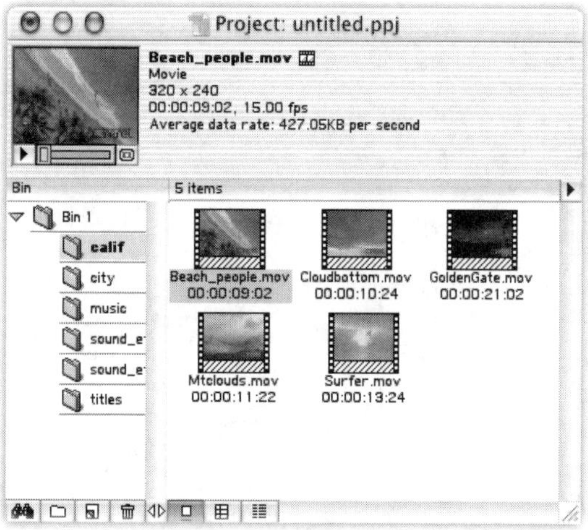

3. To save your project, choose File > Save, give the project a name, and click Save.

The project file doesn't contain your video and audio files themselves. Instead, it contains references (*pointers*) to all the video, audio, and image clips you've imported, as well as a log of every edit you make in your project. That means that the project file is a small, but very important, text file and that the source files are never altered directly when you edit them in Premiere. If you're using Windows (or plan to use the project file on Windows), make sure to add the file extension

".ppj" when you name your project file so that it is recognizable as an Adobe Premiere file to your system software and to other applications. Back up your project files frequently.

Premiere can also automate the saving process for you. It will place your backup files in a folder called Project-Archive inside the Premiere folder.

Using Auto Save

1. Choose Edit > Preferences > Auto Save.

2. Check the Automatically Save Projects check box, and specify how often you want Premiere to save the project.

3. Enter the number of copies of all projects that you want Premiere to save in the Project Archive folder in the Maximum Files in Archive box. When it reaches the maximum number of files you've specified, Premiere will delete the oldest projects to make room for newer ones.

4. Enter the number of versions of each project that you want Premiere to automatically save in the Maximum Project Versions box.

5. Click OK to close the dialog box.

The Monitor Window: Playing and Editing Clips

The first thing you want to do in the Monitor window is to set it up in Dual View mode. At the top of the window, you'll see some buttons. Click the Dual View button on the left (**Figure 5.7**) to change the setting to two, side-by-side, monitor windows.

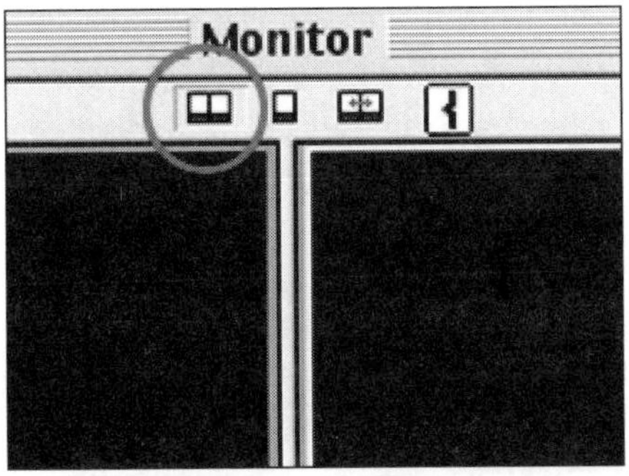

FIGURE 5.7
Click the Dual View button on the left to display side-by-side monitor windows, a convenient way to work.

The left side, called the Source view, shows the source clips; the right side, or Program view, plays back your edited version of the clips. To play a clip that is already in the Project window, drag it to the Source view. When you play your edited sequence, you'll see it play in the Program view, on the right. The VCR-like controls at the bottom of both Monitor views offer Play, Stop, Frame Forward, Frame Back, Loop, and Play In to Out buttons (the latter plays the clip from the In and Out markers you've set). The readouts below the screens show clip duration on the left and timecode (in hours: minutes: seconds: frames) on the right (**Figure 5.8**). A blue Edit Line marker provides random access to any frame in the clip.

FIGURE 5.8
Premiere's Monitor window displays the source clip on the left and the edited movie on the right. VCR-like controls at the bottom of each view allow you to control playback. Editing buttons along the bottom allow you to select sequences within clips and place markers at specific frames within clips.

The bread and butter of any editing project is making choices about what to keep and what not to keep. To do that, you've got to be ready to choose selections of frames from longer video clips. The Mark In and Mark Out buttons, which look like brackets beneath the Source and Program views' controller bars, are Premiere's tools for selecting the parts of a clip you want to use. The Mark In button marks the start of the selection and the Mark Out button (surprise!) marks the end of it (**Figure 5.9**).

FIGURE 5.9
Use the Mark In and Mark Out buttons to bracket the frames that you want to use in your edited movie. A clip pop-up window at the bottom left lets you call up any clip that you've already opened up in the Source view.

1. Use the Play button or the slider under the Source window to find the point where you want your segment to begin.

2. Click the Mark In button. The white In marker will appear at the top of the Monitor window, and a corresponding black In marker will appear in the Source window's timeline.

3. Click the Play button or click-drag the Edit Line to find the point where you want the segment to end and click the Mark Out button.

Now that you have marked the beginning and end of your selection, Premiere will only use the portion of the clip between those two points and ignore everything else. Notice that the Clip Duration readout below the Source view changes as you change the In and Out points: Premiere considers the duration of the clip to be the time from your marked In point to your marked Out point. You can change the In and Out points at any time: Just find a new spot in the clip and click the Mark In or Mark Out button again. You can also just click and drag the existing In and Out points in the Source view. The Clip pop-up menu at the bottom of the Monitor window's Source view allows you to quickly call up any clip that you've already opened there.

TIP ▸ *Click the "Play In to Out" button to confirm that your In and Out points are where you want them. The Loop button will "Play In to Out" repeatedly.*

The Timeline Window: Sequencing Your Clips

Once you've made your editing selections and created just the clips that you want to use, the next step is to arrange them into a sequence of clips that play back in a certain order. Premiere's Timeline window is the tool you'll use for that task. In it, you arrange your clips in the sequence that will become your movie. The Timeline window shows you clips as they are arranged in time, at a scale you select. Its default setting is for two video tracks and three audio tracks, but, assuming you have enough RAM, you can use up to 99 video tracks and 99 audio tracks. For our movie, we'll use 4 video tracks and 6 audio tracks, which makes it possible to create video transitions and use a layered soundtrack.

You can add a clip to the Timeline in several ways: click and drag the clip from the Monitor window's Source view to the Timeline window; click and drag the clip from the Project window to the Timeline window; or click and drag the clip from the Monitor window's Source view to the Program view—which automatically adds it to the Timeline (**Figure 5.10**).

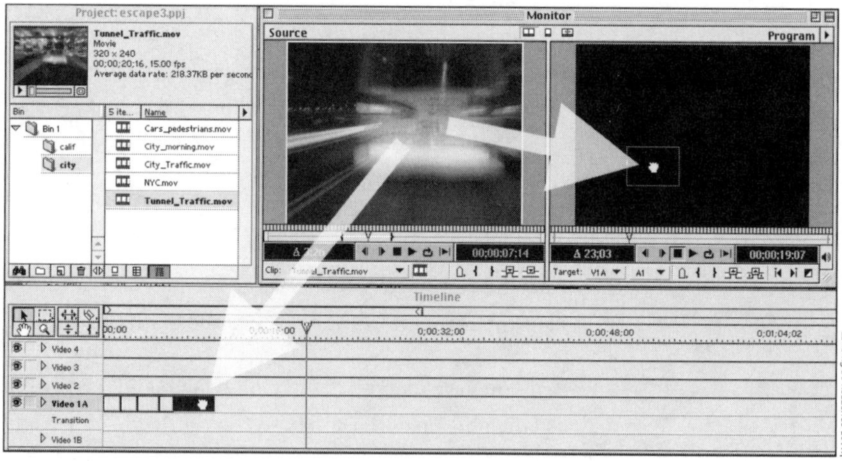

FIGURE 5.10
You can add clips to the Timeline window either by clicking and dragging them from the Source window directly to the Timeline window (the left arrow) or by clicking and dragging them from the Source view to the Program view.

IMAGE COURTESY OF CINENET

Making Your Movie: Escape.mov

If you do all of the exercises in this chapter, you will end up with a 30-second commercial promoting California as a travel destination. I call this little Web spot *Escape*. You can find a copy of the finished movie (escape.mov) in the Chapter5_Editing folder on the CD. As you can see from the movie, this spot is all about breaking free from the workaday world and vacationing in California. The first half of the spot shows the misery of the daily grind, and the second half conveys the glories of the Golden State.

The chapter is written so that you can build everything yourself. However, if you don't want to take the step-by-step tour, you can take shortcuts through the process and view the movie at various stages of completion. You'll find these partially completed versions of the movie in the Chapter5_Editing folder. Just drill down this path: Chapter5_Editing/Escape_Practice_Files/Projects. Within the Projects folder you'll see escape1.ppj, escape2.ppj, and so on, as well as the final completed version. During this tutorial, just look for the CD icon and the "Escape Shortcut" heading for your cue to use these presaved project files.

Marking the End Point

While this may seem like putting the cart before the horse, your first step in making the *Escape* spot will be to mark the end point of the movie in the Timeline window, so that you can make the commercial exactly 30 seconds long. When you play a clip in the Timeline window, you'll notice that the numbers in the timecode readout in the Program view change as the clip plays. Similarly, if you click and drag the Edit Line marker back and forth in the Timeline window, these numbers change. This area is known as the Program Location field—it tells you exactly where you are in the clip.

1. To navigate precisely to the 30-second point, do one of the following:

   Manually drag the blue Edit Line in the Timeline window to exactly 30 seconds, as shown on the timeline that runs along the top.

   Or

   Highlight the numbers in the readout of the Program Location field in the Program view, type in new numbers so that it reads "00:00:30:00" and then press the Enter key (**Figure 5.11**). This will move the Edit Line in the Timeline window to the 30-second mark exactly.

FIGURE 5.11
Entering a new timecode in the Program Location field moves the Edit Line to that spot in the Timeline window below.

2. Now that you've specified the end point, you need to place a visible marker in the Timeline window: Make sure the Edit Line is in the right place ("00:00:30:00") and then click the Marker button in the Program view. The Marker menu will appear (**Figure 5.12**). Select the number "0" in the submenu. You can also use Timeline > Set Timeline Marker to accomplish the same thing.

FIGURE 5.12
Use the Marker menu to place a marker at the 30-second point in the Timeline window.

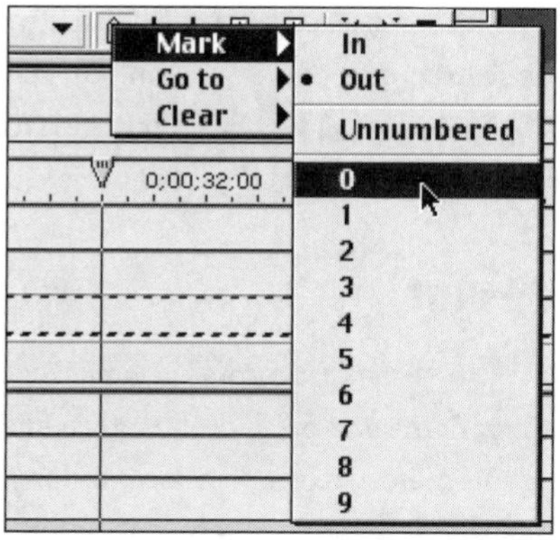

The visible indicator in the Timeline window ensures that your clips and music won't extend past the maximum length that you want for your movie (**Figure 5.13**).

FIGURE 5.13
The marker you just set is visible at exactly 30 seconds in the Timeline.

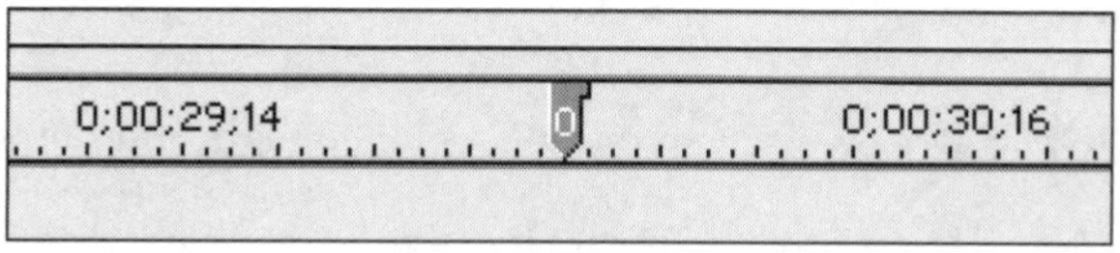

Creating a Sequence in the Timeline

The next step in making a movie is using your editing skills to select the frames that you want to use, and then arranging them in Premiere's Timeline so that they play in sequence. Here's how:

1. Open NYC.mov from the Project window's city bin by either double-clicking it or dragging it into the Source view. Using the Mark In and Mark Out buttons, select a 1- to 2-second sequence from it that you like. Drop your edited clip into the Video 1A track at the left side of the Timeline window.

2. Do the same thing with City_morning.mov, Cars_pedestrians.mov, and City_Traffic.mov. You'll now have four short clips in the Timeline window. It doesn't matter how long each clip is, as long as these four add up to about 6 seconds in length.

3. Open Tunnel_Traffic.mov, select a 4-second sequence, and drop that into the Timeline window (**Figure 5.14**).

TIP ▸ *Premiere's Timeline Window Options dialog box lets you customize the appearance of the Timeline window by selecting the icon size, track format, audio display, zero point, and timescale. Select it by choosing Window > Window Options > Timeline Window Options.*

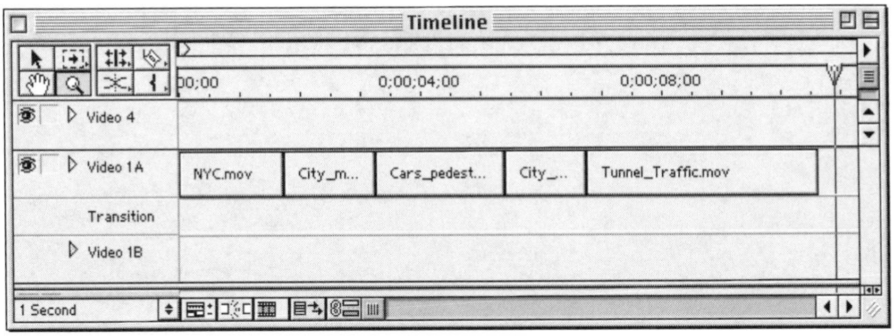

FIGURE 5.14
Once you have these clips in the Timeline window, it should look like this.

"Escape" Shortcut

To skip to this point in the making of the 30-second *Escape* commercial, open the escape1.ppj project file in the Projects folder within the Escape_Practice_Files folder by double-clicking on it or selecting File › Open.

Relinking Projects and Offline Clips

There are some important things to know about how Premiere operates when you open a project (.ppj) file. If nothing has changed about the location of the source files, preview files or project file associated with that particular project, then the project will generally open without any further ado. However, if one of these files has changed its location in the file structure of the hard disk or is missing, Premiere will first attempt to find the file on its own and then ask you to help it locate the files that it needs (**Figure 5.15**).

If any file in the project (including the .ppj project file) has been moved or changed since the last time the project was open, Premiere presents you with the Locate File window.

Since the practice files I am sharing with you include .ppj (project) files, you will inevitably be confronted with Premiere's Locate File window when you try to open one of them.

If Premiere finds the correct file, you can just click the Select button and be on your merry way. If the file is missing entirely, you can either click Skip, which eliminates the file from the project (bad idea), or you can click Offline, which places a salmon-colored "placeholder" for the file in the Timeline (good idea). The Offline option is useful because it retains all of your editing work even though the original source file is missing. This gives you the option of locating or re-creating the missing file at a later time. Clicking Skip Preview Files is often a good idea, since preview files can always be re-created (as long as you have all the source files).

FIGURE 5.15
Premiere will ask you to find the files that it needs to assemble a project if any of those files have been moved or changed since the last time that project was open.

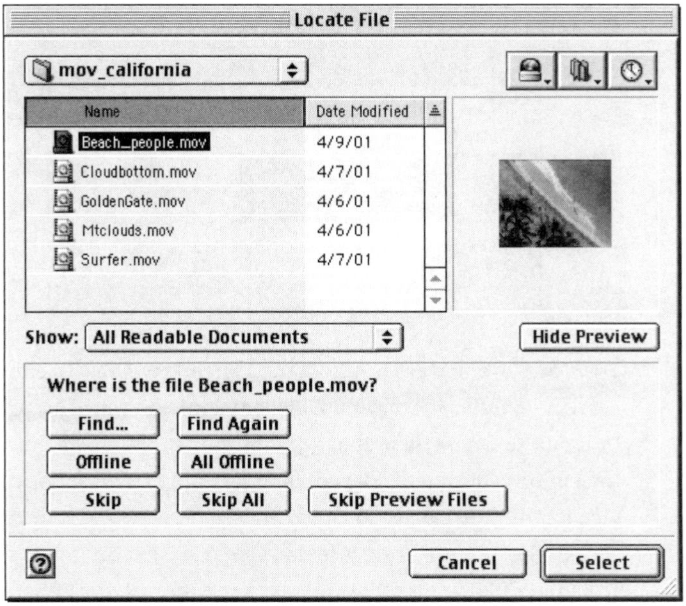

4. Press the A key on your keyboard to rewind Premiere to the first frame of your edited sequence.

5. Click the Play button or tap the spacebar to see your new sequence play back in the Monitor window's Program view. Notice how the blue Edit Line moves across the ruler at the top of the Timeline window. You can click and drag on the Edit Line to quickly get to any point in your sequence of clips.

6. If necessary, you can rearrange the order of the clips by sliding them around in the Timeline (**Figure 5.16**). Figuring out what sections of your video clips to use and the order in which to use them is the bread and butter of video editing. Make sure that you don't unintentionally leave gaps in your movie, which will appear as black areas on the timeline: Slide (click and drag) the clips next to each other until they "snap" together.

TIP ▸ *When you drag a clip over an existing cut point (where two separate clips touch ends), Premiere shows a little right-arrow icon indicating that if you drop the clip there, it will make an "insert edit"—in other words, move the clip(s) on the right further to the right (later in time) to make room for the new clip.*

Figure 5.16
You can rearrange clips in the Timeline window by sliding them to where you want them to go.

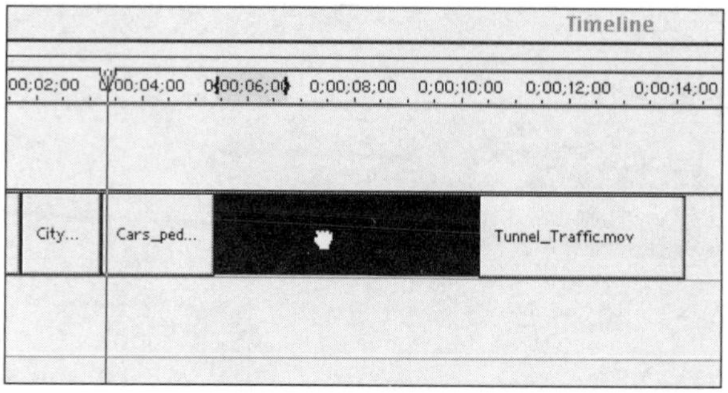

There are several ways to adjust the Timeline window to either zoom in on more detail or to pull back to get the bigger picture on your editing progress. The Time Unit pull-down menu in the lower left corner of the Timeline lets you select the time units you want displayed, ranging from 1 frame (close up) to 8 minutes (the big picture). You can use the plus (+) key on the top of your keyboard to get a closer view or the minus (-) key to get a wider view. You can select the Zoom tool in the Timeline window's toolbox (it looks like a magnifying glass) and then click in the part of the Timeline that you want to see in more detail. And you can select the Navigator palette by selecting Window > Show Navigator and sliding the time-unit slider to the left or right to set the timeline to the right scale for your project. As you make any of these changes, watch the ruler at the top of the Timeline window; it will change its units as you change the scale at which you view your movie.

Editing Clips in the Timeline

Your five-clip *Escape* sequence should now be about 10 seconds long (ending at the Program Location of about "00:00:10:18." To fine-tune your movie, you can make changes to your clips' duration in the Timeline window directly by changing their In and Out points:

1. Mouse over the right or left edge of the clip in the Timeline. As you do so, your cursor will change to a red "bracket" icon with an arrow on one side of it, depending on which edge you're moving.

2. Click and drag the edge of the clip as needed to shorten or lengthen the clip (**Figure 5.17**). Make sure that there are no gaps between your clips. If you are lengthening a clip with this method and you can't drag it any further to the left, you have come to the end of the original length of the clip. You can either capture a longer clip or choose Clip > Speed to change the clip's playback speed (decreasing the speed will make the clip longer).

3. Press the A key on your keyboard to rewind Premiere to the first frame of your edited sequence.

4. Click the Play button or tap the spacebar to view the changes you've just made.

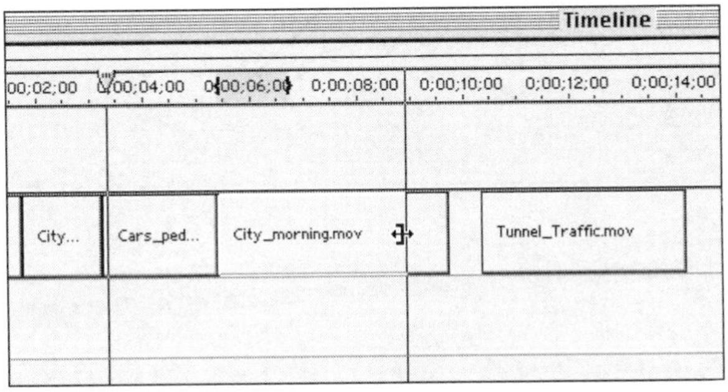

FIGURE 5.17
You can adjust the Out Point of a clip in the Timeline by clicking and dragging the edge of that clip.

Another way to make adjustments to the In and Out points of a clip that is already in the Timeline is to double-click the clip in the Timeline. This will open the clip in the Source view of the Monitor window. There you can make changes to the In and Out points, and then click the Apply button. If double-clicking opens your clip in a separate clip window, choose Edit > Preferences > General and Still Image, and uncheck the Open Movies in Clip Window check box. This will reset Premiere's default so that double-clicking a clip opens it in the Source view.

Adding Transitions to Your Project

A transition is a visual effect that makes a change between clips appear more gradual than a cut. Technically, Web video usually works better without transitions. But sometimes, like in this *Escape* spot, the nature of the movie requires a few transitions. Here, we're using a dissolve effect to give an ethereal feel to our California fantasy section. Here's how to add transitions to your project:

1. Open the following clips from the "calif" bin in the Project window, and then click-drag them to the Monitor window's Source view. You don't have to edit these—they're the right length already.

   Beach_people.mov
   Surfer.mov
   Mtclouds.mov
   Cloudbottom.mov
   Goldengate.mov

2. Drop these clips into the Video 1A track in the same order. Start at about 00:00:11:18 in the Timeline (**Figure 5.18**). To get there, type "00:00:11:18" into the Project Location field in the Program view and press Enter. The Edit Line marker will jump to that spot in the Timeline window.

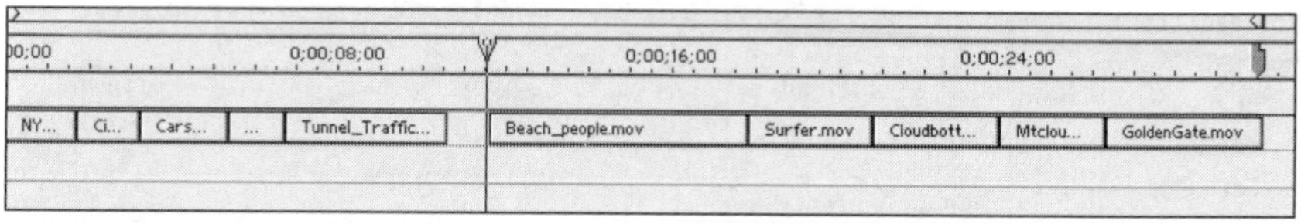

Figure 5.18
The second set of clips (those depicting California) should start at around "00:00:11:18."

"Escape" Shortcut

To skip to this point in the making of the 30-second *Escape* commercial, open the escape2.ppj project file in the Projects folder.

At this point, all your clips are arranged on the Video 1A track. (The Video 1 track is actually composed of three "subtracks": Video 1A, Transition, and Video 1B.)

1. Drag the Beach_people.mov clip into the Video 1B track.

2. Move Surfer.mov over to the left slightly, so that it overlaps in time with Beach_people.mov.

3. Click the Next Edit or Previous Edit button in the Program view until the Edit Line is lined up just at the beginning of the overlap. (Take a look at **Figure 5.8** to refresh your memory as to where these buttons are located.)

4. Click the Add Default Transition button in the Program view. This adds a blue transition clip in the Transition track, exactly where the two clips overlap (**Figure 5.19**).

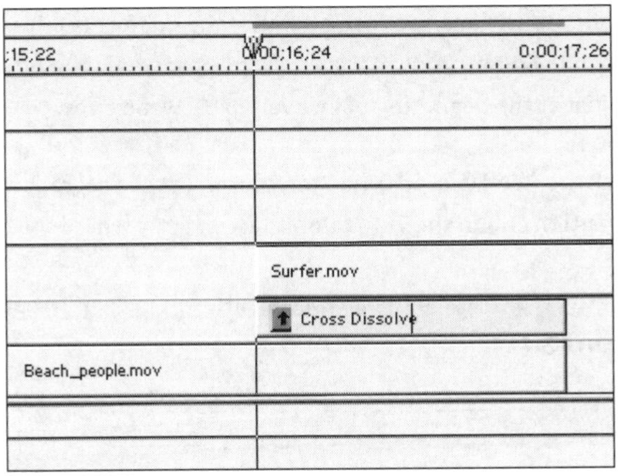

FIGURE 5.19
A close-up view of the overlapping clips, with the inserted transition in the Transition track.

5. Move Mtclouds.mov to the Video 1B track at about 00:00:08:25 (that will leave a gap between it and Beach_people.mov).

6. Move Goldengate.mov to the Video 1B track at about 00:00:22:10 (that will leave a gap between it and Mtclouds.mov).

7. Slide Cloudbottom.mov to the left to about 20:10, so that it overlaps in time with Mtclouds.mov. You should now see a checkerboard pattern like that shown in **Figure 5.20**.

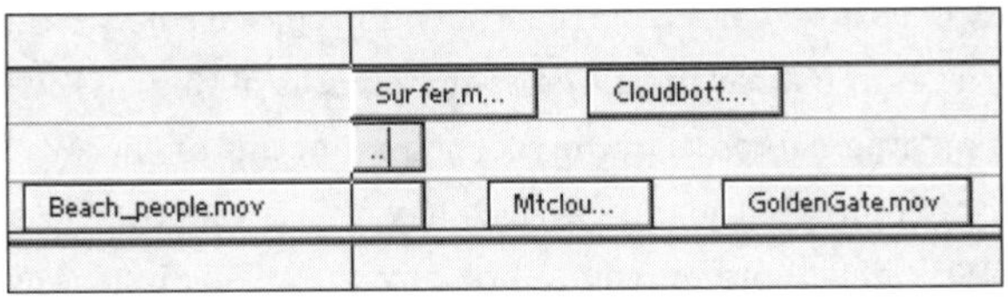

FIGURE 5.20
This checkerboard pattern of overlapping clips makes your movie ready for adding transitions in the overlap between clips.

"Escape" Shortcut

To skip to this point in the making of the 30-second *Escape* commercial, open the escape3.ppj project file in the Projects folder. To see the transitions and all other effects from here on out, you'll need to press the A key to rewind and then hit Enter so that Premiere can render the effect each time you open one of the saved project files.

8. To add transitions between all five of the California clips, click the Next Edit or Previous Edit buttons in the Program view until the Edit Line marker is lined up just at the beginning of an overlap between clips.

9. Click the Add Default Transition button in the Program view. This adds a blue transition clip in the Transition track, exactly where the two clips overlap.

10. Repeat steps 8 and 9 to place a transition at each of the other overlaps (**Figure 5.21**).

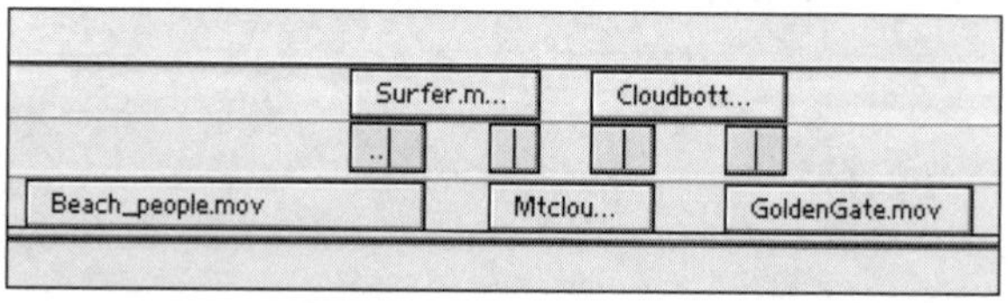

FIGURE 5.21
Here's a close-up of what the Timeline looks like when you've added transitions to all five "California" clips.

NOTE ▸ The more an individual frame of video looks like both the preceding frame and the subsequent frame, the easier it is for the compression software to do its job. In a cross-dissolve in which every pixel of the image changes with every frame of video, the compression software has to work overtime to compress the image—and the higher the compression, the greater the loss in image quality. In a wipe, only part of the frame has to change at a time. So wipes are more suitable for Web video. But as creative people, we can't be enslaved by technology. We don't usually choose visual effects like transitions based solely on their technical virtues. Sometimes it just has to be a cross-dissolve, as in this case, where we're trying to create an ethereal mood in the second part of this movie. We'll pay the price later when we compress the movie—but, hey, this is supposed to be a learning experience! (Still, if you prefer, you can replace the cross-dissolves with wipes, or just straight cuts.)

TIP ▸ *To change the transition from the default cross-dissolve to another type of transition, such as a wipe, select Window > Show Transitions. This brings up the Transitions palette, which groups transitions by category. Open the Wipe bin. Scroll down to Wipe. Click and drag it on top of the cross-dissolve transition in the Timeline window. This will replace the cross-dissolve with the wipe transition.*

11. Rewind the Edit Line back to the beginning of the California sequences to play the section of your movie with the overlapping clips and transitions. You will still see cuts, but not the transitions that you've placed there. To create any visual and audio effects such as transitions you must first *render* a preview to actually see the effect.

Previewing (Rendering) a Transition

To display a transition effect in your movie, Premiere first must render it. That means that Premiere has to generate the effect before you can see it. In this case, the effect contains the overlapping clips and the transitions, which will be written to your hard disk. (The Premiere term for rendering is *previewing*. These two terms are interchangeable.)

1. To preview your transitions, stretch the yellow Work Area bar at the top of the Timeline window over the section of the Timeline that contains the overlapping clips and the transitions (if it isn't already stretched).

2. Press the Enter key (Windows) or the Return key (Mac) to see Premiere go to work rendering a preview file. Watch the area between the yellow Work Area bar and the ruler: Premiere will draw a green line over the transition areas, indicating that it's saving a new file to your hard disk.

Adding Audio

One of the most important skills in video editing is designing the interplay between picture and sound. Good sound can enhance less-than-perfect video and give your movies a professional polish. Let's add some sound effects and music to this Web video commercial:

1. Open the bin called Sound_Effects_A1 and add the citytraffic.wav clip to the Audio 1 track in the Timeline.

2. You will see that it is much too long for its intended use: as background sound for the first half of the clip.

   Trim the end of the citytraffic.wav clip (**Figure 5.22**), either in the Monitor window's Source view or in the Timeline window, so that it ends right where the tunnel_traffic clip ends (approximately 00:00:10:17).

"Escape" Shortcut

To skip to this point in the making of the 30-second *Escape* commercial, open the escape4.ppj project file in the Projects folder.

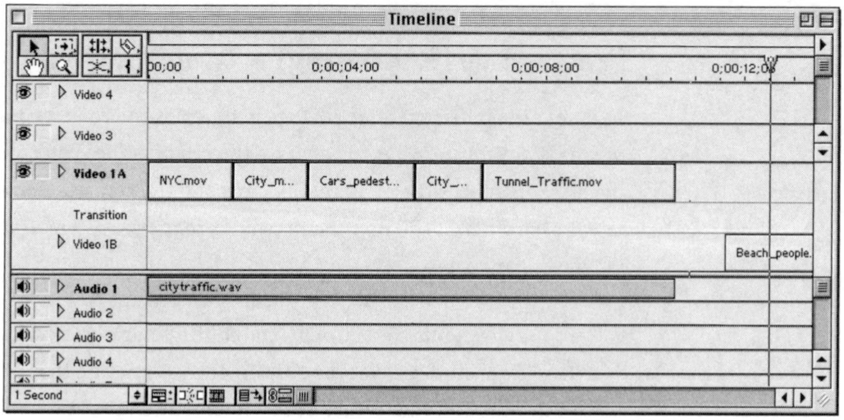

Figure 5.22
To sync the sound to the picture, trim the citytraffic.wav clip so that it ends right where the tunnel_traffic clip ends.

3. Now add the other clips in the Sound_Effects_A1 folder to the Timeline (**Figure 5.23**). Since many of these clips will overlap in time, you'll need to create several different audio tracks to accommodate them. To add new audio tracks, choose Timeline > Add Audio Track. Another way to do this is to Control-click (Mac) or right-click (Windows) in the dark gray area below the audio tracks, then choose Add Audio Track from the context-sensitive menu. The following list indicates at what point in time the clips should *start*.

   roadconstruction.wav (at 00:00:00:00)
   trafficjam.wav (at 00:00:03:23)
   telefony.aif (at 00:00:04:13) (located in Sound_Effects_B)
   zoomby.aif (at 00:00:05:13) (located in Sound_Effects_B)
   speed.wav (at 00:00:06:09)

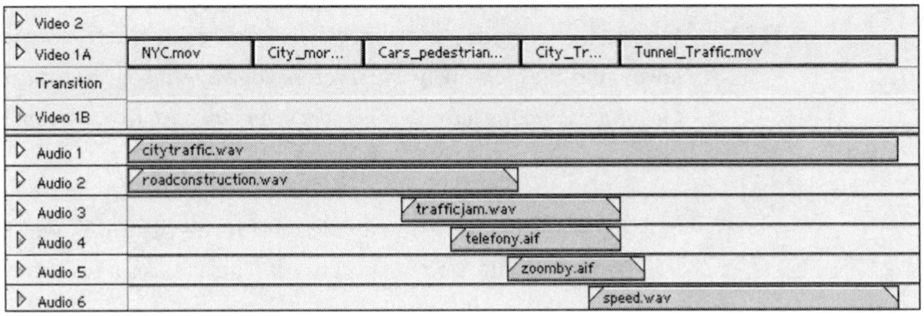

Figure 5.23
Here's what the various sound effects clips in six separate audio tracks should look like once you've added them.

Note that the speed.wav clip should end at about 00:00:10:18, exactly at the same time as citytraffic.wav and tunnel_traffic.mov. To achieve the desired abrupt end to the first half of the spot, they must all end at exactly the same time. If necessary, trim the longer clips to achieve this effect.

"Escape" Shortcut

To skip to this point in the making of the 30-second *Escape* commercial, open the escape5.ppj project file in the Projects folder.

Adjusting Volume

Some of the sound clips are too loud, so you'll have to *mix* them by adjusting their relative loudness. The simplest way to do this is to adjust the *gain level*, or overall volume, of the audio clips in the Timeline. Here's how to do it:

1. Click the triangle button to the left of the Audio 1 track. This displays a red timeline control called the *volume rubberband*. By changing its slope, you can control the volume of a clip—here citytraffic.wav—over time.

2. Click the Fade Adjustment tool, which is located at the upper left of the Timeline window and looks like a line with an up and down arrow above and below it. When you hold down your mouse for a moment, you'll see a sub-menu of three choices; choose the button with a line with an up and down arrow above and below it.

3. Click and drag vertically on the red rubberband to adjust the volume for the entire clip. (Hold down the Shift key to get a numeric readout of your current adjustment level, and adjust the gain of citytraffic.wav to about 63 percent.)

TIP ▸ *When you're using any of the special tools in the upper-left corner of the Timeline window, always put the tools away when you're done by clicking on the arrow-shaped Selection tool or pressing the letter V. This sets Premiere back to normal operation mode.*

4. To create a fade-in and a fade-out for the citytraffic.wav clip, click the rubberband at about the 1-second mark. This creates a little red point (or box) called a *handle*.

5. Click the beginning of the rubberband at the leftmost end of the clip to create another handle, then drag that box down to level 0 (**Figure 5.24**).

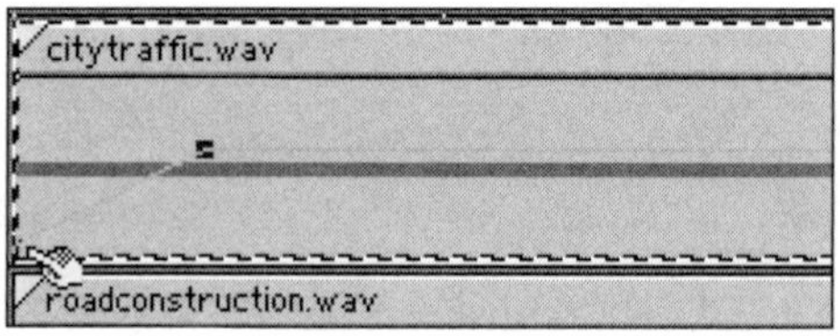

Figure 5.24
Dragging down the starting gain-level handle makes the volume louder as the clip plays.

TIP ▸ *Premiere has a sophisticated (and complicated) tool to automate this mixing process called the Audio Mixer. Go to Window > Audio Mixer to check it out.*

6. Now reverse this process at the other end of the same clip to create a fade-out (**Figure 5.25**).

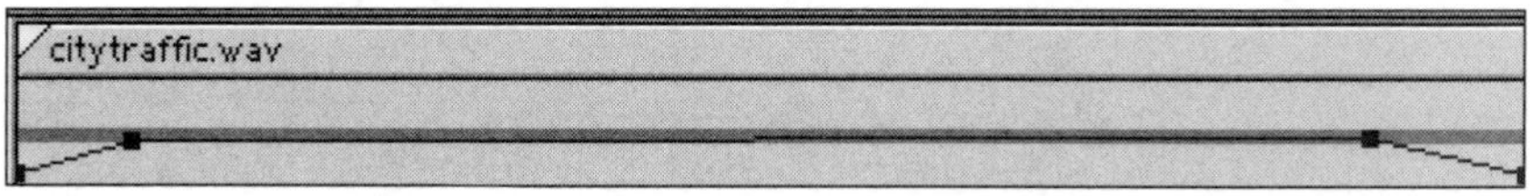

Figure 5.25
Here's what the fade-in and fade-out look like on the citytraffic.wav clip.

7. Now make similar gain-level and fade-in and fade-out adjustments to the other sound effects clips. This is a trial and error process. You'll have to play this section of the Timeline over and over to get it right.

Editing with Markers

Premiere's Source Markers help you synchronize sound to video (and video to sound) precisely by allowing you to mark a specific point in time both on an individual clip and in the Timeline window. Each clip can contain up to 10 numbered markers and up to 999 unnumbered markers. Here's how to use them:

1. Move the Edit Line to the very end of the tunnel_traffic.mov clip in the Timeline.

2. Tap the right arrow on your computer's keyboard six times to move the Edit Line six frames later in time (to the right).

3. Select the Marker button under the Monitor window's Program view and choose "1" from the numbers 0 through 9 in the submenu. This will place marker #1 on the frame in the Timeline. When you mark a frame, Premiere also puts a white box with that marker's number inside of it at the top of the Monitor window.

   Notice that the frame marker and its number are now visible in the Timeline. You will use this marker to sync-up two important clips.

4. Find the sound-effect clip called slam.aif in the Sound_Effects_B bin, and Option–double-click it (Ctrl–double-click for Windows users).

5. This opens the *waveform* of the clip—a graphical rendering of a sound file (**Figure 5.26**).

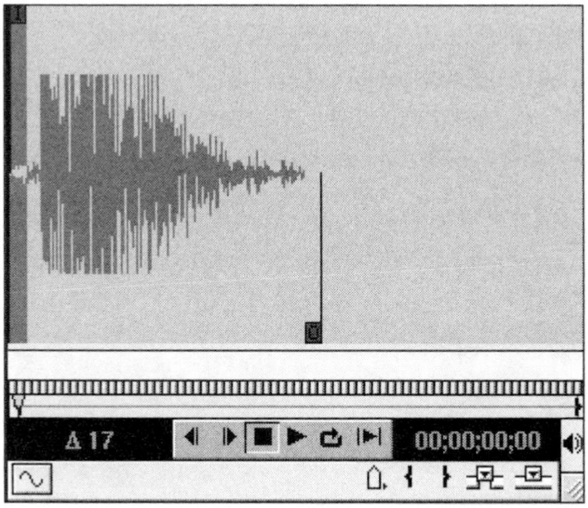

Figure 5.26
The waveform view gives you a graphical representation of your sound file.

To expand or condense your view of the waveform, click the Waveform button, located at the lower-left corner of the Audio-Clip window. Condensing the view shows you less detail but more of the waveform. Expanding it shows you more detail but less of the whole clip.

6. Tap the right arrow twice to move the Edit Line two frames to the right.

7. Mark that frame (the actual beginning of the sound) with the #1 marker (**Figure 5.27**).

Figure 5.27
The expanded waveform view, with the #1 marker.

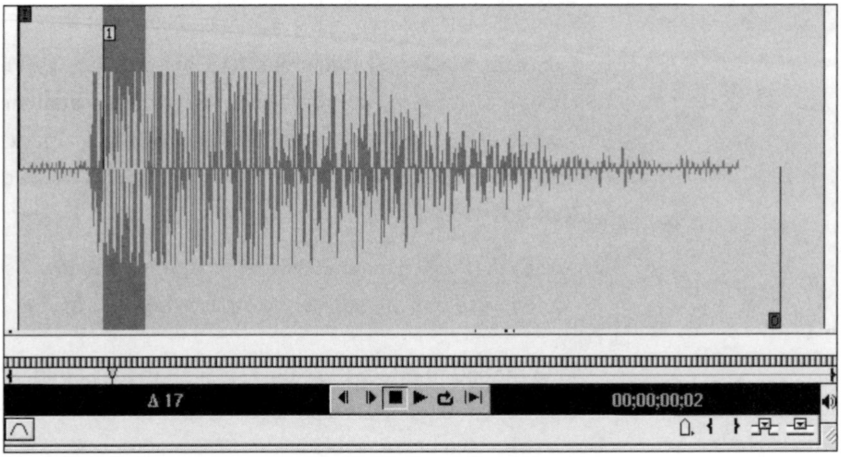

8. Close the expanded waveform view.

9. In the main part of the Timeline window, move the slam.aif clip so that its #1 marker "snaps" into alignment with the marker in the Timeline (**Figure 5.28**). To do this, you will have to set the Timeline view to an extreme close-up (zoomed-in) view. I used 4 frames in the pop-up menu.

   If the clips/markers don't snap into alignment by moving as if they're magnetized, toggle "snap to edges' on by clicking the Snap to Edges button at the bottom of the Timeline, or use the Timeline > Snap to Edges menu item to make sure this feature is turned on.

FIGURE 5.28
An extreme close-up view of the "slam.aif" clip in the Timeline, with the marker that was placed in the Timeline and the clip marker in alignment.

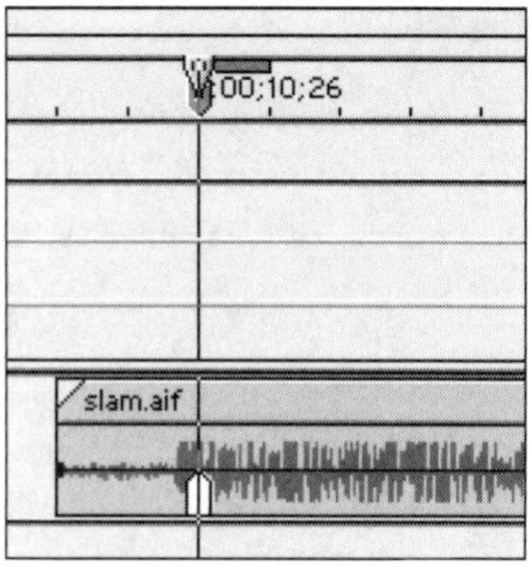

"Escape" Shortcut

To skip to this point in the making of the 30-second *Escape* commercial, open the escape6.ppj project file in the Projects folder within the Escape_Practice_Files folder in the Chapter 5 folder you copied to your hard drive, or find it on the CD.

10. Open the music clip called calif_theme_comp.aif from the music bin and add it to the Audio 1 track of the Timeline, exactly at the end of the slam.aif clip. The Out point should be exactly at the 30-second mark in the Timeline.

Adding Titles

Another skill that is useful for editing both Web video and standard "television" video is that of creating and compositing *titles*. And I don't mean thinking up a name for your movie! Titles are graphics (usually containing text) that are combined in some way with a background video clip. They are useful for presenting information (such as the name of the program, end credits, subtitles), as well as for enhancing a particular mood or message with superimposed text and graphics. The most common type of title (and the kind we are going to create in the following exercise) is a *keyed* title. *Key* is a video term for a foreground image that blocks out portions of a background image and thereby appears to be layered on top of it.

Making Titles Readable on the Web

Having readable video titles is important in any movie, but it takes some particular care to create them in Web video because the smaller frame sizes and the degraded image quality of compressed Web movies can play havoc with text. Here are some things that help:

- Make Big Subtitles

  The film and TV veterans among you may have some assumptions about titles that don't work for Web video. For example, in traditional television, subtitles and name identifications are always contained within the lower third of the frame. This will not work for a movie that is only 160 by 120 pixels—it will just be too small to read. The smaller the frame size of your final Web movie, the larger the relative size of the subtitle will have to be.

- Choose Fonts Carefully

  Simpler and bolder text will work better in Web video than complex and delicate text. Choose *san serif* (no curlies) typefaces over *serif* (curly) typefaces. (For example, Arial and Helvetica work better than Palatino or FrenchScript.) Also, the bold or "black" versions of these fonts make them easier to read.

- Use Contrasting Colors

  Obviously, if the color of your title is exactly the same color as the background image, no one will be able to read it. That's why many people use plain white text on darker backgrounds, or plain black on lighter backgrounds. If you're using a reference background image as we do in the exercise below, you might want to use the Title window's Eyedropper tool in conjunction with the Color Picker to find a suitable contrasting, yet complementary color.

Creating Titles in Premiere 6.5

Premiere 6.5's new Adobe Title Designer window could easily be a stand-alone application. Fortunately it's built into Premiere at no extra charge. The Adobe Title Designer allows you to create vector-based text and graphics, which means that each text or graphic object can be manipulated separately, and can be scaled to any size without any loss in visual quality. You can also change the size, shape, and color of any of these text and graphic objects. And titles are editable, ready to be altered and re-used in your other Premiere projects, if you like. In Premiere 6.5, you can apply a variety of attributes to titles (such as sheens and textures), use various templates to help you design titles, freely manipulate the title shapes, and create custom title styles that you can save and load later for use with other title documents.

WARNING ▸ If you're using the Premiere 6.0 tryout version, be aware that the Adobe Title Designer is a new feature in Premiere 6.5. However, you'll still be able to create, import, and edit titles in the Premiere 6.0 Title window, though its interface differs from the examples shown below (and it offers fewer features). You can use the pre-built Premiere 6.0 titles provided in the book's CD by navigating to the Chapter5_Editing/Escape_Practice_Files/Titles folder, then browsing through sample titles. For additional information on using titles in Premiere 6.0, see Antony Bolante's *Premiere 6 for Macintosh and Windows: Visual QuickStart Guide* (2001, Peachpit Press).

To make the titles for escape.mov, open a new Title window:

1. Choose File > New > Title (**Figure 5.29**).

FIGURE 5.29
Premiere's Adobe Title Designer allows you to create editable titles.

A quick alternative way to open a Title window is the Create Item button at the bottom of the Project window. Click it, choose Title from the menu that appears, and click OK (**Figure 5.30**).

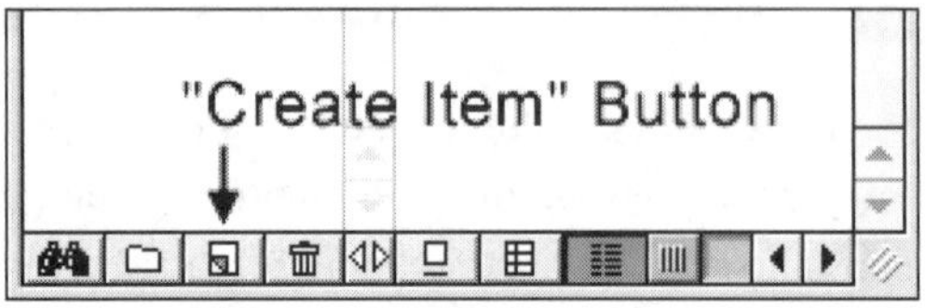

FIGURE 5.30
The Create Item button, at the bottom of the Project window, gives you another way to open a Title window.

This opens a new, blank Title window (**Figure 5.31**).

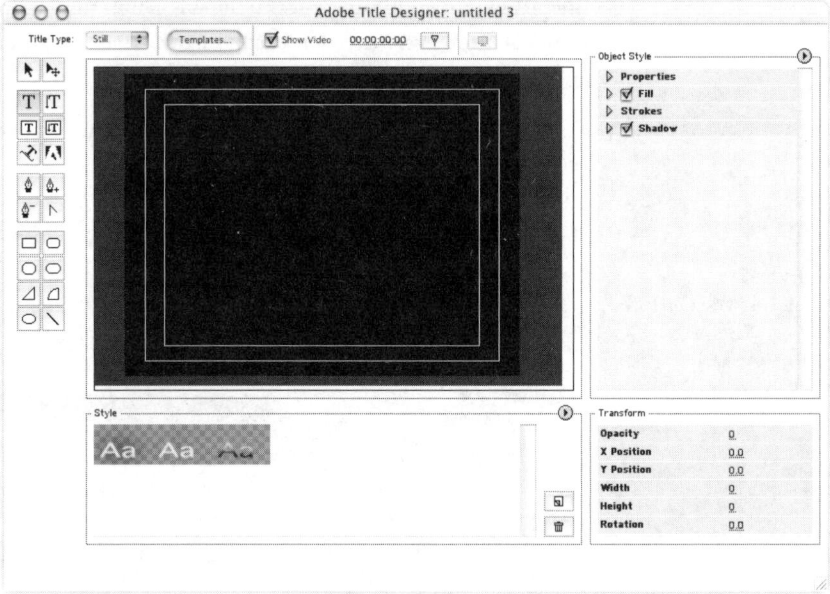

FIGURE 5.31
Premiere's Adobe Title Designer window has so many features, it could be an application unto itself.

At this point, you can either create a title from scratch by working directly in the title area or use one of the included templates to modify the title area and guide your title design. We are going to create some titles from scratch, so that you can better learn the capabilities of this titling tool.

TIP ▸ *To check out the prebuilt templates, Choose Title > Templates or click the Templates button at the top of the window.*

2. Most of the tools on the left side of the Title window are for adjusting the shape and color of the text and graphics you create. Many of these tools will be familiar to those of you who already use draw tools in programs like Adobe Illustrator and Macromedia FreeHand.

3. Click the Type Tool button in the toolbar to activate it (it looks like the letter T).

4. With the Type tool selected, mouse over the canvas. The cursor should change to an I-beam shape, indicating that the Type tool is active. Click on the canvas area and type *Escape*. The letters should appear in the light gray color as you type (**Figure 5.32**).

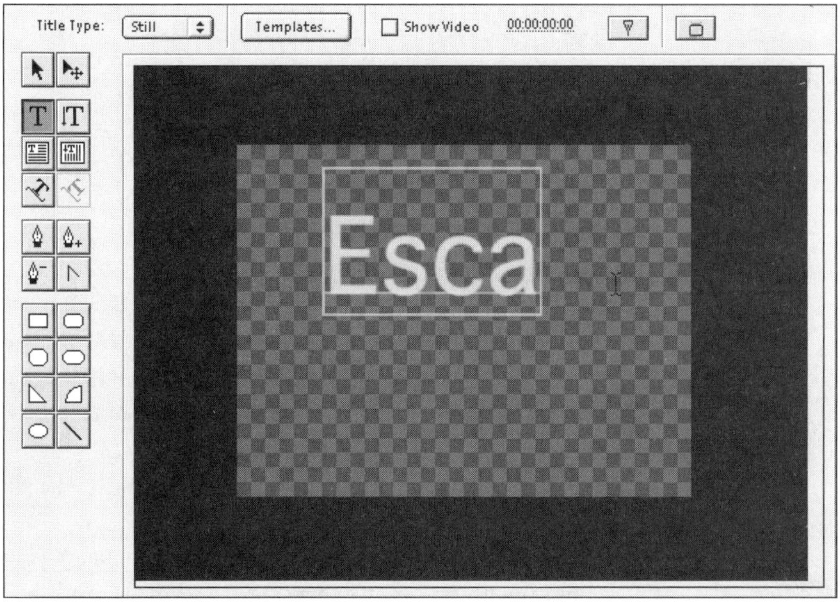

FIGURE 5.32
Click on the canvas area and type *Escape*.

Note that each additional text or graphic object that you create can also be moved independently.

5. Click and hold on the Font pop-up menu under Properties, and choose Arial Black Regular (or a similarly wide font) from the resulting menu (**Figure 5.33**).

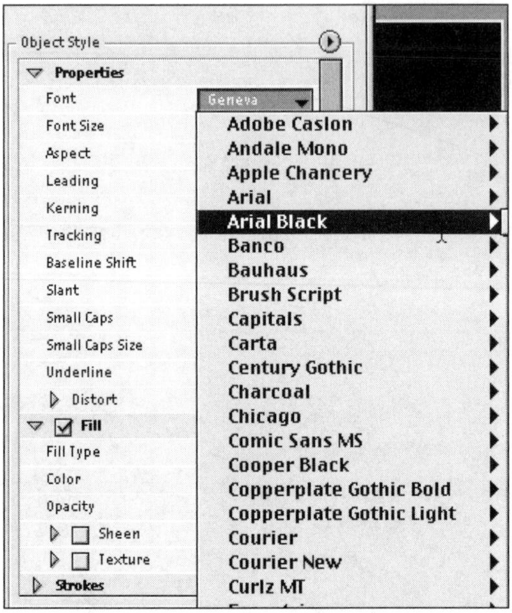

FIGURE 5.33
Choose the font from the pop-up menu.

Next, we'll adjust the size of the *Escape* text. Premiere 6.5 now uses special controls for adjusting the values. These new controls are underlined, interactive values called *hot text* controls.

6. Adjust the Font Size value to "48" by doing one of the following:

- Place the cursor over the Font Size hot text value. When the cursor becomes a finger with arrows on either side of it (Windows) or a hand (Mac OS), drag the value either to the left or down to decrease it, or to the right or up to increase it (**Figure 5.34**).

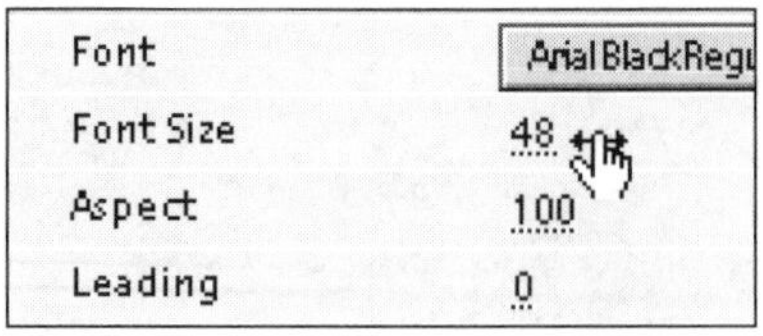

FIGURE 5.34
Adjusting the font size using Premiere 6.5's new hot text control (on the Mac OS, the cursor will appear as a hand when you place it over the Font Size hot text value).

TIP ▸ *Hold down the Shift key as you drag, and the value will change in increments of ten.*

or

- Click the hot text value to select it, and enter "48" as the new value.

TIP ▸ *Don't forget to save your work periodically. Unlike most other work inside Premiere, titles are saved separately from Premiere project files. In version 6.5, they will automatically appear in the Project window after being saved. Take the time now to choose File > Save to save your work thus far.*

7. Click and drag the title from the Project window into the Video 3 track of the Timeline, just above the slam.aif clip (**Figure 5.35**).

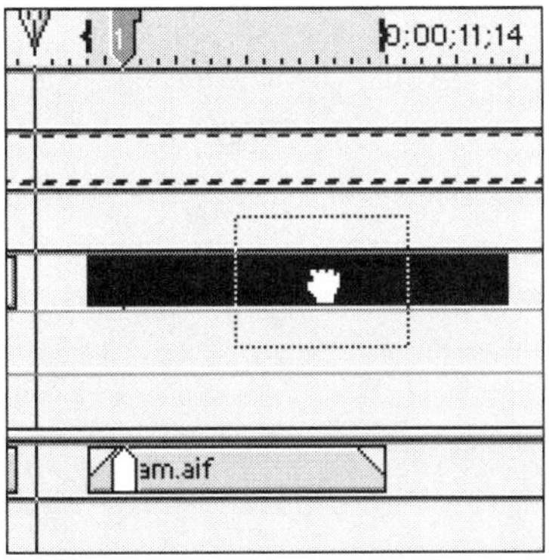

FIGURE 5.35
Once you've created your title, just drag it into the Video 3 track of the Timeline.

8. Adjust the title in the Timeline so that the left edge of the title lines up with the marker in the slam.aif clip.

TIP ▸ *Rather than creating all of the titles necessary for this 30-second commercial from scratch, just use the ones in the Titles bin that you already imported into the Project window from the Chapter5_Editing folder.*

Adjusting the Position of the Title

As I mentioned above, any text or draw object can be moved around in the Adobe Title Designer by simply clicking and dragging it with the Selection tool or the Move tool. Sometimes, though, you need to see how your title will look with the video itself. To adjust the color and position of a title precisely, you can use clips in the Timeline as a temporary background reference. (In the following example, you will adjust the title for the mtclouds.mov clip.)

1. With the *Escape* project open in the Timeline, double-click the title called climb_a_mountain2.ptl to open it in the Adobe Title Designer. This particular title is intended to go over the Mtclouds.mov clip.

2. Click the Show Video check box at the top of the Adobe Title Designer window (**Figure 5.36**).

3. Do one of the following:

- Click once on the Timecode hot text to the right of the Show Video check box, enter "1928" (for 19 seconds, 28 frames), and press Enter.

  or

- Click and drag on the hot text value until it shows "00:00:19:28."

TIP ▸ *Here is yet another way to load a background image from the Timeline: In the Timeline, position the Timeline marker on the frame you want; then, in the Title Designer window, click the Timeline Marker button (just to the right of the Timecode hot text).*

Figure 5.36
With the Show Video check box checked, you can quickly show any frame from your current Timeline as a temporary background image.

TIP ▸ *With the Show Video check box selected, you can find a good spot in the Timeline to put your title. Just click and drag on the Timecode hot text to quickly scrub through the whole Timeline until you find a good spot.*

Either way, you should now see the Mtclouds.mov clip in the background of the Title window. This background frame of video will not appear in your final title. It's merely a reference for you to see how the title will appear over the video clip so that you can make the proper adjustments. Notice how the light color of the text blends into the lighter areas of the background, making it difficult to read (**Figure 5.37**). In this case, the text practically disappears in the clouds.

Image courtesy of Cinenet

Figure 5.37
This title is hard to read against the cloudy background.

4. The best way to make the title more readable is to move the title to a different part of the frame (**Figure 5.38**). Of course, in video it's possible that the background is constantly changing. You just have to experiment to find the right place.

Image courtesy of Cinenet

Figure 5.38
To make your title readable, you may have to try moving it to a different part of the frame.

For the Web, Ignore Safe Title and Safe Action Boxes

You can turn the Safe Action and Safe Title frames on or off in the Adobe Title Designer by choosing Title > View > Safe Title or Title > View > Safe Action.

Fortunately as Web video producers, we can ignore the two frame outlines. These are the Safe Action and Safe Title areas that are important for television only (which cuts off the outer edges of every program). One of the tenets of Web video production is "filling the frame" with close-ups and large titles and graphics. If you are making a movie for the Web *and* TV, however, make sure your titles stay inside the inner Safe Title box (**Figure 5.39**).

IMAGE COURTESY OF CINENET

FIGURE 5.39
You only need to be concerned with these Safe Title and Safe Action boxes if you are making your program for TV.

Changing the Color of the Title

You can easily change the color of the title by selecting it in the main title window (so that the gray box appears around it) and then clicking on the Color chip under Fill Type and choosing a new color in the Color Picker (**Figure 5.40**).

Another way to pick a new color for your title is to use the Eyedropper tool:

1. Make sure your text is selected (you'll see a gray box).

2. Select the Eyedropper tool (just to the right of the Color chip).

FIGURE 5.40
Click on the Color chip to open the Color Picker, or click the Eyedropper to select a color in the image.

3. Click any color on your computer screen with the Eyedropper (**Figure 5.41**). In this case, I chose the dark gray/blue of the foothills in the Mtclouds.mov clip.

FIGURE 5.41
Choose a color for your title from the background video by using the Eyedropper tool.

Adding a Drop Shadow

Another popular technique for making video titles stand out from the background is to use a drop shadow:

1. Select the text in the Title window so that the gray text box appears around it.
2. Click the Shadow check box at the bottom of the Object Style menu to turn on this feature.
3. You can adjust the look of the drop shadow by changing the Color, Opacity, Angle, Distance, Size, and Spread (**Figure 5.42**). Just click and drag on the hot text value for each parameter, or click once on the hot text and enter a new value.

TIP ▸ *If you don't see a drop shadow, click on the Shadow Color chip swatch to open the Color Picker and make sure that it's set to pure black (Red=0, Green=0, Blue=0).*

FIGURE 5.42
Drop shadows can help video titles stand out from the background.

Adding a Graphic Background to the Text

The final option for making the title readable is adding some kind of graphic element behind the text (**Figure 5.43**):

1. Deselect the text in the canvas.

2. Click the Rectangle tool.

3. Under Object Style, make sure the Fill check box is checked, and that Fill Type is set to Solid.

4. Click on the Color chip, choose a dark (almost black) color, and click OK.

5. Click and drag over the text to create a dark-colored rectangle. (You may have to adjust the shape of rectangle to fit the shape of the text.)

6. Select the rectangle and choose Title > Arrange > Send to Back.

FIGURE 5.43
Adding a filled rectangle behind the text is one technique for making the text pop out.

7. If the contrast between the rectangle and the background is too stark, you can adjust the opacity (transparency) of the rectangle (**Figure 5.44**). Select the rectangle so that the gray handles appear around its edges. Then adjust the Opacity hot text value (downward) until you get to the desired transparency level.

Figure 5.44
You can lighten up your filled rectangle by adjusting the Fill > Opacity setting.

Adding a Title to the Timeline

1. Now you can add the title to the Timeline to see how it looks over a moving background and to adjust the timing and positioning. Choose File > Save to save your work. The completed title will appear automatically in the current bin of the Project window.

2. Click and drag the title into the Video 2 or Video 3 track of the Timeline, just above the Mtclouds.mov clip. You will have to click and drag the edges of the clip to stretch it across the desired length of time.

Adding Fade Effects to a Title

In general, I don't recommend using fade effects for the same reason I don't recommend using dissolve or fade transitions: Too many changing effects—and the resulting compression requirements—will degrade the visual quality of your presentation.

But in this particular spot, we've established a pattern in which the titles quickly fade in and then fade out. You can adjust the opacity of video clips using the rubberbands in the video tracks as you did when you adjusted the gain level in the audio tracks.

1. Click the triangle buttons next to the Video 2 track, then click and drag in the Timeline to create and position the little red handles. Once you've done that, click and drag these points to create short ramp-up and ramp-down fades (**Figure 5.45**).

FIGURE 5.45
Adjust the opacity of the clip to quickly fade in and fade out.

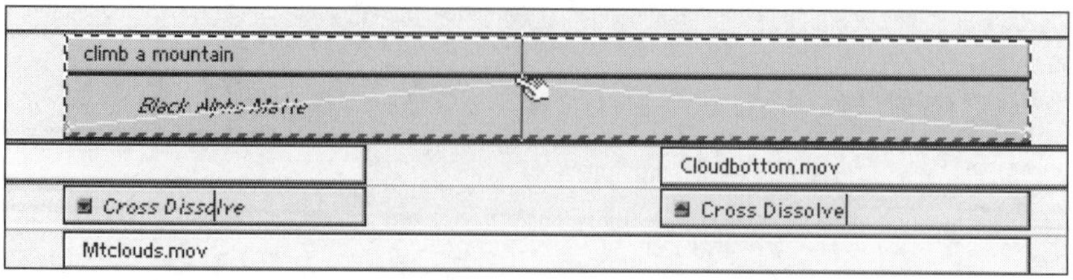

2. Stretch the yellow Work Area bar over the length of the clip and press the Enter key to have Premiere render the clip with the title superimposed on the moving background.

   Notice that Premiere automatically makes a pure white (or a pure black) background of the title window transparent. It applies a transparency mode called Alpha Matte by default to everything created in the Title window.

TIP ▸ *If you need to make a change in the title once it's in the Timeline, simply double-click the title to open the Title window.*

Mass-Producing Titles

This *Escape* movie calls for quite a few titles. The easiest way to mass-produce similar-looking titles in Premiere is to change an existing title and choose File > Save As to save the new title. However, in the case of this project, you can just open the pre-built project file, with all of the titles already in the Timeline.

"Escape" Shortcut

To skip to this point in the making of the 30-second *Escape* commercial, open the escape7.ppj project file in the Projects folder, located in the Escape_Practice_Files folder. Remember, though, if you want to see the titles and effects, you'll have to first rewind (by pressing A and then pressing Enter on your keyboard) so that Premiere can render them. The escape7.ppj project uses Premiere 6.0 titles that can be used in either Premiere 6.0 or Premiere 6.5.

Note: The "Escape_Practice_Files" folder contains two folders of titles:

- "Titles" contains Premiere 6.0 titles (which will open in Premiere 6.0 and Premiere 6.5)
- "Titles_New" contains the same titles, but in the Adobe Title Designer format (which requires Premiere 6.5).

Special Effects

Premiere comes with so many video effects (also known as video *filters*) that it would take a second book to describe them properly. Here's a list of the *categories* of video filters you can choose from: Adjust, Blur, Channel, Distort, Image Control, Perspective, Pixelate, QuickTime (which lets you choose from QuickTime's numerous library of effects), Render, Sharpen, Stylize, Time, Transform, and Video. And this doesn't even count the *dozens* of third-party plug-in filters available for Premiere! Not only can you combine multiple visual filters to create unique effects, but they are also *keyframe-able*, which means that their effect can be adjusted over time.

Here are a few of the most useful filters for Web video:

Black & White Filter

Let's start with a simple one. Since an important goal of this *Escape* spot is make the imagery in the first half of the timeline unappealing and lifeless, why not make it colorless? This is easy to do using the Black & White filter that is found in the Image Control bin of the Video Effects tab.

1. Choose Window > Show Video Effects to open the Video Effects palette.
2. Click the triangle button next to the Image Control bin to open it (**Figure 5.46**).

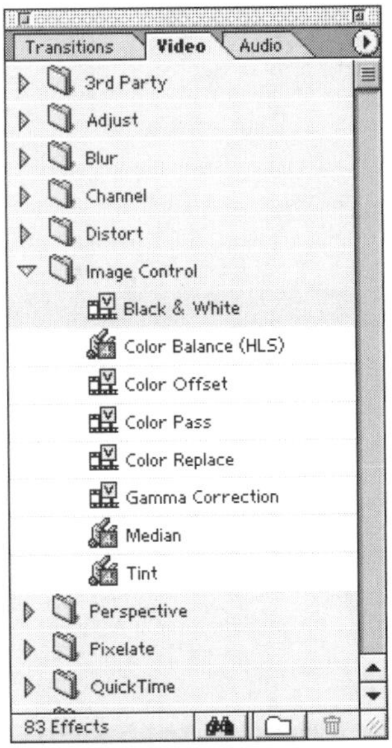

Figure 5.46 The Image Control bin in the Video Effects palette.

3. Click and drag the Black & White filter from the Image Control bin onto the clips you want to de-colorize. (In this case, that means the first five clips in the Video 1A track.)

Once filters are applied, clips exhibit a green label; and if you click the triangle button to expand them, a text label appears, indicating their new status (**Figure 5.47**).

Figure 5.47
The "city" clips that you've drained of color now have labels indicating their new, dreary black-and-white look.

Levels Filter

Next up is a filter that Premiere inherited from its older sibling, Adobe Photoshop. The Levels filter is essentially a color-correction and exposure-correction tool. We'll use it in this example to make the colors in the California clips as vibrant as possible.

1. Choose Window > Show Video Effects to open the Video Effects palette.

2. Click the triangle button next to the Adjust bin to open it.

3. Click and drag the Levels filter on to the target clip(s) in the Timeline. In this case, it will be the last five clips. This will automatically open the Effect Controls palette (**Figure 5.48**).

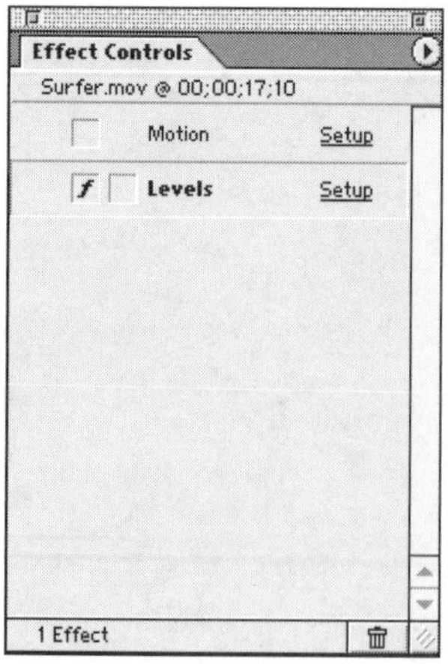

Figure 5.48
The Effect Controls palette lets you heighten the vibrancy and contrast of your clips.

4. Click Setup on the Effect Controls palette to open the Levels Settings dialog box.

5. There are triangular sliders under the histogram in the center of the screen (**Figure 5.49**): The left one is for blacks, the middle one is for grays, and the right one is for whites. The histogram shows you a graph of the colors in the clip: The *x*-axis represents the brightness values in the clip from the darkest to brightest; the *y*-axis shows the total number of pixels with that value. Slide the left triangle toward the center and the right one toward the center (as shown in the figure) so that the bulk of the information in the histogram is between those two sliders. Then slide the gray one in the center, if necessary, so that it is under the highest point of the histogram. The result is usually a sharper image with brighter colors because you've just narrowed the range of color values in the clip and increased the contrast between them.

6. Repeat this process for each of the California clips.

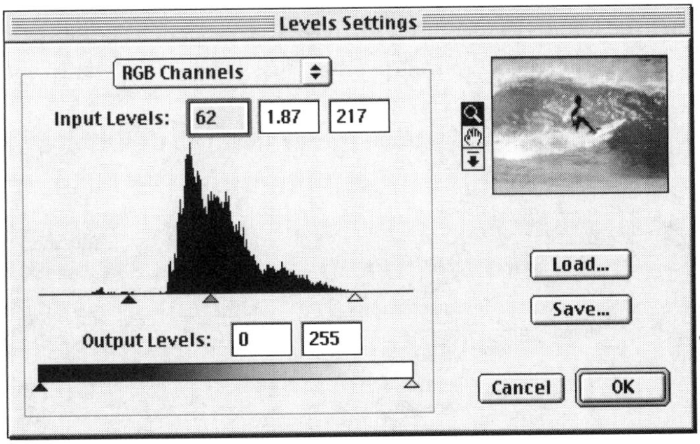

IMAGE COURTESY OF CINENET

FIGURE 5.49
The Levels Settings shows you a graphical representation of the color values in your clip and allows you to increase their brightness and contrast.

"Escape" Shortcut

To skip to this point in the making of the 30-second *Escape* commercial, open the escape8.ppj project file in the Escape_Practice_Files /Projects folder.

Transparency Settings

When you create a title, Premiere automatically makes everything except the text part of the title transparent. Premiere has many other types of transparency settings—all are different ways to make part of a video track transparent so that you can composite (merge) several layers of video at one time. These settings are also known as *keys*, for the keyhole effect they create. One key that I like to use for Web video is Multiply, which uses the bright areas of one video clip (the bottom) to make the bright areas of another (the top) video clip transparent. In this case, the result will be a transparent "California" title text, a slightly more magical way to introduce the second half of our spot than if it was just a solid color title.

1. Choose Window > Show Effect Controls (if the Effect Controls palette isn't already visible).

2. Select the to_california.ptl title in the Timeline.

3. With the to_california.ptl title still selected, click on Transparency Setup in the Effect Controls palette. This will open the Transparency Settings window.

4. Choose Multiply from the Key Type menu (**Figure 5.50**).

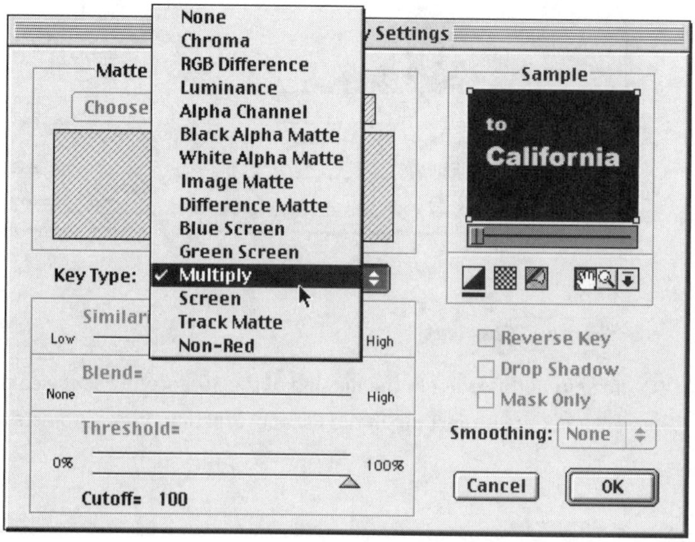

FIGURE 5.50 Choose the Multiply setting from the Key Type menu to make title text transparent.

5. Click OK.

6. Stretch the yellow Work Area bar over that section of the Timeline, and then press the Enter key. You should see the beach_people.mov clip playing through the text of the to_california.ptl title (**Figure 5.51**).

IMAGE COURTESY OF CINENET

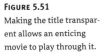

FIGURE 5.51
Making the title transparent allows an enticing movie to play through it.

Saving Your Movie

You're almost done. If you've followed this tutorial step-by-step and built your own Timeline, it will look a lot like mine, though probably not exactly—and that's as it should be (**Figure 5.52**).

Now that you've completed your movie, save it. You'll use it in the next chapter as raw material for Web compression. Be sure to keep an uncompressed copy for backup purposes—and because it will always look better than anything you make for the Web.

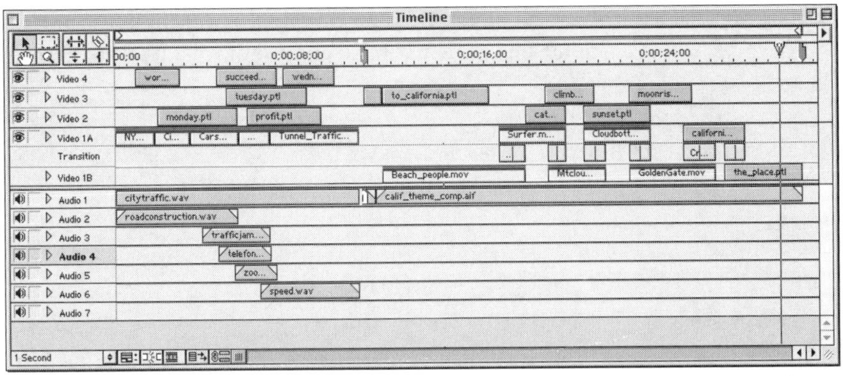

FIGURE 5.52
This shows my version of the completed *Escape* timeline. If you built your own, it will probably look a little different.

Outputting Your Finished Project to DV Tape

This pertains only to Premiere projects that have been captured and edited at full-screen (for example, 720 × 480 pixels) and full-motion (for example, 29.97 frames per second) using the DV codec. Even if your video is intended exclusively for the Web, it's still a good idea to output a copy of your edited movie to videotape. This will provide you with a high-quality backup copy. Remember: videotape is cheap; your time is precious.

1. Connect your DV camera or deck to your computer using a FireWire cable. Connect a video monitor or television to your DV device so that you can see the movie as it plays. Insert a blank tape into the DV device.
2. Play your movie from the Timeline window. If everything is connected properly, you should see your movie playing on the video monitor or television that is connected to your DV device. If you don't see the movie playing, check to see that the FireWire connections are properly made, that the DV device and monitor or television are turned on, and that your Premiere Project Settings are correct.
3. Click the Timeline window once to make it active. Press the A key to rewind the cursor to the first frame of the Timeline.
4. Set your DV device to Record mode.
5. Press the spacebar (or click the Play button under the Monitor window's Program view) to play your movie from the Timeline. The DV device will now record your movie to the DV tape.

Alternatively, you can choose File › Export Timeline › Print to Video. This allows you to add a color bar test pattern and a few seconds of black leader to your tape just before the movie starts.

You've now successfully made the movie that will soon (trust me) be up on the Web for all to see. In the next chapter you'll compress it, with your target audience in mind, and get a first-hand glimpse at what it takes to make Web video work well.

WEB VIDEO SPOTLIGHT

SFMOMA.org

San Francisco's Museum of Modern Art (SFMOMA) is one wired museum! It has interactive kiosks in almost every gallery, an extensive and constantly updated Web site, and its own line of interactive multimedia publications (**Figure 5.53**). To find out more about its Web video program, I spoke with the museum's Susie Wise, producer of interactive educational technologies, and Stuart Rickey, video producer.

SFMOMA's Web video projects are actually a part of several interactive multimedia projects that were designed to coincide with the opening of the new museum building in 1995. "Making Sense of Modern Art" and "Voices and Images of California Art" were gallery kiosk and CD projects featuring outstanding artists (such as Matisse, Pollock, Kahlo, and Rivera) and their works the museum exhibits. Spurred by the existence of remarkable archival footage of some of these artists, the SFMOMA team decided to produce video clips about the artists and their work. By the late 1990s, it was clear that the Web was *the* cutting-edge medium, and so the museum created its vibrant Web site, incorporating the multimedia works that originally had been created for kiosks and CD.

Wise describes their creative process: "We'll first figure out a series of questions or topics that a typical gallery visitor might have about an artist and his or her work. Sometimes these questions can be answered in text and pictures, sometimes in video." SFMOMA video clips are created from both archival and originally produced footage. Wise says, "We've had a huge range of experiences in terms of licensing and

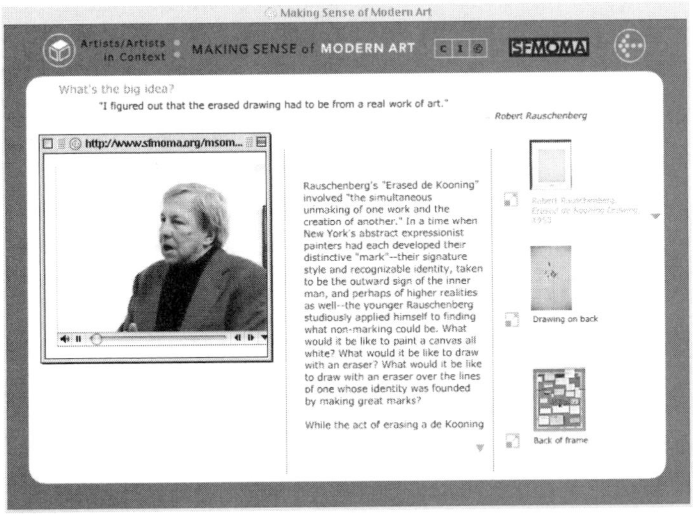

FIGURE 5.53
The San Francisco Museum of Modern Art's Web site features multimedia presentations of artists and their work.

permission issues for archival footage; sometimes there's no problem, sometimes the usage fees are too high, sometimes the rights holders have a fear of their footage being disseminated on the Web." As a result, the museum team has dedicated itself to creating a video archive of originally produced interviews with artists and scholars. Often, several points of view are presented in video clips, but the team firmly believes that showing the artists at work is always better than interviews with scholars. Before the team starts any video production, they create a single interactive page that combines HTML, pictures, Flash, and video; the final page appears both in the gallery kiosks and on the Web site.

Rickey explains that during a video production, they shoot for multiple media. "We made a decision early on not to dumb down the content for a 56K modem. There's a difference between being enslaved by the limitations of the [Web] medium and being aware of it," he says. The SFMOMA Web site uses a QuickTime Streaming Server and a QuickTime alternate system to detect the viewer's selected connection speed and serve the appropriate stream. The Web streaming files range from a 56K modem version that has a frame size of 192 by 144 pixels and is compressed at 26 kilobits per second (Kbps), to a DSL version that has a 248 by 186 frame and is compressed at 120 Kbps. The gallery kiosk (non-Web) versions of the movies are allowed a much higher data rate: They are compressed at 1200 Kbps but have the same frame size as the DSL version. All movies are compressed with the Developer version of the Sorenson Video codec and Discreet's Cleaner 5 software.

Since 1999 the museum has standardized its video production system on DV. Rickey shoots with a Canon XL-1 mini DV camera, and on occasion he will rent a Sony DSR 300. These cameras offer excellent picture quality, even at low light levels. As he puts it, "If you have budget issues, spend the money on the camera, not the lights." In postproduction, Rickey uses Macintosh computers running Apple Final Cut Pro, Adobe After Effects, Adobe Photoshop, and Cleaner 5.

Here are Stuart Rickey's Web video tips:

- Always shoot on a tripod.
- No wide shots.

  "I tend to shoot a medium shot or closer, with no panning or zooming."
- Use uncomplicated backgrounds.

  "I like dark, out-of-focus backgrounds. This allows the subject to pop out more. I generally use a soft key light from one side and a fill light (one stop lower) from the other side."

- Use a long lens for interviews.

  "I shoot from 15 to 20 feet away and use a long focal length to throw the background out of focus. Not only does this help the codec focus bits on the subject, it also makes for less background. Plus, people generally look better in a long lens."

- Put all the camera's settings into manual mode.
- Remove or reduce pans or zooms over still images as necessary.

  Many of the SFMOMA clips involve animating still images. Rickey does this in After Effects. To reveal different parts of a painting or photo, Rickey will pan or zoom on it. Sometimes this animation will work only for the DSL version of the movie. The 56K version will require Rickey to "freeze" the image to avoid unsightly compression artifacts.

- Use sound blankets to minimize echoes.

  The museum's galleries present a particular challenge, since they are large spaces with hard surfaces. "Sometimes we'll cover the entire floor," says Rickey.

- Always have interviews transcribed verbatim with timecode.

  Since many SFMOMA clips are shot as (sometimes very long) interviews, verbatim transcripts are critical for the video editor to quickly find particular sections of videotape.

- Juice the gamma 20 percent.

  "We have concluded that the world is Windows," says Rickey. He points out that displays on Windows computers are darker than on Macintosh screens. He first adjusts the video so that it looks right on his Macintosh, and then he boosts the gamma (the gray levels) on all of his movies by about 20 percent and slightly increases the contrast to +5.

When asked about the choice of the QuickTime media player, Rickey says that as a consumer he finds QuickTime has the most subtle and least distracting interface of the Big Three players. "We want the audience to focus on the content of the video clips, not on the player."

Both Wise and Rickey acknowledge that streaming Web video technology has its limitations. "Streaming at low bandwidths is a work in progress," says Rickey. But at SFMOMA, the content will always be paramount. Wise offers this final piece of advice: "Remember it's about storytelling...and keep it short."

To see some examples of SFMOMA's Web video clips

1. Go to `www.sfmoma.org/msoma/index.html`.
2. Click the red Start Program link.
3. After the intro, click Artists in Context.

(All of the following clips are accessed from the main Artists in Context screen. You can always get back to this screen by clicking the top of the "box" icon in the upper-left corner of the screen.)

- Click "The Sixties and Seventies."
  Click "Serra" (at the five o'clock position on the circle).
  Click "How was this work made?"
- Click "Rauschenberg Case Study."
  Click "Erased de Kooning" (at one o'clock on the circle).
  Click "What's the big idea?"
- Click "Post-Revolutionary Mexico."
  Click "Frida Kahlo" (at four o'clock on the circle).
  Click "How is Kahlo's painting different from Diego Rivera?"
- Click "Late 20th Century."
  Click "Robert Gober" (at two o'clock on the circle).
  Click "What's going in this gallery?"

Also check these other SFMOMA sites for video clips:

`www.sfmoma.org/msoma` (Making Sense of Modern Art)

`www.sfmoma.org/espace/viola` (Bill Viola)

`www.sfmoma.org/anderson` (Art as Experiment. Art as Experience)

`www.sfmoma.org/adams` (Ansel Adams)

`www.sfmoma.org/hesse` (Eva Hesse)

CHAPTER SIX

The Big Squeeze: Compression

Finally, the moment has arrived. You've created a good-looking movie, and now you're going to use powerful compression software to throw out most of it. By the time you're done with this chapter, you'll have a much smaller movie that you can distribute over the Web, as well as a clear sense of the trade-offs that Web video requires, at least for the moment. You don't have to be a computer geek to make good Web movies, but you do have to know what connection speed your target audience is likely to have, how you want to deliver your Web movie, and how you want to balance the trade-off between movie quality and movie size.

Understanding the Tools

Adobe Premiere offers several tools for compressing and optimizing movies for the Web. Its native tool for the job allows you to export a movie for the Web by selecting a frame rate, frame size, data rate, and compression algorithm (codec) for both audio and video in the Export Movie Settings dialog box. Premiere also ships with several third-party plug-ins that link stand-alone compression products directly to Premiere. These export plug-ins save you both time and hard drive space by letting you compress your edited movie directly from Premiere's Timeline using preset export settings. Without these export plug-ins, you would have to make a high-quality intermediate movie that you would then import into stand-alone compression software (which you'd also have to buy separately). Perhaps the most important benefit of the export modules is that they prevent accidental recompression; it's all too easy to mistakenly choose a lower-quality setting as you make an intermediate file for importing into the compression software.

To complicate matters somewhat, some of these plug-ins are operating-system–specific. The most versatile one (Save for Web/Cleaner 5 EZ) works only with Mac OS 9 (unless you are using an earlier version of Premiere, such as 6.0, in which the plug-in also works in Windows.

Here's a quick look at which plug-ins are supported by Premiere 6.5.

	Windows XP, ME, 2000, 98SE	Mac OS 9	Mac OS X
Advanced RealMedia Export	Yes	Yes	No
Advanced Windows Media Import/Export	Yes	No	No
Save for the Web/Cleaner 5 EZ	No	Yes	No
QuickTime Export (MPEG-4)	No	Yes	Yes

TIP ▸ *You can, and should, export your movie without any additional compression as a high-resolution video file. You might do this to create a backup version of your movie, to combine it with other video material in another software program, or to compress it with another tool created specifically for media optimization. But whatever your goal, one of the best tools for this job is Discreet's Cleaner 5, which provides you with access to dozens of options designed to optimize compression performance. However, Sorenson Squeeze, RealSystem Producer Plus (recently renamed to Helix Producer Plus), and Windows Media Encoder are all also very good, and may be better choices than Cleaner if you're only concerned with one or two formats.*

Understanding the Compression Process

No matter which export method you choose, you're going to compress your movie by using an encoder that analyzes each pixel in your movie and decides what to throw out and what to keep based on settings that you select. It is impossible to give you the exact settings that will make your movie shine on the Web. There's definitely an element of art to compression. Your choices will depend on the video you've shot, your own sense of aesthetics, your target audience's connection speed, and many other factors. But this chapter offers a set of Web-specific compression choices, along with comments on each, to help get you started (see "Codecs for Web Movies" later in the chapter).

All of your choices really boil down to controlling one or more of these four parameters: frame rate, frame size, spatial quality (how the movie looks visually), and temporal quality (or how smoothly it plays back). You can think of it as a four-way seesaw: You can give weight to one or more of these, but that will mean sacrificing one or more of the other factors.

Inside a Codec

Codecs plug into the media players in the modular way that fonts plug into word processors. Like fonts, each codec offers its own set of characteristics. But all Web video and audio codecs perform the same task—to reduce the data rate of your movie so that you can deliver it over the Web within a reasonable amount of time and so that it will play back well. Digital video (DV or DVCam version), which is compressed as it's shot, has a data rate of 3.6 MB per second (Mbps). In order to deliver your movie over the Web, you're going to have to get that data rate down to something between 5 kilobytes per second and 50 kilobytes per second (Kbps). The trick, of course, is to significantly reduce the video signal without throwing out so much data that your movie becomes a grainy blob. That means codecs must throw out an awful lot of data without destroying your movie. Most do it by analyzing data both within and between frames.

One thing codecs take advantage of is the way that human eyesight works. The human eye is much more sensitive to changes in the *luminance*, or brightness, of a signal than to changes in the *chrominance*, or color, of that signal. So most video codecs take advantage of this fact by simply throwing out much of the color information.

Codecs use many techniques, such as color averaging, to economize on the data needed to describe a frame of video. *Spatial compression* (also known as *intraframe* compression) removes redundant information within individual frames. For example, picture an image of a sandy (white) landscape with a blue sky: Instead of describing the image by saying, "pixel 1 is blue, pixel 2 is blue, pixel 3 is blue," and so on, spatial compression says, "pixels 1 through 480 are blue." More specifically, the codec divides each frame of video into small rectangular blocks, and then averages the colors in each block (**Figure 6.1**).

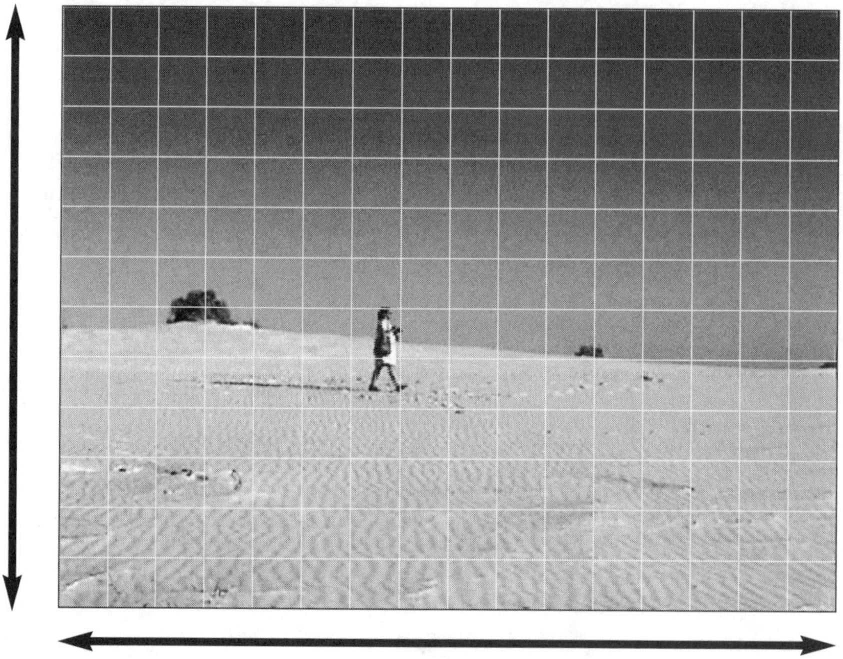

Figure 6.1
Spatial compression divides each frame into rectangular blocks and then averages the color information in each block to reduce the data rate of the overall file.

Most codecs further divide every rectangular block into smaller blocks, and then count the different colored pixels in each block. Let's say the codec finds 19 blue pixels, 5 green pixels, and 1 red pixel in one of those blocks. The software will average the colors and pronounce this particular block to be "blue," effectively throwing out the green and red information (**Figure 6.2)**. Of course, no compression scheme is quite this simple. In practice, stray pixels are best prevented by careful preprocessing of the video (before compression). Most compression software packages also have n*oise reduction* features that are user-adjustable.

FIGURE 6.2
Spatial compression software also divides every rectangular block into smaller blocks, and then counts the different colored pixels in each smaller block to effectively average the colors within each large block.

Temporal compression (also known as *interframe* compression) removes information that is repeated over time, from frame to frame. Temporal compression takes advantage of the fact that any given frame is probably similar to the frames before and after it. Instead of storing the entire frame, the codec stores just the differences between it and the preceding frames. It saves a *keyframe*, which is a complete frame, at regular intervals to refresh the image. Keyframes have a maximum interval (specified in either frames or seconds), but generally they're inserted as needed rather than inserted at regular intervals. In the other frames, called *delta frames*, it saves only the information that has changed since the last keyframe (**Figures 6.3** through **6.10**).

FIGURE 6.3
This is a keyframe, which shows the complete image.

FIGURE 6.4
This is a delta frame, which shows just the part of the image that has changed since the previous keyframe—in this case, the woman entering the image.

FIGURE 6.5
This delta frame shows the woman's progression as she walks across the sand—notice the lengthening shadow.

FIGURE 6.6
This keyframe refreshes the complete image, this time with the woman *in* the picture.

FIGURE 6.7
This delta frame again shows just the new information in the image—the woman moving toward the right of the frame.

Figure 6.8
This delta frame shows her progressing further to the right.

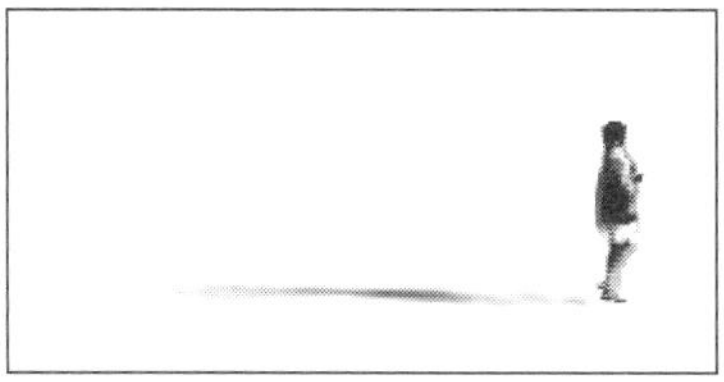

Figure 6.9
This keyframe refreshes the entire picture, making it easy to see how far the woman has progressed.

Figure 6.10
This delta frame shows only the shadow the woman has left after exiting the frame.

To see all this spatial and temporal compression in action, play the whitesands-walk.mov movie in the Chapter6_Compression folder on the CD.

TIP ▸ *All the project files for the projects in this chapter are kept in the Chapter6_Compression folder on the CD.*

Using Premiere to Compress Your Movie

You can use Premiere to compress a movie for the Web and avoid bothering with third-party plug-ins altogether. Before version 6 came along, in fact, that was your only choice. While the plug-ins make compression easier by offering you presets for specific Web delivery scenarios, they usually serve only one or two of the main operating systems (Windows and Mac OS). Using Premiere directly is the only export method that works on all operating systems that Premiere supports. Plus, using it is a good learning experience: Fine-tuning the export settings requires you to make critical compression choices yourself. Understanding what you're doing helps to demystify the black art of compression. And what you learn by doing it applies to the third-party plug-ins that now come with Premiere—and any other video compression or editing tool you might use down the road.

We'll make a progressive-downloading QuickTime movie suitable for viewing over a 56K modem (*progressive downloading* means the movie can start playing before it has fully downloaded from server to hard drive).

Choosing Your Options

Choosing the Project Settings

1. In the Timeline, drag the yellow Work Area bar over the entire escape.mov film that you created in Chapter 5.

2. Choose File > Export Timeline > Movie to open the Export Movie window. Click the Settings button to open the Export Movie Settings dialog box (**Figure 6.11**).

3. Choose the File Type for the file to be exported. Use the QuickTime mode to export a QuickTime movie.

TIP ▸ *When you first launched Premiere, you had to choose your project settings. For our exercises, you used the WebVideo_Exercises preset that came on the CD. But you can make other choices, and if you do, you'll see different choices in the File Type pull-down menu here. For example, if you're working on Windows, you may choose Video for Windows, QuickTime for Windows, or some proprietary format as the Editing mode. On a Mac, you get QuickTime or a proprietary format as your Editing mode. (Proprietary formats are third-party codecs that work only with a specific capture card, such as the Pinnacle DV500.) In the case of Video for Windows, you can export your movie as an AVI or Windows Media file.*

Figure 6.11
The Export Movie Settings dialog box.

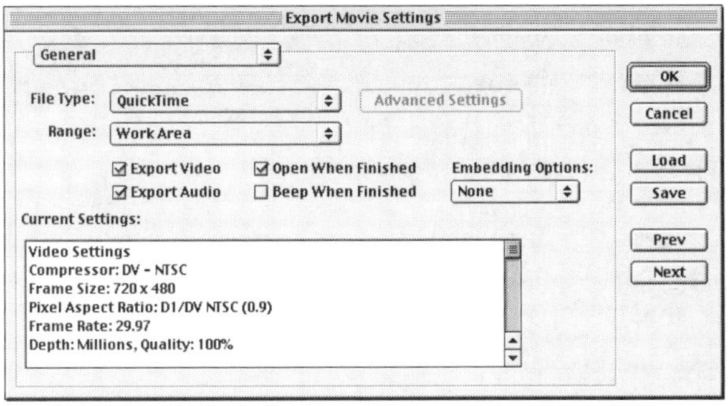

3. Use the Range pop-up menu to pick one of the following:
   - Entire Project (this will export everything in your Timeline)
   - Work Area (this will export the area of the Timeline that you have indicated with the yellow Work Area bar)
4. Make sure both the Export Video box and the Export Audio box are checked.

Choosing the Video Settings

1. In the Export Movie Settings dialog box, click Next to access the Video section of the dialog box.
2. Click the Compressor pull-down menu, and choose Sorenson Video 3 from the list of video compressors, or codecs (**Figure 6.12**).

   Sorenson Video 3 is the best choice for making QuickTime Web movies, because it produces low data rates and relatively good quality.

Figure 6.12
Premiere offers these video codecs when you export in the QuickTime format.

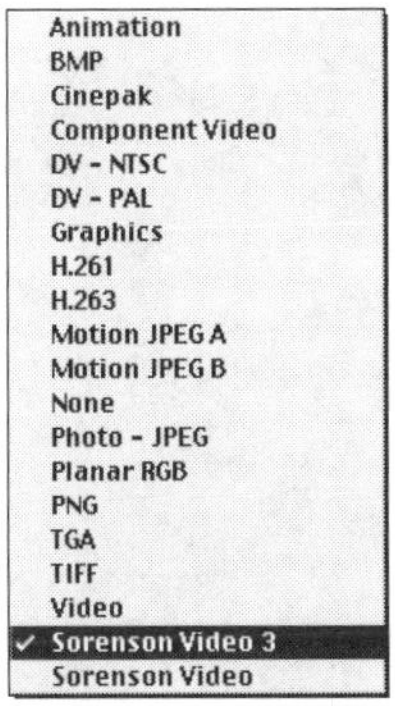

TIP ▸ *If you don't see Sorenson Video 3 on the list, you'll need to download the most current version of QuickTime from* `www.apple.com/quicktime/download`.

3. Pick Millions for the Depth setting.

   Other codecs allow you to decrease the colors here, but decreasing won't give you much of a reduction in your movie's data rate.

4. Change the frame size of your movie to 160 × 120.

   Reducing the frame size of your movie will reduce the data rate, too. A 160 × 120 movie has only 6 percent of the pixels contained in a 640 × 480 movie, the standard for full-screen display on a computer monitor, and only 25 percent of the pixels contained in a 320 × 240 movie, such as the source clips for the *Escape* project. The frame size is one aspect of Web video optimization that is totally under your control. Just remember the four-way seesaw: If you want to keep the frame bigger, you can, but the other three variables will have to be reduced instead to maintain the same quality (**Figure 6.13**).

For an illustration of what happens when you change the frame size, look at the Frame_Size folder in the Chapter6_Compression folder on the CD. In it, you'll see four QuickTime movies, each with a different frame size: 240 × 180, 320 × 240, 400 × 300, and 640 × 480. The frame size is the only variable; all other parameters, such as the 10 frames per second (fps) frame rate, were held constant during compression. The point here is to show the trade-offs you make when you change any of these variables: The larger the frame size, the more the spatial (visual) and temporal (motion) quality will suffer.

FIGURE 6.13
Reducing the frame size is a good way to make your movies look better at a specified data rate.

5. Reduce the Frame Rate setting to 10.

Reducing the frame rate from 15 fps to 10 fps theoretically reduces your movie's data rate by 30 percent, but it also makes your movie play back less smoothly (read *positively jerky*; this is just one of the sacrifices we must make to play our movies on 56K modems; see **Figure 6.14**). To minimize the jerkiness, divide the frame rate by whole numbers. If you were compressing DV-NTSC video, which plays at nearly 30 fps, you would divide by, say, 2, 3, or 4 to get frame rates of 15, 10, and 7.5, respectively. The data rate reduction might not be proportional to the reduction in frame rate. This depends on the codec you are using and the type of footage in your movie. For example, with the Sorenson Video 3 codec and a static "talking head" shot, cutting the frame rate in half may only reduce the data rate by 20 percent.

As an illustration of what happens when you change the frame rate, look at the frame_rate folder on the CD. In it, you'll see four QuickTime movies at four separate frame rates: 30 fps, 15 fps, 10 fps, and 7.5 fps. The only variable in these movies is the frame rate; all other parameters (such as the 320 × 240 frame size) were held constant during compression. The movie plays back more smoothly at 30 fps, but the visual quality suffers.

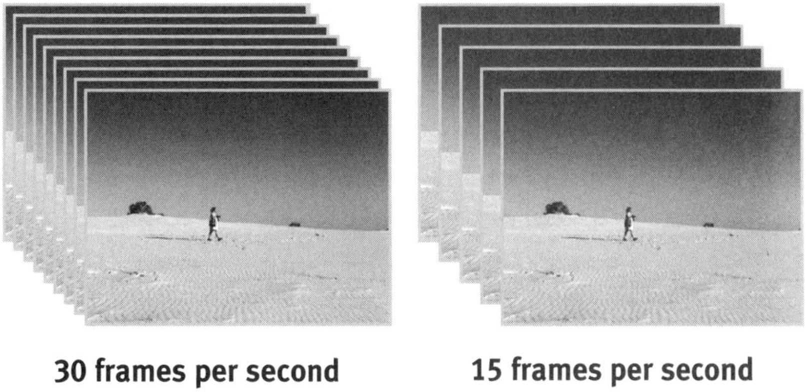

FIGURE 6.14 Reducing the frame rate reduces the data rate of the movie, but it also reduces the motion quality, making the movie play back in a more jerky fashion.

Setting the Video Data Rate

Choosing your codec and then specifying the effective data rate is usually the most critical step in compressing your Web movies. If you set the data rate too high—higher than the connection speed of the viewer—a streaming movie won't play smoothly on the target computer, and a progressive-downloading movie will require a longer wait for the viewer. If the data rate is too low, the movie will have unnecessarily low quality. (See "Kilobits vs. Kilobytes," below, for an explanation of what these two units, both used to measure data rates, really mean.)

Kilobits vs. Kilobytes

A very annoying little bugaboo of making Web video is that there are two different units of measurement for data rates. Most Internet connection speeds and data rates are expressed in *kilobits* (such as "56 *kilobits* per second"). File sizes and data rates are sometimes expressed in *kilobytes* (such as "100 *kilobytes* per second"). Adobe Premiere uses kilobytes.

These terms are not interchangeable: 1 kilobyte = 8 kilobits. (On top of this, the "kilo" in kilobytes is 1,024 and the "kilo" in kilobits is 1,000, but let's not go there!) An occupational hazard of Web video is that you will constantly be converting back and forth between *kilobits* and *kilobytes*, as you'll see when we get to the math exercise below.

In this book, we use the following abbreviations:

- kilobits = Kb
  kilobits per second = Kbps
- kilobyte = KB
  kilobytes per second = KBps

The one exception to the rule (and there's always an exception, right?) will be for modem data transfer rates. For instance, the most typical dial-up modem used today is 56 Kbps; however, since this is so widely referred to by the shorthand term "56K," that's the way we will refer to it:

- 56 Kbps modem = 56K modem

Although 56K modems can technically receive data at 56 Kbps (or 53 Kbps in the United States), you probably know from personal experience that your modem usually connects at data rates that are less than that. Since most viewers will be able to reliably connect at 40 Kbps, you should use total (video and audio) data rates of 40 Kbps or less for minimal delay.

You could just set the data rate at around 40 Kbps and leave it at that. Since this is a progressive-downloading movie, you can either make the data rate a little lower, to ensure that the movie plays back smoothly as it downloads from the Web, or a little higher, to preserve higher quality—albeit at the expense of making the viewer wait a little longer (while the media player buffers more media).

But remember, the data rate you enter here is only for the video portion of the movie. You also need to leave some room for the audio portion, since that too has to travel across the Web to your audience's computers (see "Choosing the Audio Settings," below).

You need to calculate the data rate for the video portion of your movie given the codec you've chosen—in this case, Sorenson Video 3. Fortunately, the folks who make the Sorenson codec have devised a formula to get the best performance out of their codec:

$$\frac{\text{Data rate (in KBps)} = \text{width} \times \text{height} \times \text{fps}}{48{,}000}$$

So, in our example, the formula would go like this:

$$160 \text{ width} \times 120 \text{ height} \times 10 \text{ fps} = 192{,}000$$

$$\frac{192{,}000}{48{,}000} = 4 \text{ KBps}$$

To get the equivalent data rate measured in kilobits, multiply by 8:

$$4 \text{ KBps} \times 8 = 32 \text{ Kbps}$$

NOTE ▸ This formula is just a rough rule of thumb to get you started; your results will obviously vary depending on the type of footage you have.

Now we know we'll have only 8 Kbps left over for the audio portion if we want to stay around the 40 Kbps data-rate ceiling that we set for ourselves.

To set the video data rate:

1. Still in the Export Movie Settings dialog box, select the Limit Data Rate To check box, and enter "5" in the "K/sec" field.

   This sets the data rate at 5 Kbps. With the Sorenson codec, you can set the data rate one of two ways: via the Data Rate setting, as in this step, or via the Quality slider in the lower left corner. If you specify a data rate in the Data Rate settings, as we have here, the Quality slider setting will be ignored.

I can find no use for the Quality slider, a vestige of the original QuickTime interface. It's just not precise enough for Web video, and I recommend against it. (But in case you're interested, here's how it works: Higher numbers on this slider will give you higher spatial quality and higher data rates. Lower numbers will give you lower quality and lower data rates. To use it, you would turn off all Data Rate settings, set a Quality level, compress the movie, look at the results, and then, based on the quality you see, adjust the slider again. Using the Quality slider allows the codec to increase the data rate as needed to maintain the quality setting you choose with the slider. This often results in data "spikes.")

2. Select Square Pixels from the Pixel Aspect Ratio pull-down menu.

   All Web video uses square pixels, so even if your source footage was D1/DV NTSC, you will want to convert it to square pixels at this point.

3. Leave the Recompress box unchecked.

   If by chance some sections of the Timeline were already compressed with exactly the right settings for your Web movie, then leaving this box unchecked would ensure that those sections will simply be copied, rather than compressed a second time. In all likelihood, your footage will need to be compressed anyway, in which case you can ignore this check box. Recompression is a bad idea—it means the quality is potentially reduced twice.

Choosing the Audio Settings

1. In the Export Movie Settings dialog box click the Next button to open the Audio Settings window. The audio track to your movie is compressed by audio codecs, which, like video codecs, each have their own distinctive effect.

   Here are appropriate settings for our 56K *Escape* movie:

   Rate: 22,050 Hz
   Reducing the sample rate from 44,100 to 22,050 cuts the data rate in half.

   Format: 16-bit Mono
   Changing the file from stereo to mono cuts the data rate in half again.

   Compressor: QDesign Music 2
   This codec is a real mainstay of Web audio in the QuickTime format. It can compress music and sound effects at a rate of up to 100:1 with excellent results.

TIP ▸ *If your soundtrack is made up of voices rather than music, you might find that the speech-optimized Qualcomm PureVoice codec gives you better results than QDesign Music at very low data rates.*

2. When you choose QDesign Music 2 in the Compressor menu, an Advanced Settings button appears to the right of the Compressor field (**Figure 6.15**).

   Click the Advanced Settings button next to QDesign Music 2. This opens the QDesign codec interface, where you can adjust the data rate. Choose "10 kbits/s" from the list (**Figure 6.16**). Click OK.

   This will make the total combined video and audio data rate for our movie about 50 Kbps, which is close enough (for a progressive-downloading movie) to our 40 Kbps target. For a progressive-downloading movie, a higher data rate simply means that the viewer will have to wait a little longer to download (into QuickTime's buffer) before it starts playing.

FIGURE 6.15
If you're optimizing a movie for Web delivery, use these audio settings in the Export Movie Settings dialog box.

FIGURE 6.16
Choose a data rate for the audio track of your movie.

3. Select "1 Second" on the Interleave pull-down menu. This setting controls how often audio information is loaded into RAM and inserted among frames of video. A low value needs less RAM, a larger value requires more RAM.

4. Under Processing Options, set Enhance Rate Conversion to Best. This will give you higher quality audio. The only cost is that it will take a little longer to compress the movie.

Choosing the Remaining Settings

1. Click the Next button to open the Keyframe and Rendering section (**Figure 6.17**). The only setting to change is the number of frames between each keyframe. Enter 100 here.

   If you want to provide quick random access for viewers, the rule of thumb is 1 keyframe every 10 seconds, and our frame rate is 10 fps. You could lower the number to increase *random access* (the ability of the viewer to jump quickly to any point in the movie). You only need to raise this number if you see a *keyframe flashing* effect (a noticeable difference in the quality of keyframes versus delta frames) in your compressed Web movie.

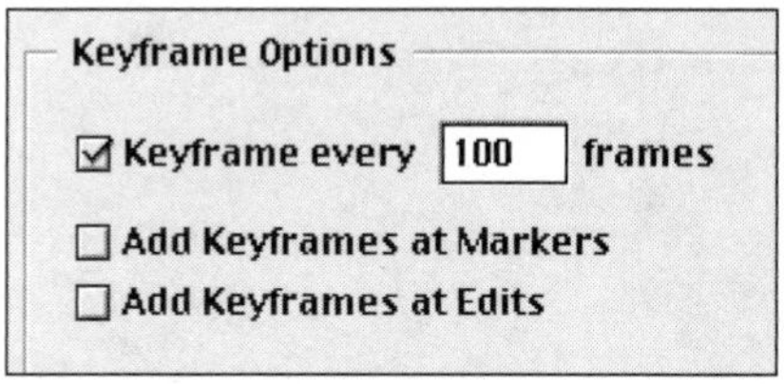

FIGURE 6.17
If you're optimizing a movie for Web delivery, the rule of thumb is 1 keyframe every 10 seconds.

TIP ▸ *Premiere allows you to add keyframes at Markers (that you add in the Timeline) and at every edit point in your movie, if you find those to be necessary.*

Check out the two versions of the *Escape* movie in the "keyframes" folder on the CD. One has very frequent keyframes (every 5 frames), the other has very rare keyframes (every 500 frames). You will notice that the clip with rare keyframes plays quite smoothly, but random access (jumping to a particular frame) is limited. The frequent keyframes movie shows signs of visible keyframe flashing.

2. Click the Next button on the Keyframe and Rendering dialog box to open the Special Processing window. Click Modify to open the Special Processing controls (**Figure 6.18**).

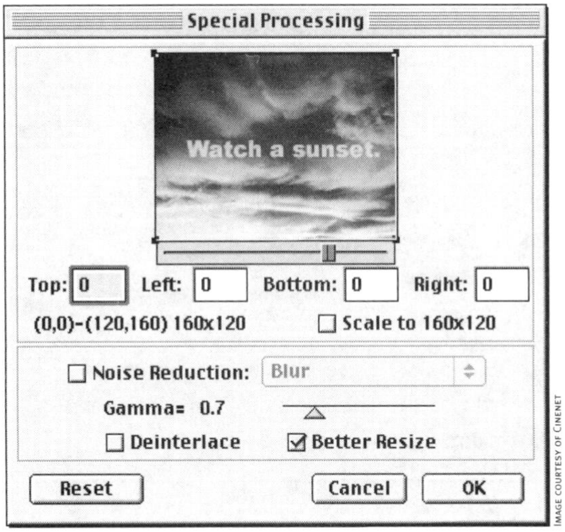

FIGURE 6.18
These are the Special Processing options you can choose from the Export Movies Settings dialog box.

Features of the Special Processing Window

CROPPING: You can manually or numerically cut off the edges of the movie. This cropping tool is good for eliminating any unwanted pixels at the edge of the frame, especially the black lines that often appear in freshly captured footage from an analog source. You don't want your codec to waste precious bits on unwanted video noise! The footage you used for the *Escape* project doesn't have any noise, so you can leave this field set to 0.

This cropping tool also offers you another way to get creative with the shape of the movie. To see a couple of examples, look in the Wide_v_Tall folder on the CD.

NOISE REDUCTION: *Blurring* usually helps the video codec apply spatial compression, because it makes pixels look more like their neighbors. You can choose from three different kinds of blur. (Try just plain Blur for starters.)

GAMMA: Gamma adjusts the midrange (gray) brightness levels, without changing the very bright (white) or very dark (black) levels. Computer monitors are generally darker than television screens, and computers running the Windows OS are usually set darker that Mac screens. To brighten the image, move the slider to the left. (Try 0.7 to start.)

DEINTERLACE: The Deinterlace setting converts the two video fields that make up a frame of NTSC video into one frame. You don't need to do this if you shot your video on a camera that offers progressive scan mode and you used this feature. You also don't need this for our *Escape* movie because the source footage has already been deinterlaced.

BETTER RESIZE: If you're scaling your frame size (and you are), then choose this option, which uses higher-quality scaling at the cost of a little extra compression time.

3. Click OK to close Special Processing window.

4. Give your new movie a descriptive name and click Save (**Figure 6.19**).

   Premiere will export and compress your movie.

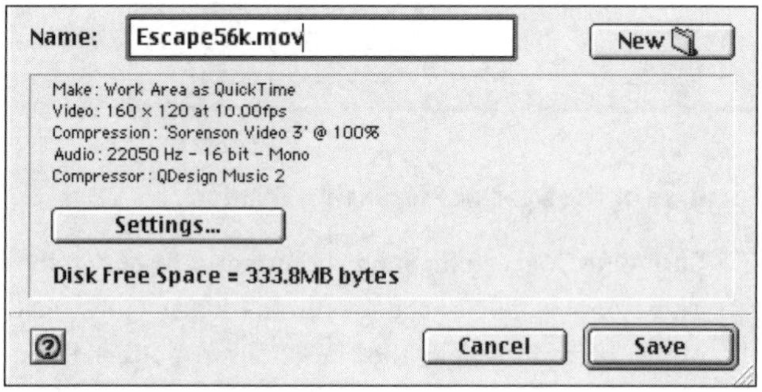

FIGURE 6.19
The final step: saving your movie. This step both compresses and exports your movie.

To see the movie these settings produce, open escape_qt_56k.mov on the CD.

Watching the Result

If this is the first time you have compressed a movie for the Web, brace yourself. You may be disappointed. The rich images and audio that you so carefully edited will be reduced to a jerky, pixelated mess. Don't despair! This was just the first attempt. Video compression is both a science and an art, and it requires plenty of trial and error. One standard technique is to compress a 5- to-10-second portion of the final movie repeatedly, changing one parameter (such as frame rate or noise reduction) at a time. You will learn more with each change you make and eventually improve the result. Then, once you're happy with the settings, you can compress the whole movie. Plus, there are still many other things you can do to present your Web movie in the best possible way. Read on!

Making Several Different Versions of a Progressive Download Movie

One way you can improve the presentation of your movie is to publish several versions of it on the Web. Although a significant portion of the Web-surfing public uses 56K dial-up modems, viewers with higher connection speeds can see better-looking incarnations of your movie if you offer different versions of it. As you've seen in several Video Spotlights in this book, your Web site can have a menu of different versions for each movie. For example, you might want to make a 56K modem version, one ISDN version at around 120 Kbps, and one DSL/cable-modem version at 500 Kbps.

To give you an idea of what our *Escape* project would look like at these data rates, the CD contains three versions of the movie (56 Kbps, 120 Kbps, and 500 Kbps) for *each* of the Big Three media players: QuickTime, RealOne Player, and Windows Media Player. You can find them in the Escape_Compression_Examples folder in the Chapter 6 _Compression folder on the CD. (There's also a version of each of the QuickTime movies using the professional editions of the Sorenson and QDesign codecs.)

Remember the four-way seesaw: In these example movies, I increased the frame size and frame rate when the higher data rate allowed it, but for an apples-to-apples comparison, I set the maximum display size at 320 × 240 for all of the movies. One other note: In order for you to be able to compare your own compression tests with these movies, I have used the same (quarter-resolution) source files that you used to make your *Escape* movie; just bear in mind that full-screen, full-motion source files would provide better results.

Making Adjustments: Premiere's Data Rate Analyzer

If you're a numbers person, you'll find Premiere's Data Rate Analyzer a useful way to assess the trade-off between a movie's quality and its data rate. Here's how to use it:

1. Open your compressed movie in Premiere. Then, do one of the following:

- Select the clip in the Project window or the Timeline.

  or

- Double-click the clip to open it in the Monitor window.

2. Choose Clip > Properties.

   This text-filled window has all the essential information about the clip, including the average data rate, the frame rate, and the codecs used (**Figure 6.20**).

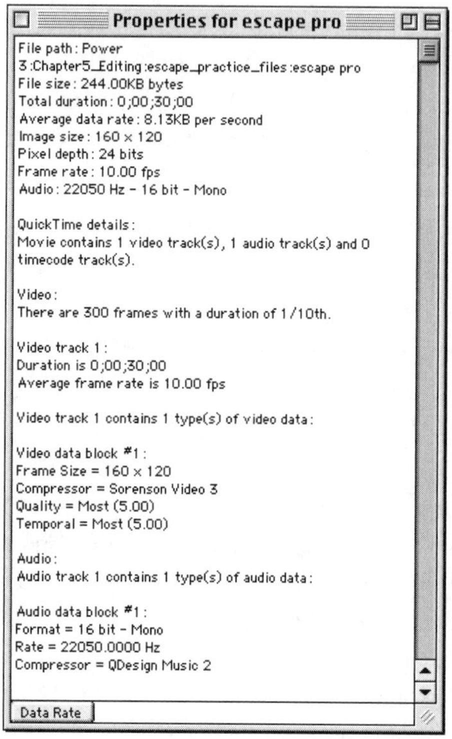
Properties for escape pro
File path: Power
3:Chapter5_Editing:escape_practice_files:escape pro
File size: 244.00KB bytes
Total duration: 0;00;30;00
Average data rate: 8.13KB per second
Image size: 160 x 120
Pixel depth: 24 bits
Frame rate: 10.00 fps
Audio: 22050 Hz - 16 bit - Mono
QuickTime details:
Movie contains 1 video track(s), 1 audio track(s) and 0 timecode track(s).
Video:
There are 300 frames with a duration of 1/10th.
Video track 1:
Duration is 0;00;30;00
Average frame rate is 10.00 fps
Video track 1 contains 1 type(s) of video data:
Video data block #1:
Frame Size = 160 x 120
Compressor = Sorenson Video 3
Quality = Most (5.00)
Temporal = Most (5.00)
Audio:
Audio track 1 contains 1 type(s) of audio data:
Audio data block #1:
Format = 16 bit - Mono
Rate = 22050.0000 Hz
Compressor = QDesign Music 2
Data Rate

FIGURE 6.20
The information-rich Clip Properties window tells you a lot about what's really going on in a compressed movie.

3. Click the Data Rate button at the bottom of the window.

   This opens the Data Rate Graph (**Figure 6.21**), which plots the amount of data allocated for every frame in the movie. The time is shown at the top of the graph. The tall red columns indicate keyframes. The shorter blue columns indicate delta frames. The squiggly white line indicates a running average of the data rate. This Data Rate Graph gives you an accurate snapshot view of how the data is being allocated in your movie, which is often more useful than just getting the average data rate. It can help you assess any adjustments you might need to make in your compression techniques.

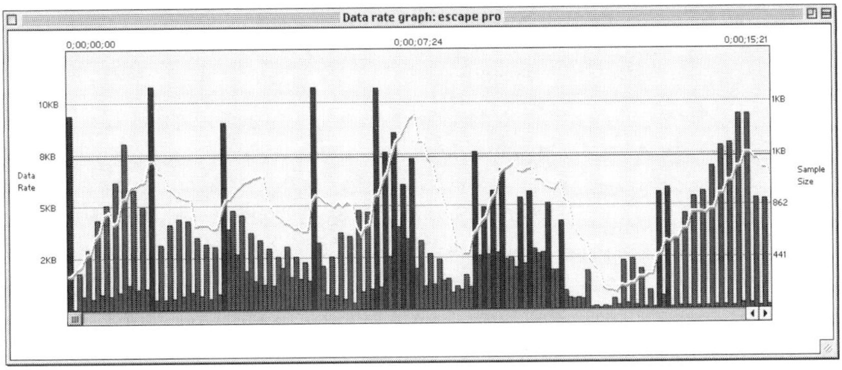

FIGURE 6.21
The Data Rate Graph gives you an accurate snapshot of how the data is being allocated in your movie, rather than simply an average data rate.

Codecs for Web Movies

While Premiere 6.5's "Save for Web/Cleaner 5 EZ" feature (Mac OS 9 only) picks the video and audio codecs for you, all the other export and compression methods require you to make that decision yourself. The following video and audio codecs are designed for low-data-rate movies—and in most cases that includes Web movies. All three media players can *auto-update* codecs; that means that when your copy of the media player encounters a movie that requires a new codec, or a new version of a codec, it will automatically update its collection of codecs for your computer.

(Note: There are other codecs available for the Big Three media players, especially QuickTime. But the list below contains only the codecs that you would consider for making *Web* movies. Also, many of these codecs are free; we provide prices for those that aren't.)

Video Codecs for Web Movies

- Windows Media Video

  This is the primary video codec for Windows Media. The current version is Windows Media Video 9. Since it comes preinstalled on the many PCs running Microsoft Windows, this is a media player format and codec that cannot be ignored. Fortunately, the current version also happens to deliver high quality in both the streaming and downloading forms.

- RealVideo

  This is the primary video codec for RealNetworks/RealOne Player format. The current version is RealVideo 9. While it can be used for downloading files, its primary use is streaming (single- and multi-bit rate encoding) using special streaming servers. While older codecs ("RealVideo 8," "G2," and "G2+SVT") also come with the RealVideo installation, RealVideo 9 is really the only one to use.

continued ›

- Sorenson Video

  Although QuickTime works with a wide variety of codecs, Sorenson is QuickTime's flagship video codec. Use it for high-quality QuickTime Web video, both progressive downloading and RTSP streaming. The current and most advanced version is Sorenson Video 3. A basic version of Sorenson comes free with the standard QuickTime installation. A more powerful and elaborate Professional Edition is available with the Sorenson Squeeze product for $299.

- Sorenson Spark

  This codec is a proprietary enhancement of the H.263 video codec that plays inside the Macromedia Flash Player 6. This codec is a proprietary enhancement of the H.263 video codec that plays inside the Macromedia Flash Player 6. The standard Spark codec ships with Macromedia Flash MX. A professional version (Sorenson Spark Pro) comes with the Sorenson Squeeze for Flash compression tool ($299). It features variable bit rate (VBR) compression and many other advanced features.

- H.263 (also known as I263)

  A widely used codec for videoconferences and live Webcasts, H.263 is good for movies with data rates below 64 Kbps and relatively low motion. Several different media players can view files encoded with this codec. The H.261 codec is a low-quality version of H.263.

- VP3

  This codec (from On2 Technologies) is very good for broadband connections of 250 Kbps or above. It has made a name for itself as the codec that allows relatively large frame sizes. Although this codec is not a part of QuickTime's standard installation, your copy of QuickTime Player will auto-update as soon as your browser encounters a VP3-encoded movie for the first time. RealOne Player can also play VP3 movies with an additional plug-in.

- ZyGoVideo

  This relatively new codec works with progressive download movies only. It comes with a free basic version or an advanced version for $79. OK quality-wise, it does not currently compare favorably with the codecs listed above.

Audio Codecs for Web Movies

Here are your options for compressing audio for the Web.

- Windows Media Audio

  Windows Media Audio is the primary codec for audio compression in Windows Media movies, including standalone audio files. It is well suited for low data rates (especially around 8 Kbps to 64 Kbps). The current version is Windows Media Audio 9.

- ACELP

  This is another audio codec available for Windows Media Player movies. It is optimized for voice-only files and is appropriate for low data rates (under 20 Kbps).

- RealAudio

  RealNetworks pioneered streaming audio over the Internet and continues to be a major delivery platform for streaming radio Webcasts and live audio-only events. They have an audio-first procedure for compressing video/audio movies: First you set the data rate for the audio, then the video portion gets whatever is left over. RealAudio is the only codec available for the audio portion of RealVideo movies.

- QDesign Music Codec

  This codec is optimized for instrumental and vocal music, but it can reproduce any type of sound at very low data rates (under 20 Kbps). I recommend it for any Web movie that includes music. The current version is QDesign Music 2. Like the Sorenson video codec, it requires relatively fast computers for playback. QDesign Music comes in both a basic (free) version and a professional version, which allows variable bit rate (VBR) encoding.

- Qualcomm PureVoice

  This codec is designed specifically for compressing the human voice at extremely low data rates. This codec does not accurately reproduce sounds other than voice (music, sound effects, and so on). There are two modes for PureVoice: PureVoice Full Rate is for audio-only files, or a file with a total data rate of 40 Kbps or more. PureVoice Half Rate is most useful when making movies that also include video at low data rates.

continued ›

- MP3

  The MP3 (MPEG Audio Layer-3) audio format has become *very* popular in recent years, and has spawned an entire software and hardware industry. It allows variable bit rate (VBR) encoding and offers excellent quality, especially at higher bit rates. MP3 is available as a QuickTime codec. Keep in mind, however, that QuickTime can decode, but not encode, MP3.

- AAC

  AAC (Advanced Audio Coding), like MP3, is an audio codec that does very well with music. It provides significantly higher quality at lower data rates through the use of VBR encoding and signal processing technology from Dolby Laboratories. It is a part of the new MPEG-4 standard for the Internet, wireless devices, and digital broadcast. AAC requires QuickTime 6.

Professional Codecs

There are at least three codecs that also come in professional editions: Sorenson Video 3, Sorenson Spark Pro, and QDesign Music Encoder.

- Sorenson Video 3 Professional Edition

  This codec comes with Sorenson's $299 Squeeze compression software and has a number of important features for providing high-quality Web video at very low data rates. If you have this version, you can access the pro features by clicking the Configure button in the Video section of Premiere's Export Movie Settings.

  The pro edition features include:

  Bidirectional Prediction: This feature creates a special type of delta frame that can lower the data rate to around 15 percent without reducing quality. (Note: One characteristic of this feature is that it duplicates the first frame and drops the last frame, so if you have important information on the last frame, such as a title, don't use this feature.)

  Playback Scalability: With most codecs, if a Web movie is delivering more data than the viewer's computer can handle, the movie will stutter (freeze) until the computer can recover, resulting in jerky playback. Playback scalability prevents that by simply reducing the frame rate of the movie on the fly.

  Automatic Keyframes: This option detects differences between frames and inserts keyframes as necessary. A slider (rare versus frequent keyframes) lets you control this feature.

Minimum Quality: This feature drops frames to maintain a quality threshold that you determine with a "least versus best" slider.

Image Smoothing: This is a filter that is automatically applied to low-data-rate movies during playback to remove blocky compression artifacts. You can (should) turn it off in high data rate movies.

Variable Bit Rate Compression: Another important feature of the Professional Edition is two-pass Variable Bitrate Rate (VBR) compression in which the codec first analyzes the entire movie and, in the second pass, allocates the data rate according to the needs of the different parts of the movie. This option is currently only available when Sorenson Video 3 Professional is used in conjunction with Cleaner 5.1 or Sorenson Squeeze. Use this option for progressive-downloading movies only.

Other SV3 Professional features include a quick compression mode; force block refresh for streaming movies; a password protection system; alpha channels, and color watermarking.

- Sorenson Spark Pro

  This is the professional version of the codec that allows you to put video inside of streaming Flash animations. Unlike the other professional codecs, it does not work with Premiere. (It costs $299 with Sorenson Squeeze for Macromedia Flash MX.)

- QDesign Music Encoder Professional Edition

  The $399 pro version of the QDesign Music codec offers a wider selection of data rates for audio compression (8 Kbps to 128 Kbps as opposed to the standard edition's 8 Kbps to 48 Kbps range). This version also includes Autopilot technology, which (like Sorenson's VBR) intelligently optimizes the quality of the audio track. Other settings include favoring either quality or speed, and fine-tuning both for different types of sound and to remap the audible portions of a sound file.

Compressing with the Save for Web Feature

One of the easiest ways to compress a movie for the Web is to use Premiere's Save for Web feature. It allows you to compress your movie directly from the Timeline by selecting preset options from pull-down menus or via an easy-to-use wizard.

TIP ▸ *Unfortunately, in version 6.5 of Premiere, the Save for Web feature is* only *available for Mac OS 9. If you are using Premiere 6.5 for Windows, you might want to consider getting a copy of version 6.0 just to use this handy feature. If you are using Premiere 6.5 for Mac OS X, you might want to try using Premiere 6.0 using Mac OS 9.x in Classic mode. If you can't be bothered with using an older version of Premiere just to compress your movie, stick with the old-fashioned method of using Premiere to compress your movie. Or read on further in this chapter to learn how to compress your movie for specific media player formats.*

All you have to know is what format you're compressing for, whether you're going to be delivering your movie over the Web as a downloading movie or as real-time streaming video, and the connection speed of your target audience.

1. With your Timeline open, choose Save for Web from the File menu's Export Timeline pull-down menu to launch Cleaner 5 EZ (**Figure 6.22**).

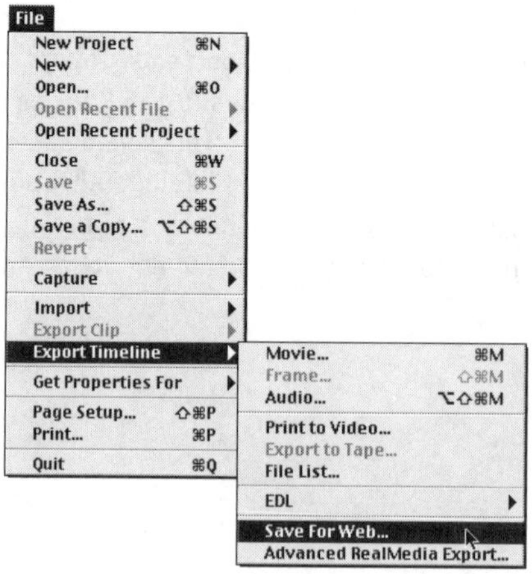

FIGURE 6.22 Choosing File > Export Timeline > Save for Web will open the Cleaner 5 EZ export plug-in module.

2. Pick Select Work Area from the Export pull-down menu to export just the section of the Timeline that you've marked with the yellow Work Area bar (**Figure 6.23**).

Figure 6.23
Cleaner 5 EZ's main window lets you select how much of your project to export, as well as pick your compression settings.

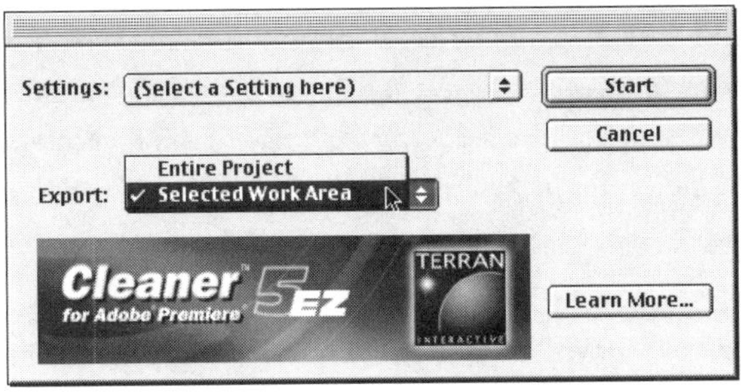

3. Select one of the first six categories of Web movies from the pull-down menu that appears (**Figure 6.24**). (See "Special Delivery: Downloading or Streaming," below, for an explanation of your options.)

Figure 6.24
Choose from the six types of Web movies that appear on the pull-down menu to get started saving your movie to the Web.

4. Once you select a format and a delivery method, a submenu appears with the next set of relevant choices (**Figure 6.25**). Cleaner 5 EZ wants to know what connection speed your target audience is using.

Figure 6.25
When you select QuickTime Progressive Download as a primary setting, you have a choice to create QuickTime Alternates. These are multiple versions of your movie. As you will learn in the next chapter, you can have QuickTime select the version that will look the best depending on the user's connection speed.

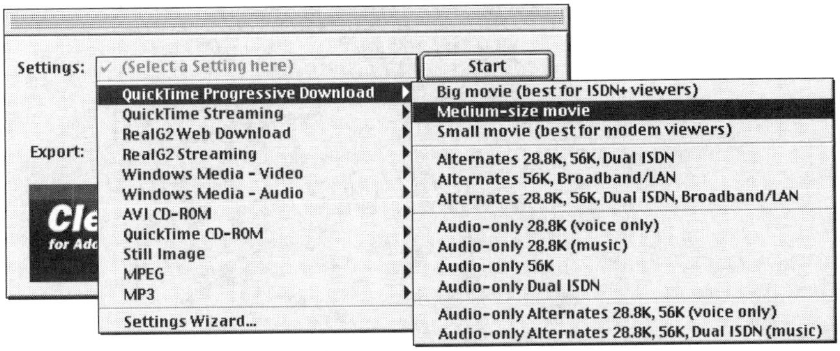

TIP ▸ *If you select RealG2 Streaming as a primary setting, the SureStream option combines several different streams into one file. During playback, RealOne Player and RealServer (now known as Helix Universal Server) continually communicate and can switch between streams to deliver the highest-quality stream that the viewer's connection can support.*

5. Click Start, select a destination for your file, and Cleaner 5 EZ begins to compress your movie. The Output window will appear and display frames of your movie while it works (**Figure 6.26**). You can click the expansion buttons on the left of the output settings to view detailed graphs and progress bars.

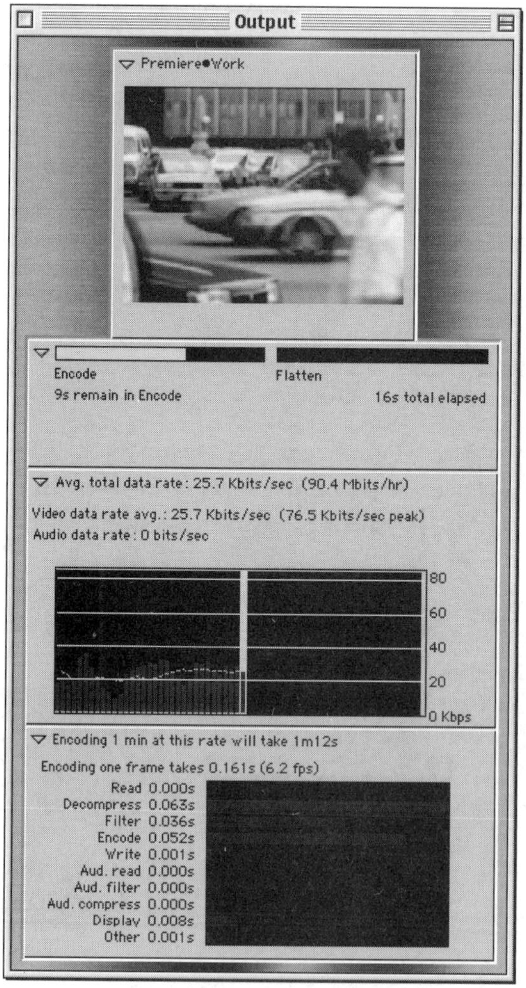

Figures 6.26
A progress bar at the bottom of the Output window indicates both the time elapsed and the time remaining as your movie is compressed.

Special Delivery: Downloading or Streaming?

You have to decide how you're going to deliver your movie before you can optimize it for the Web.

A *downloading* movie copies from a Web (HTTP) server to the destination computer's hard drive, rather than directly to the computer screen, as do movies that stream from an RTSP server. QuickTime, Real, and Windows Media Player movies can all be set up as *progressive downloading* movies, where the file starts playing before it has completely downloaded.

Streaming video sends your movie to the viewer on an as-needed basis. No movie file is ever stored on the viewer's computer. It requires a dedicated server (that you'll have to install yourself or pay your Web hosting service for); and if the viewer's connection isn't fast enough, or network traffic is congested, frames may be skipped. Still, this is the best choice for longer clips or live events.

The other subcategory of downloading movies, *downloadable* movies, is relatively rare. These are files that you place on a Web server specifically for copying. These movies must be completely downloaded before they can start to play back. The viewer copies the file and then opens it with a media player. In a sense, these movies aren't true Web video, since they're not being played from the Web at all. The most popular example of this subcategory is movies compressed with the MPEG-1 codec that are shared via email. Producers sometimes inadvertently make downloadable movies when they mean to make progressive downloading movies (for reasons too arcane to bother with here).

Using Cleaner 5 EZ's Settings Wizard

If you'd rather get a guided tour to Cleaner 5 EZ, the Settings Wizard is for you. You'll end up in the same place, with more or less the same results, as you would have using Cleaner 5 EZ's settings, but the Wizard explains each of the steps and makes some educated guesses for you as you go.

1. Choose Settings Wizard from Cleaner 5 EZ's Settings menu to launch the Wizard.

2. Choose WWW for your Delivery Medium and click Continue.

3. Select QuickTime as your delivery format (**Figure 6.27**). If you choose Real here, you can choose between either RealTime Streaming or Progressive Download options. Progressive Download delivery for the RealPlayer is similar to QuickTime's delivery method, except that you don't have the option of creating alternate versions of your movie that the player can match to the viewer's connection speed. If you choose Windows Media, you can choose between Windows Media Server (that's essentially streaming) and Web Server (that's downloading).

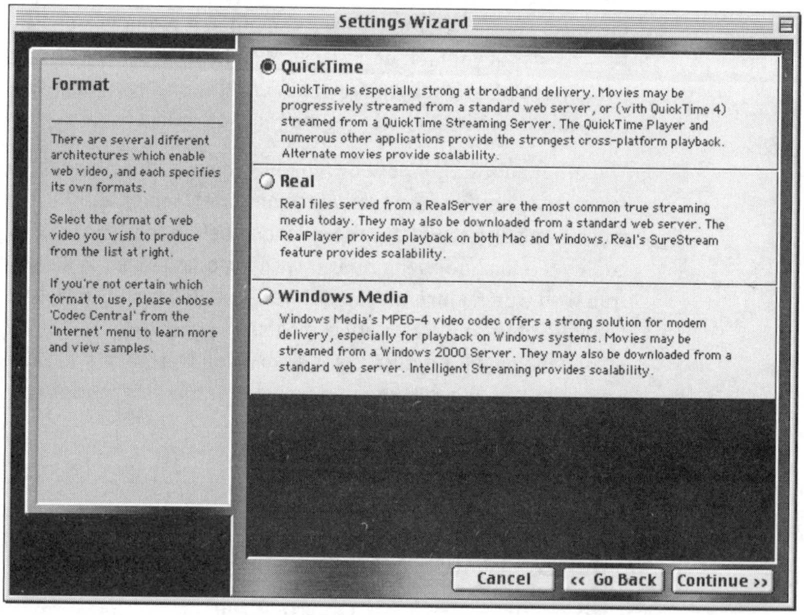

FIGURE 6.27
Select QuickTime from the Setting Wizard's choice of movie delivery formats.

4. Choose "Progressive Streaming (high quality)" and click Continue.

5. You'll now be presented with the Alternates list, a feature unique to QuickTime (**Figure 6.28**). The Wizard is asking you to identify the likely connection speeds of your target audience. It will compress a version of your movie for each selection you make, and QuickTime will display the movie that will look the best on a given user's system. Select "56k," "ISDN," and "T1, Cable Modem." Click Continue.

FIGURE 6.28
The Alternates window allows you to make alternate versions of your movie that are optimized for different connection speeds.

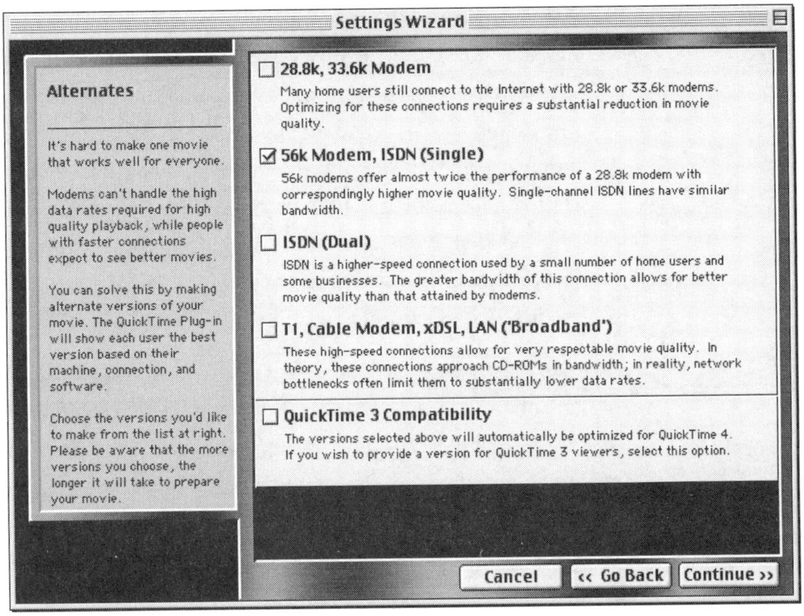

6. Choose Audio & Video Equally Important and Soundtrack Contains Range of Material to help Cleaner 5 EZ select the proper audio codec to compress your audio track (**Figure 6.30**). Click Continue.

FIGURE 6.29
The Soundtrack window asks you to both weigh the importance of the audio against the video in your movie and characterize whether the sound is mostly speech or music. Your choices will determine how much your audio is compressed.

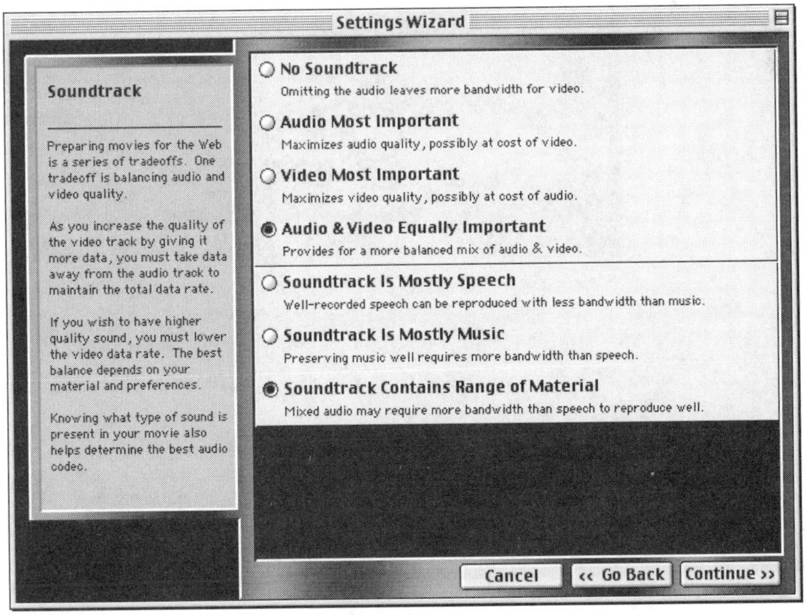

7. The Optimize window requires you to balance image quality, image size, and motion smoothness against one another (**Figure 6.30**). To get the low data rate that Web video requires, you have to make sacrifices—and here's where. The higher the image quality you want to achieve, the lower the frame rate will be, which means your movie will play back less smoothly. If you choose Large Image size, then both image quality and motion will suffer as a result. Choose Slide Show if you want to completely sacrifice motion to preserve image quality and size. Do not check any box if you want to leave the default setting. Click Continue.

To get an idea what each of these parameters will do, have a look at the movies in the "optimize" folder on the CD. The movies in that folder are identical except that a different Optimize Window setting was chosen for each movie: image quality, image size, motion smoothness, and slide show.

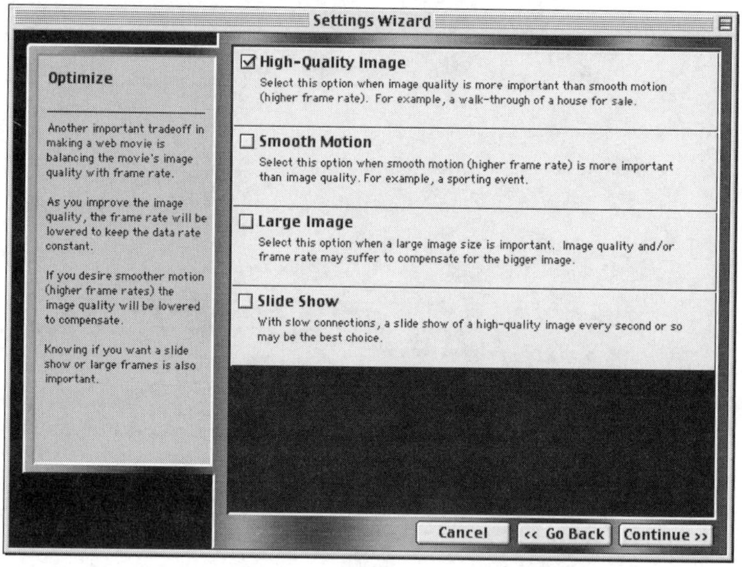

Figure 6.30
The Optimize window lets you prioritize image quality, image size, and motion smoothness.

8. In the Options window you decide how you want your movie to start playing. Select Show Controller and Start Playing Automatically and click Continue.

9. You're done! When making QuickTime movies, the Wizard displays a summary of its choices based on the information you've selected (**Figure 6.31**). You can adjust any of the settings (although the whole point of the Wizard is that you don't have to) and save them for reuse. When you click Finish, you'll

be prompted to pick a destination file, and your movies will be compressed. (This scenario used QuickTime as the example, but the process works just as well for Real and Windows Media.)

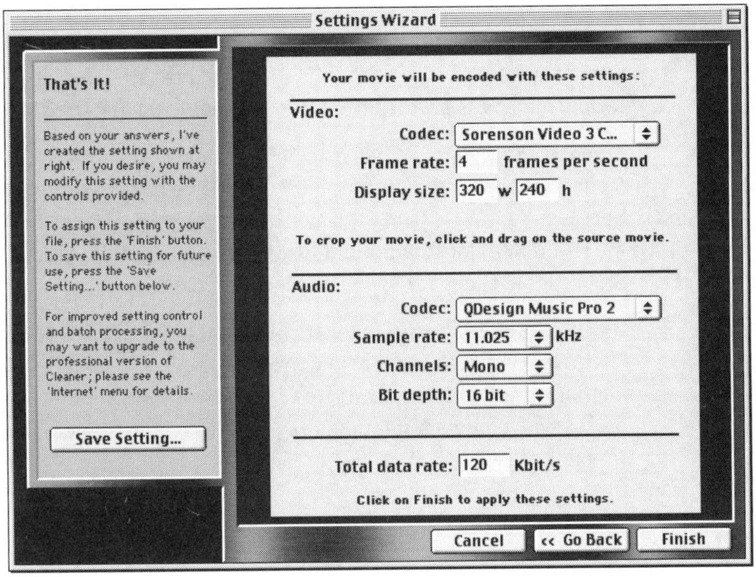

FIGURE 6.31
At the end of the Wizard interview, your settings are displayed in this window. You can adjust them or save them for future use.

If you would like to see movies that resulted from the Wizard settings I just described, have a look in the Settings_Wizard folder on the CD.

Going Pro

Although Cleaner 5 EZ makes compression easy and produces great results, it isn't the right tool for everyone. If you're serious about Web video, you'll want the full version of Cleaner 5—the all-purpose format converter tool ($599).

Here's why:

- You get much more control over your compression project in Cleaner 5's Advanced Settings mode (which is only available in the full version). It offers virtually every compression option on the planet.
- The full version of Cleaner 5 allows you to use advanced features of professional editions of certain codecs to create much higher quality output.
- The full version has a slew of other useful features, including batch processing, dynamic preview, settings modifiers, high-quality scaling, video and audio filters, DV capture, metadata annotations, EventStream interactivity authoring, and StreamPublisher, an automated FTP transfer utility.

Other Format Converters

Besides Cleaner 5, there are three new entries in the format converter category: Canopus ProCoder ($699), Sorenson Squeeze ($299, or $499 when bundled with Squeeze for Macromedia Flash MX), and HipFlics ($99.95).

ProCoder includes many of the same features as Cleaner (batch processing, aspect ratio conversion, video and audio filters, frame rate interpolation, adaptive deinterlacing, multipass processing, a wizard mode, and FTP transfer tools).

Sorenson Squeeze also has many of the movie optimizing features found in Cleaner 5 and ProCoder, but it outputs only QuickTime movies using the following codecs: Sorenson (and Sorenson Pro), Qualcomm PureVoice, QDesign Music 2, Fraunhofer MP3, and IMA. Most important, the only way to get the excellent Sorenson Video 3 Professional codec (or Spark Pro) is to buy Squeeze.

HipFlics from Totally Hip Software offers an easy-to-use interface, support for all QuickTime video codecs (including Sorenson 3, VP3, and ZyGoVideo), support for multiple video codecs in a single QuickTime movie, a four-up preview display, batch processing, cropping, rotating, drag-and-drop filters, and watermarking—all for a very low price.

Compressing for RealOne Player

Premiere's Advanced RealMedia Export plug-in allows you to compress movies for RealOne Player, using software created by the company that knows that media player the best. RealOne Player's strength as a player is delivering streaming video over the Web, which it calls a SureStream file: When a viewer plays a movie, the Real Streaming Server adjusts the streaming file to match the viewer's connection speed. If the connection speed improves or degrades, the server adjusts the file accordingly, ensuring that the viewer always gets to see the best possible quality movie.

TIP ▸ *If you know that you only want to create RealPlayer files, and that you need one tool that can capture a live video signal and compress files, then RealSystem (a.k.a. Helix) Producer is the tool for you. It can also convert existing media (videotapes, live feeds, AVI files, digital images, and more) into streaming media files for live events or on-demand content. There is a free Basic version, and a $200 Plus version with many extra features. See this Web site for details:* `www.realnetworks.com/products/producer/comparison.html`.

In the Advanced RealMedia Export window, you can specify the audio format you're using, the quality of video, the connection rates for your target audience, a location for your output file, and general information about the clips that you're using. You can use existing presets or create your own.

Specifying General Export Settings

1. With your *Escape* project open in the Premiere Timeline, choose File > Export Timeline > Advanced RealMedia Export to open the Advanced RealMedia Export main window (**Figure 6.32**).

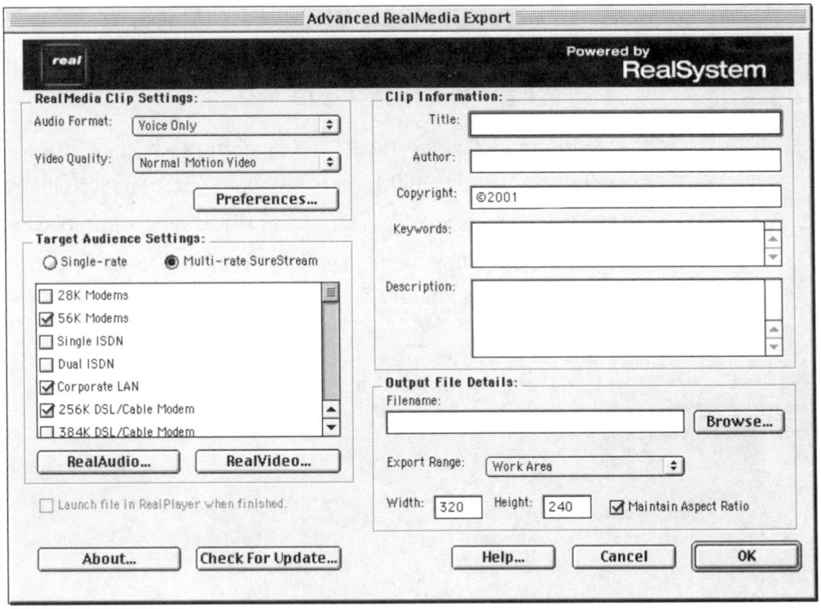

FIGURE 6.32
The main Advanced RealMedia Export window asks for basic information about your movie in order to optimize compression quality.

2. Select Music from the Audio Format pull-down menu (**Figure 6.33**). (This ensures that a codec engineered for music is used to compress the *Escape* movie, which has plenty of music in it.) The plain Music option creates a mono file (half the data rate of the Stereo Music option).

FIGURE 6.33
Since the *Escape* movie has plenty of music, select Music for the audio format.

3. Select Normal Motion Video from the Video Quality pull-down menu (**Figure 6.34**). This will balance the spatial and temporal quality of the video. It is the best setting for most clips. Smoothest Motion Video would favor temporal quality by increasing the frame rate (and decreasing the keyframe rate). Sharpest Image Video would favor spatial quality by adding more keyframes. Slide Show turns the video into a series of still images.

Figure 6.34
Normal Motion Video is the best setting for most clips.

4. Choose Multi-rate SureStream by clicking one of the radio buttons under the Target Audience Settings, and click the check boxes for 56K Modems, Single ISDN, and Dual ISDN (**Figure 6.35**).

I recommend Real for true RTSP streaming and QuickTime for progressive downloading, but if you would like to see what individual "single-rate" Real versions of the *Escape* movie look like, check out the Escape_Compression_Examples folder on the CD. There you will find a 56K version (50 Kbps), an ISDN version (120 Kbps), and a DSL/cable modem version (500 Kbps).

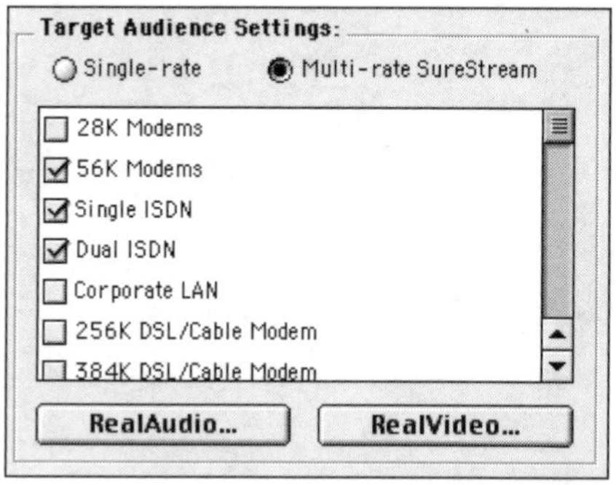

Figure 6.35
The Target Audience Settings section shows "Multi-rate SureStream" selections.

You're not likely to want to make any adjustments to the Advanced RealMedia Export plug-in's default values for your target audience, because they work well. But if you do, click the RealVideo and RealAudio buttons located beneath the scrolling connection speed checklist to view or adjust the default data rate settings for any preset, based on the connection speed of the target audience.

5. Enter information about the title, author, and copyright holder, along with keywords, and a description of your movie in the Clip Information section of the Advanced RealMedia Export window (**Figure 6.36**). This *metadata* (data *about* data) is detectable by some search engines. Since RealMedia clips do not contain text the way normal Web pages do, the only way your audience can search for your clip is through the keywords that you specify.

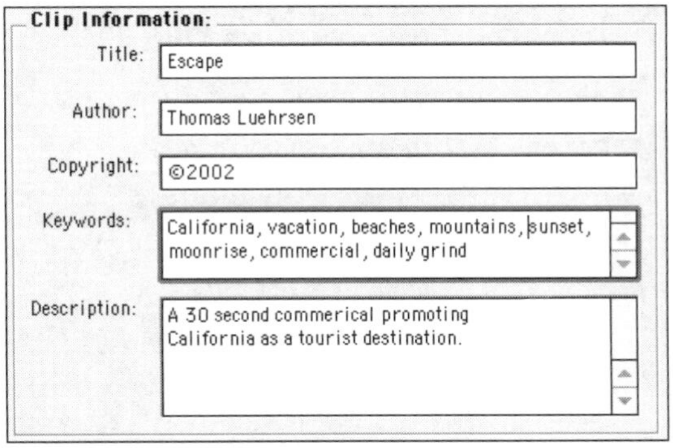

Clip Information:
Title:
Escape
Author:
Thomas Luehrsen
Copyright:
©2002
Keywords:
California, vacation, beaches, mountains, sunset, moonrise, commercial, daily grind
Description:
A 30 second commerical promoting California as a tourist destination.

FIGURE 6.36
If you would like to make your RealSystem movie findable by a Web search engine, add textual information such as this.

6. To enter a location for your file, fill in the blanks in the Output File Details section (**Figure 6.37**).

7. Choose either Selected Area or Entire Project in the Export Range pull-down menu to define how much of the Premiere Timeline you want to include in the compressed movie.

8. Enter 240 and 180 in the Width and Height boxes, respectively.

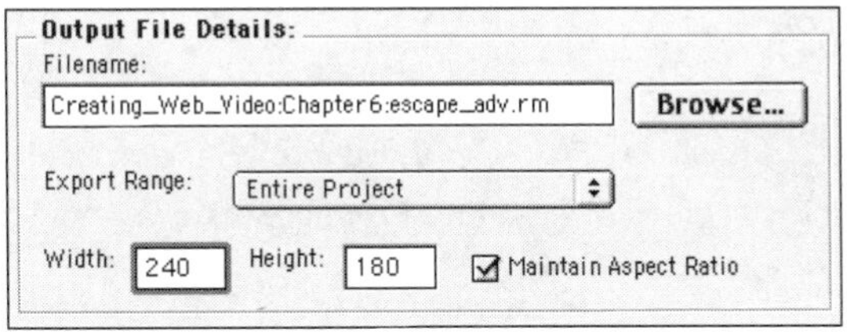

FIGURE 6.37
Enter the filename and destination, the export range, and the frame size of your movie.

9. Click OK to begin compressing. You'll get a RealVideo movie with a .rm extension.

   You can double-click the file to open it in RealOne Player and just play it from your computer's hard disk.

My version is on the on the CD; it's called escape_adv.rm. However, since this is a SureStream movie, you would need a RealServer (now Helix) to see it in all its adjustable glory. Unless you have software that can emulate an Internet connection, you'll only see the biggest stream (in this case, "Dual ISDN") when you play it from your hard disk.

Compressing for Windows Media Player

Advanced Windows Media Export allows you to compress movies for Windows Media Player. It is only available to Window users. Like Real technology, Windows Media codecs are primarily geared toward true (RTSP) streaming with on-the-fly adjustable data rates, but you can make downloading Windows Media files as well. Since Cleaner 5 EZ is only available for older versions of Premiere and Windows (and Mac OS 9), the advanced Windows Media Export is a handy way to make Web movies for the Windows Media Player.

TIP ▸ *Premiere's Advanced Windows Media Export module has many of the same features and underlying code as Microsoft Windows Media Encoder, a tool dedicated to creating movies and audio for Windows Media Player. The full Windows Media Encoder can convert both live and prerecorded audio, video, and computer screen images to Windows Media Format for live and on-demand delivery. Unlike the other tools mentioned in this book, the Windows Media Encoder and Premiere's Advanced Windows Media Export module work only on the Windows operating system. Like Cleaner, Windows Media Encoder has a wizard mode that guides users through the process of setting up an encoding session, target bandwidths, and quality options. The full version of Windows Media Encoder can be downloaded for free at* `www.microsoft.com/windows/windowsmedia/download/default.asp`.

1. Choose File > Export Timeline > Advanced Windows Media to open the Windows Media Export Plug In for Adobe Premiere main window (**Figure 6.38**).
2. Select a Profile from the scrolling list that best describes the connection rate of your target audience. Windows Media Profiles are similar to *presets* in Premiere and *settings* in Cleaner. They contain all the technical details required to compress a particular Web movie and they include information on the type of content being compressed, the desired video and audio quality, the target data rate, and the codecs used to compress the movie. Choose "Video for dial-up modems or single channel ISDN."

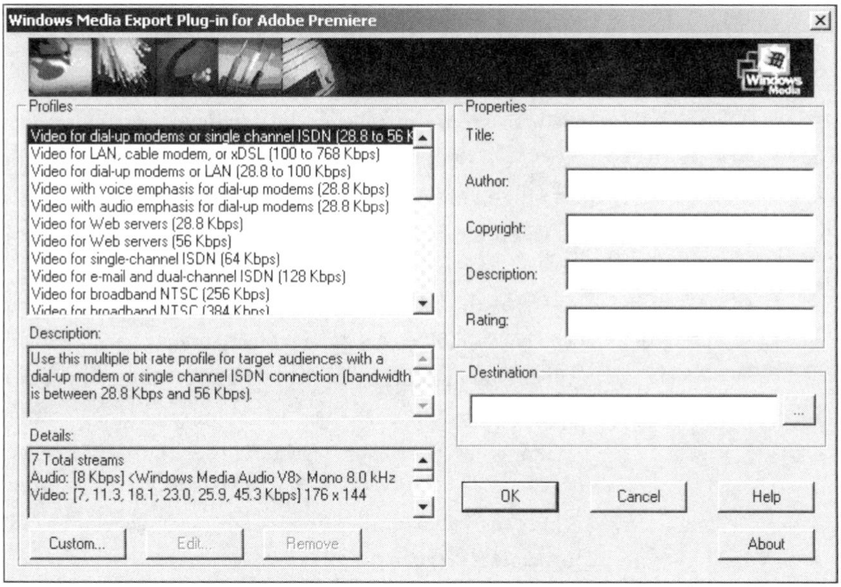

FIGURE 6.38
Here's the main window of the Advanced Windows Media Export Plug-In for Adobe Premiere.

3. Fill in the Properties section if you want to add identifying information to your movie, including title, author, copyright holder, and description of the movie.

4. Enter the filename and destination where you want the clip to be exported in the Destination section.

5. Click OK and you'll create a movie using Microsoft's default settings. The export module will render a Windows Media Player version to the destination you specified. If you chose to make a multi-bit-rate streaming movie, it will require a special streaming server to play back at variable data rates. You can now double-click your new movie to play it in Windows Media Player. (As with the RealSystem SureStream movies, if you play a Windows Media multi-bit-rate movie from your computer's hard disk, you'll only see the highest data rate stream contained in it.)

TIP ▸ *While the Advanced Windows Media Export module that shipped with Premiere 6.0 exports multi-bit-rate movies with the .asf filename extension, Microsoft recommends using the .wmv extension on all movies encoded with the Windows Media Video codec. If the movies are encoded with other third-party codecs, then they should be called .asf. You can simply rename the movie after it has been compressed.*

Creating a Custom Profile Using Advanced Windows Media Export

Want a little more control over the details of the Windows Media movies you're making? As with the Advanced RealMedia Export plug-in, the Windows Media Export plug-in provides access to the settings that underlie its preset profiles and allows you to save custom profiles for future use.

1. Let's say the "Video for dial-up modems or single channel ISDN" preset that you chose above is *not quite* perfect for your needs. You'd like to slightly increase the high-end data rate of the streams contained in your Web movie. To create a custom profile, click the Custom button at the bottom of the Advanced Windows Media Export screen. This opens the Manage Profiles window.

2. Find the "Video for dial-up modems or single channel ISDN" profile and click to select it (**Figure 6.39**).

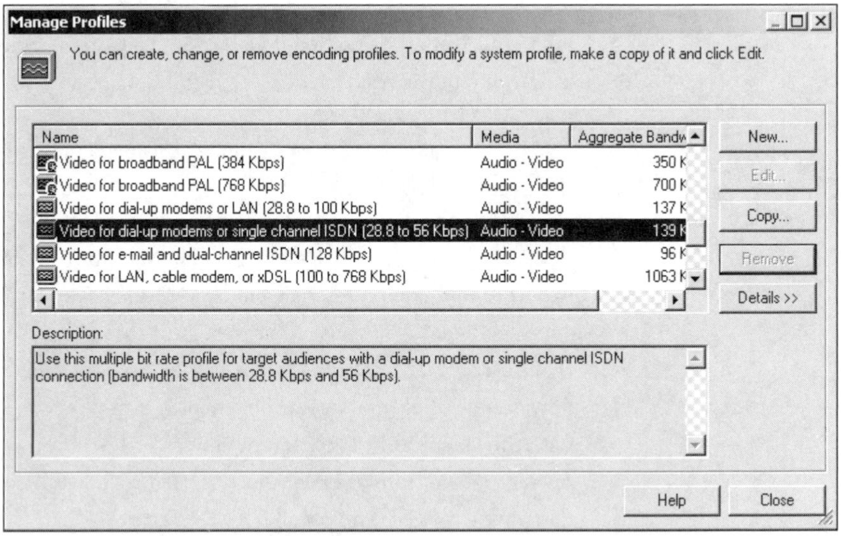

FIGURE 6.39
The Manage Profiles window is where you select the profile that you're going to modify.

3. Choose Copy, and type in a name for the custom profile you're about to create (**Figure 6.40**). Click OK.

A series of Edit Profile windows appear in which you can specify a new connection speed for your target audience, select different audio and video codecs, and adjust the frame rate, keyframe frequency, and image quality of your movie.

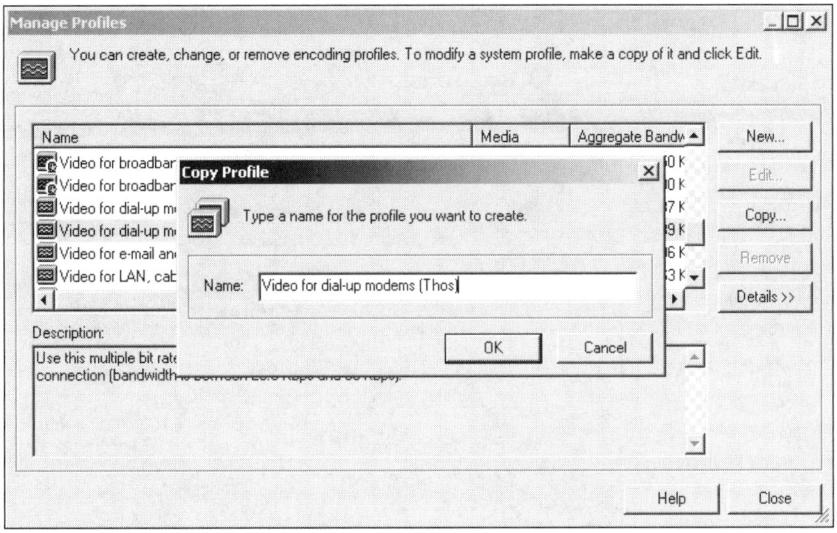

Figure 6.40
To create a copy of a profile, you give it a new name.

4. In the Audience Selection window, click the check box for "Local playback and dual-channel ISDN." This will add a higher (93 Kbps) data rate stream to the existing collection of streams for this profile. Click Next to move ahead to the next Edit Profile window, then click Finish when you're done.

When you've finished making the desired tweaks to the new Profile setting, you'll see the Profile Settings Review window, which lists all the settings in your customized profile.

5. Click Finish to create and save the profile, or Back to change the settings.

   When you click Finish in the Profile Settings Review window, you'll return to the Manage Profiles window, where your new profile will appear with a red icon (**Figure 6.41**).

6. Select the new profile and click Close to return to the Advanced Windows Media Export main window.

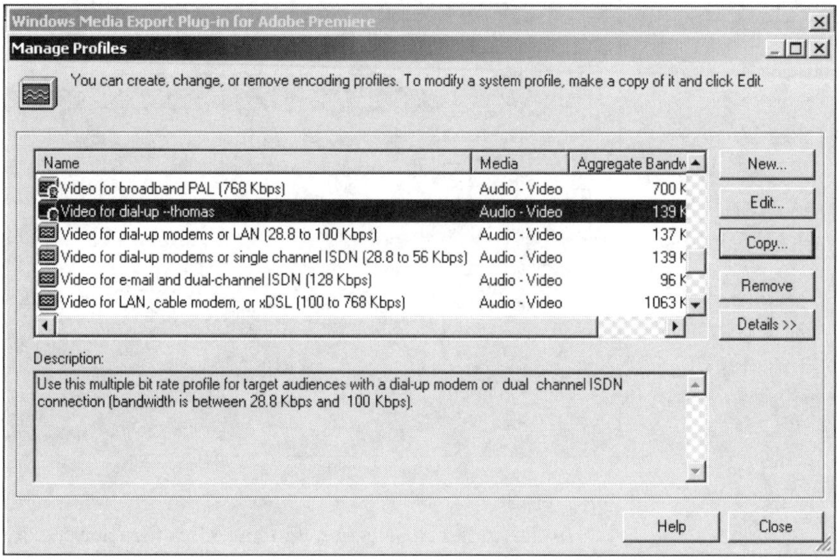

FIGURE 6.41
Custom profiles appear in red and standard profiles appear in green in the Manage Profiles window.

To see the movie that resulted from these tweaked settings, have a look at escape_adv.asf on the CD.

Congratulations! You've made Web-ready versions of the *Escape* movie using Premiere and plug-ins for RealOne Player, Windows, and Cleaner 5. Now you're ready to face the audience. In the next chapter, you'll learn how to put your movies out on the Web for the world to see.

CHAPTER SEVEN

Hard Disk Delivery

It's show time. To get your movie out to the masses, you've got to get it onto a Web page and out onto the Web. And that means learning the basic language of the Web—HTML (Hypertext Markup Language)—or at least enough of it to get your movie playing back the way you want. If you prefer to skip the HTML, the accompanying CD comes with a free 30-day trial version of Adobe's GoLive software, which lets you incorporate your movie into a Web page without doing any HTML coding at all. Of course, getting the movie to play is just the beginning. This chapter also gives you plenty of tips and techniques to make your movie look good and play back easily for as many viewers as possible.

Downloading to Viewers Everywhere

When you were compressing your movie in Chapter 6, "The Big Squeeze," you had to decide whether to deliver it over the Web as a downloadable video file or as a streaming video file. Downloading movies and streaming movies require two different types of procedures for integrating your movies into Web pages. This chapter teaches you how to incorporate downloadable QuickTime video files into Web pages; Chapter 8, "Streaming Your Way," covers how to publish RealVideo and Windows Media format movies as streaming video files.

When a viewer selects a downloadable movie, that file downloads from a Web server directly to the viewer's hard drive and then plays back. QuickTime movies play back while the file is being downloaded, so the viewer doesn't have to wait so long; that's called *progressive downloading*. That means your viewer will see your movie exactly as you intended it to be seen, without any interruptions from Internet traffic congestion. Publishing your movies this way is also simpler and less expensive: You don't need to buy and install special streaming servers, as you must to offer streaming video. And for those of you who want people to watch your movies while they're at work, corporate firewalls won't get in the way of downloading movies, as they often will with streaming video.

To see the best examples of progressive downloading, take a look at Apple Computer's movie trailer Web site (`www.apple.com/trailers/`).

The Web's Basic Language: HTML

Web servers are computers that act like waiters in a restaurant; they listen for requests from clients (Web browsers) and respond to those requests. Web servers and Web browsers communicate using a set of rules known as the Hypertext Transfer Protocol (HTTP). Servers generally respond to requests by sending out data in the form of Web pages—documents usually composed of text and graphics that are formatted in Hypertext Markup Language (HTML). That means that some HTML has to be written, or modified, in order for your movies to actually play on the Web. For those of you who already know how to write or edit HTML, I will describe the basic codes required to add video to a Web site. If you're new to Web site development and don't know HTML, I will show you how to add your movies to a Web site using Adobe GoLive 6, a Web authoring tool that is easier to use and more WYSIWYG ("what you see is what you get") than using plain-text HTML code.

HTML Basics

HTML documents are always text-only. That's why you only need a plain-text editor to do the first exercise below. Although all Web pages are created with HTML, and most Web pages display images, HTML documents don't actually contain any images or other media.

That's where the *Hyper* and the *Markup* parts of Hypertext Markup Language come in. Although HTML is only text, it can contain references to many different kinds of files and media. HTML uses commands called *elements* (also called *tags*) to tell the Web browser to display text in a certain way, or to insert an image file or movie at a particular point.

The *Language* part means that, like any language, HTML has a specific *syntax*, or set of rules, for ordering the content of a statement (or a Web page). If you don't say the words in the right order, your HTML won't be understood by a Web browser and therefore won't be viewable by your audience.

Getting Started with a Simple Page

Actually, HTML is easier to use than it is to describe. So let's get started. (If you prefer to use software that does the HTML coding for you, skip to "Using GoLive," below.) For these exercises, you will need the following:

- A simple-text editing tool such as NotePad on the Mac or WordPad if you use Windows (it's one of the accessories).
- A Web browser, such as Internet Explorer or Netscape.

Let's look at a very basic HTML document. **Figures 7.1** and **7.2** show an HTML document as it appears first in a text editor and then in a Web browser.

simple_page.html
<html>
<head>
<title>A Simple Web Page</title>
</head>
<body>
<p>This is a very simple, text-only, Web page.</p>
<p>This is about as simple as it gets.</p>
</body>
</html>

FIGURE 7.1
A simple Web page, displayed as an HTML document, includes both text and the HTML codes that tell the Web browser how to display the page.

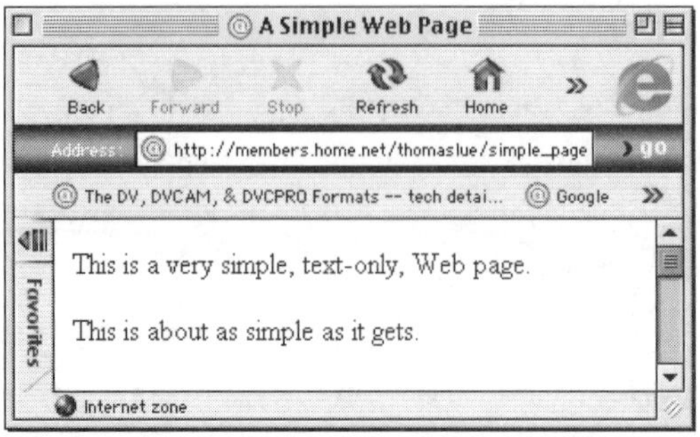

FIGURE 7.2
The same Web page as it appears in a Web browser.

What you see here is more or less the minimum coding you need for a functional Web page. The parts marked with the less-than (<) and greater-than (>) symbols are the HTML elements. They define how text is displayed in a Web browser and, as you will see below, how other media (such as image and video files) are inserted into the Web page.

NOTE ▸ HTML elements are not case-sensitive, meaning they can be written in either all capital letters or all lowercase letters—they'll work either way. This book will use the lowercase style, except when capitals are necessary for clarity.

This sample file, called simple_page.html, is included in the Chapter7_Web_integration folder on the accompanying CD-ROM. You can view it by opening it in your own browser and edit it by opening it in your own text editor. Or you can use this document as a guide for creating your own HTML document from scratch in your text editor.

Adding a Movie to a Web Page

Now that you've got a simple page under your belt, here's how to add a progressive downloading movie to this Web page. (We're using a QuickTime movie for this example, but the procedure is virtually identical for RealPlayer and Windows Media Player progressive downloading movies.)

1. Make sure that the document named simple_page.html and the movie named simple.mov are located in the same folder (directory).

2. Open the simple_page.html document in a text editor. If you can't see it in the list of available files, make sure that you've got "all files" selected as the file type to be shown.

3. Remove the line that says, "This is a very simple, text-only, Web page." And replace it with: "This is an embedded QuickTime movie." (Make sure you leave the `<p>` and `</p>` elements.)

4. Just below the last line of text (which says, "`<p>`This is about as simple as it gets.`</p>`"), add the following new line:

```
<embed src="simple.mov" width="320" height="256">
```

This `<embed>` element has three *attributes* (also called *parameters*): SRC, WIDTH, and HEIGHT. These attributes are required to tell the browser what media to display and the width and height of the media file specified in the SRC attribute (SRC stands for *source*). Here, the SRC attribute is the movie file that you want to display, simple.mov. The HEIGHT attribute specifies the vertical size in pixels of the SRC attribute. The WIDTH attribute specifies its horizontal size.

IMPORTANT ▸ In order for the controller bar to appear properly at the bottom of the movie window, you need to add 16 pixels to the height parameter. That's why we set the HEIGHT to 256 here.

Your HTML document should now look like **Figure 7.3**.

This sample file, simple_page_embed.html, is also included in the Chapter7_Web_integration folder on the accompanying CD-ROM.

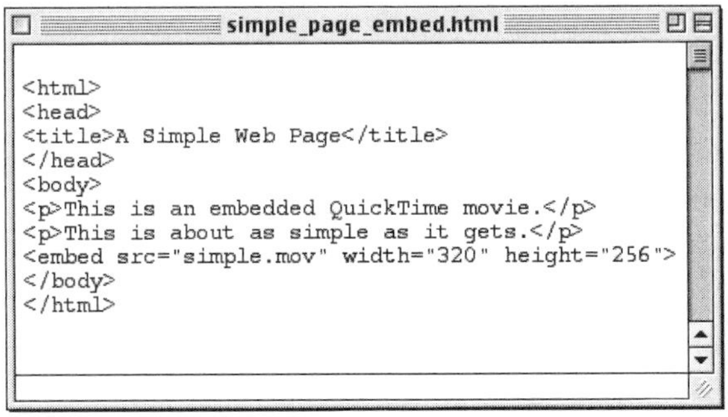

```
<html>
<head>
<title>A Simple Web Page</title>
</head>
<body>
<p>This is an embedded QuickTime movie.</p>
<p>This is about as simple as it gets.</p>
<embed src="simple.mov" width="320" height="256">
</body>
</html>
```

FIGURE 7.3 The simple Web page, as it appears in a text editor, uses the `<embed>` element.

5. Save your HTML document.

6. Open your HTML document in a Web browser. The resulting Web page should look like **Figure 7.4**.

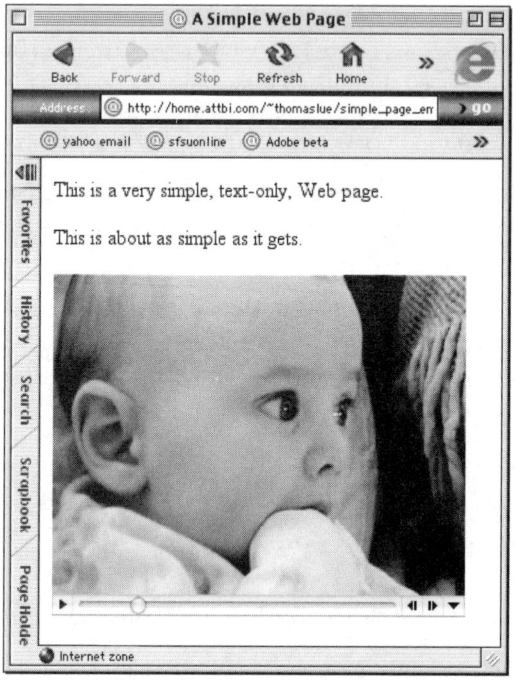

FIGURE 7.4
The simple Web page as it appears in a browser, showing the effect of the `<embed>` element.

If the movie doesn't appear in the browser window, make sure that

- You have no typos in the HTML document.
- The movie file is in the same folder as the HTML document.
- The QuickTime plug-in is properly installed in your browser.
- QuickTime is properly installed on your computer.

The QuickTime movie is now fully operational, including a Play/Pause toggle button and Frame Left and Frame Right buttons.

QuickTime Attributes

Attributes are modifiers for an HTML element, which change that element's appearance, behavior, or activity. Besides the three required attributes of the `<embed>` element (SRC, HEIGHT, and WIDTH), you can use a number of other attributes understood by the QuickTime browser plug-in to customize the playback and display of QuickTime movies. Here are a few of the more commonly used QuickTime attributes. For a comprehensive list, check out the Apple Web site: `www.apple.com/quicktime/authoring/embed.html`.

- AUTOPLAY = true/false

  When set to *true*, this parameter tells the movie to start playing as soon as the page opens and the QuickTime plug-in estimates that it will be able to play the entire movie without waiting for additional data.

- CACHE = true/false

  This parameter saves the movie to the browser's cache, so that replaying goes faster.

- CONTROLLER = true/false

  This parameter shows or hides the standard QuickTime playback controls below the movie. The default is *true*.

- LOOP = false/true/palindrome

  By default, LOOP is set to *false*, which means the movie plays just once. When set to *true*, the LOOP attribute makes the movie play continuously. Setting LOOP to *palindrome* causes the movie to play, alternately, forward to the end and then backward to the beginning.

- BGCOLOR = binhex value

  Specifies a background color for the movie. It can also be used to create a border around the movie (if you increase the height and width by a couple pixels).

- HIDDEN

  If you supply the HIDDEN attribute, the movie won't be visible on the page. The HIDDEN attribute is good for sound-only movies, which are hidden in the background.

Preparing Progressive Downloading QuickTime Movies

QuickTime's Fast Start feature makes it the best media player for progressive downloading. If you prepare a progressive downloading movie properly, the movie will play as it downloads. QuickTime's Fast Start feature figures out how much of the movie to download before it starts playing, so that there won't be any interruptions in the presentation (**Figure 7.5**).

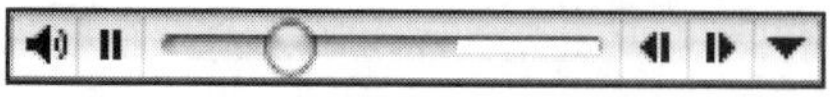

FIGURE 7.5
QuickTime's Fast Start progress bar indicates how much of the movie has downloaded to the hard disk.

For all of this to work properly, you need to make sure that the movie is truly a Fast Start movie. If your movie downloads in its entirety before it starts playing, then you know the Fast Start feature is either missing from the movie, or there is a problem with it.

Normally, Fast Start movies are created automatically when you save a new movie in QuickTime 3 or later, so the procedure below is rarely necessary. But glitches have been known to happen.

Making a Fast Start Movie out of a Regular QuickTime Movie

1. Open your movie in QuickTime Player. (Make sure you have a current version of QuickTime installed.)

2. Choose File > Save As.

3. Select the "Make movie self-contained" radio button (**Figure 7.6**). This creates a self-contained, flattened Fast Start movie. *Self-contained* means that it can be moved, uploaded, and played without requiring any other files. *Flattened* means the movie's "internal references are resolved" (in other words, it will play back smoothly!).

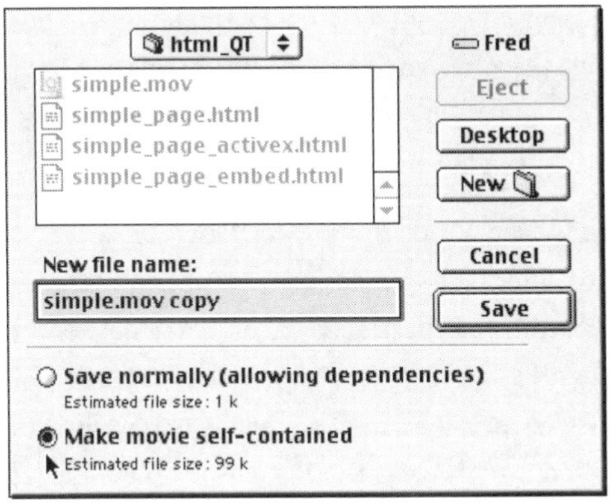

FIGURE 7.6
In the File > Save As window, selecting "Make movie self-contained" turns a regular movie into a progressive downloading one.

TIP ▸ *When creating video for the Web, the main troubleshooting issue is testing the final Web page, complete with your video, on all of the different computer platforms (Windows, Macintosh, and so on) and browsers (Internet Explorer, Netscape, and others). Web browsers usually come out with a new version every year. Since your audience will not always upgrade to the latest browser version, trying to keep your Web site compatible with older browser versions is an ongoing challenge for most Web developers. Your best course here is to systematically test your Web site before releasing it, on as many different combinations of Web browser versions and computer platforms as possible. (Yes, this means IE for Windows, IE for the Mac, Netscape for Windows, Netscape for the Mac—and in the many different version numbers of each browser!)*

Fixing the Internet Explorer Problem

Once you start testing your Web page, you're going to come across a browser compatibility problem that emerged in the Web world in the latter half of 2001. As a result, if you have viewers who use Internet Explorer 5.5 SP2 (or later versions) on Windows—a likely scenario—you must change the HTML on your site to include an `<object>` element in addition to the `<embed>` element.

When you install any of the Big Three media players on your computer, the installer adds plug-ins to your Web browser. During most of the life of the Web, the two main Web browsers have been Netscape and Internet Explorer, and different plug-in technologies have grown up around each. Sometimes the plug-ins worked with both browsers, sometimes just with one.

But Internet Explorer for Windows 5.5 SP2 and later versions no longer support any Netscape-style plug-ins, such as the plug-in installed as part of QuickTime 5.0.2 and earlier versions. One of these plug-ins worked with the `<embed>` element to enable QuickTime to play on Windows computers.

What that means is that Windows viewers using these versions of Explorer may be unable to view QuickTime movies within the browser unless the Web pages' HTML is fixed according to the procedure outlined below. If the Web pages aren't fixed, the viewer will see a "broken plug-in" icon (**Figure 7.7**). Usually, that icon indicates that the viewer's Web browser needs to have its QuickTime plug-in installed or updated; in this case, though, the problem is that the plug-in is, in effect, unrecognized.

To remedy this, the viewer's browser needs to install an ActiveX control that will provide the browser with the QuickTime plug-in. *ActiveX controls* are self-contained software applications that are automatically downloaded and executed by a Web browser, and they can do anything from presenting forms and databases to displaying graphics and movies on a Web page. ActiveX controls work only in Windows. As a Web developer, you need to set up a way for your Web site to make sure the ActiveX control is automatically installed in the viewer's browser when necessary.

FIGURE 7.7
The "broken plug-in" icon as it appears in Internet Explorer 5.5 or later versions.

Installing the QuickTime ActiveX Control

Here's what you need to do to alter (or build) any Web site to get QuickTime movies to play with newer versions of Internet Explorer on the Windows platform. When you're done you will have established a way for a Web page to see if the required ActiveX control is installed on the viewer's browser and, if it isn't, to trigger its installation.

NOTE ▸ Users of unaffected browsers on either Windows or the Mac OS can continue to use the plug-in installed with QuickTime and do not need to get the new QuickTime ActiveX control.

Here is the simple_page_embed.html Web page with the necessary changes shown in italic. You have to include this HTML code wherever a QuickTime movie is embedded in a Web site (unless you can use the procedure described in the tip in this section). You will know your fix is working when you open your site with the Windows version of Internet Explorer 5.5 or a later version and the movie plays.

```
<html>
<head>
<title>A Simple Web Page</title>
</head>
<body>
<p> This is an embedded QuickTime movie. </p>
<p>This is about as simple as it gets.</p>
<object CLASSID="clsid:02BF25D5-8C17-4B23-BC80-D3488ABDDC6B"
WIDTH="160"HEIGHT="144"
CODEBASE="http://www.apple.com/qtactivex/qtplugin.cab">
<PARAM name="SRC" VALUE="simple.mov">
<PARAM name="AUTOPLAY" VALUE="true">
<embed SRC="simple.mov" WIDTH="320" HEIGHT="256" AUTOPLAY="true">
</embed>
</object>
</body>
</html>
```

This sample file, simple_page_activex.html, is also included in the Chapter7_Web_integration folder on the accompanying CD-ROM.

Understanding the Fix

For those of you who want to know exactly how the fix works, here's a peak under the hood:

The `<object>` element is used by Internet Explorer on Windows 9*x*/NT/2000/XP platforms. The enclosed `<embed>` element is used by Netscape browsers, Internet Explorer for the Mac, and other browsers that support the Netscape QuickTime plug-in. Browsers that understand the `<object>` element ignore the `<embed>` element; conversely, those that don't understand the `<object>` element use the `<embed>` element.

The CLASSID parameter within the `<object>` element uniquely identifies which ActiveX control to use. The value "clsid:02BF25D5-8C17-4B23-BC80-D3488ABDDC6B" tells Internet Explorer to use the newly created QuickTime ActiveX control.

If the viewer does not already have the ActiveX control installed, the CODEBASE parameter (`CODEBASE="http://www.apple.com/qtactivex/qtplugin.cab"`>) tells the browser where to find it for downloading. Internet Explorer will automatically offer to download and install the ActiveX control for the user, after which the movie can be played without restarting the browser.

The `<object>` element can use any `<embed>` attributes QuickTime understands. You can also include the following attribute just after the AUTOPLAY attribute:

```
PLUGINSPAGE=http://www.apple.com/quicktime/download/
```

If QuickTime is not already installed, this will prompt the viewer to download and install QuickTime and will provide an automatic link to the appropriate site for doing so.

Because a browser will use either the `<object>` element or the `<embed>` element, but not both, most of the element attributes must be included in each instance. For example, that's why the AUTOPLAY attribute is repeated: once for the `<object>` element and once for the `<embed>` element.

TIP ▸ *If you are adjusting an existing Web site for this new problem, it might be sufficient to add the* `<object>` *element to the opening page—also called the* front door *or* home page*—of your site. Most Web sites' pages are easily accessible through links from other sites. (For example, search engines such as Yahoo and Google will search individual pages of Web sites and then link to them.) You could, however, design your site in a way that requires a visitor to enter the site through a single front door. This means that no matter what page on your site the viewers are trying to get to, they must first visit the front door. Once the* `<object>` *element on the front door causes the viewer's browser to install the ActiveX control, all subsequent pages with the original* `<embed>` *elements will work properly. If you can't be certain that the front door will always visited (as in the case of the search engine example), then all your pages should be adjusted to include these* `<object>` *elements.*

Using Web Authoring Tools

If all that HTML coding makes your head spin, fear not. There is an alternative to writing all of the HTML code by hand. Web authoring tools let you view and/or modify Web page layouts and source code side by side. Like a word processor, they are WYSIWYG tools. You don't have to know how to write HTML; you just have to know what you want on your Web page.

The accompanying CD-ROM includes a 30-day "tryout" version of Adobe GoLive for you to use in doing these exercises.

If you want to delve deeper into GoLive, try these books: *Adobe GoLive 6 for Macintosh and Windows: Visual QuickStart Guide*, by Shelly Brisbin (Peachpit Press), or *Real World Adobe GoLive 6*, by Jeff Carlson and Glenn Fleishman (Peachpit Press).

Installing GoLive

Here's how to install the tryout version from the CD-ROM:

1. Once you've inserted this book's CD-ROM into your computer, go to the Tryout Software folder. Open the folder that describes the operating system you're using (Macintosh or Windows). Open the Adobe GoLive 6.0 folder.

2. Open the Installer folder and double-click the GoLive6_Tryout icon and follow the instructions for decompressing it (if necessary).

3. Double-click the Setup file in the uncompressed GoLive folder, and follow the installer's instructions.

Using GoLive

1. Open Adobe GoLive.

2. When the blank untitled.html page appears, type in some text similar to that shown in **Figure 7.8**.

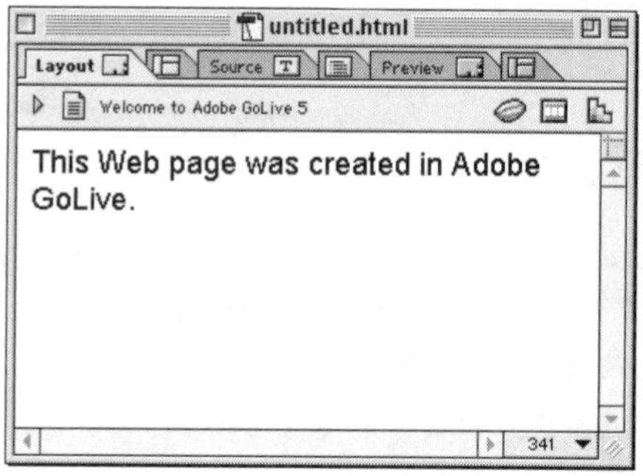

FIGURE 7.8
A new Web page, created in Adobe GoLive, with text typed in.

3. Choose File > Save and give the page a name (such as GoLive_video.html).

4. Add a QuickTime movie by dragging the QuickTime plug-in icon from the Objects palette to your new Web page (**Figure 7.9**).

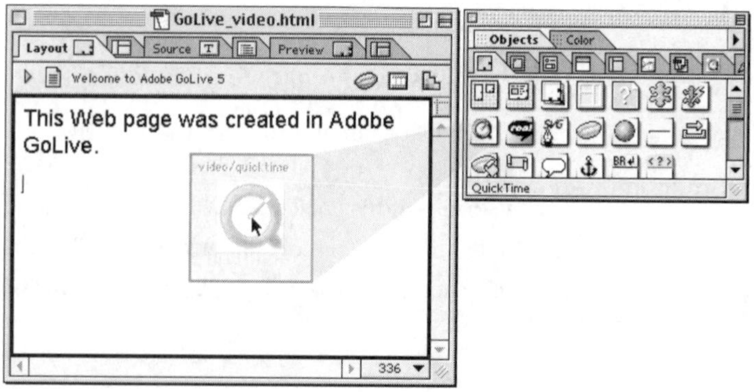

FIGURE 7.9
Drag and drop the QuickTime plug-in icon into place on your page.

5. With the "video/quicktime" placeholder icon still selected in the new Web page, click on the Browse button of the context-sensitive Inspector palette (**Figure 7.10**). (If the Inspector palette isn't open, choose Window > Inspector to open it.)

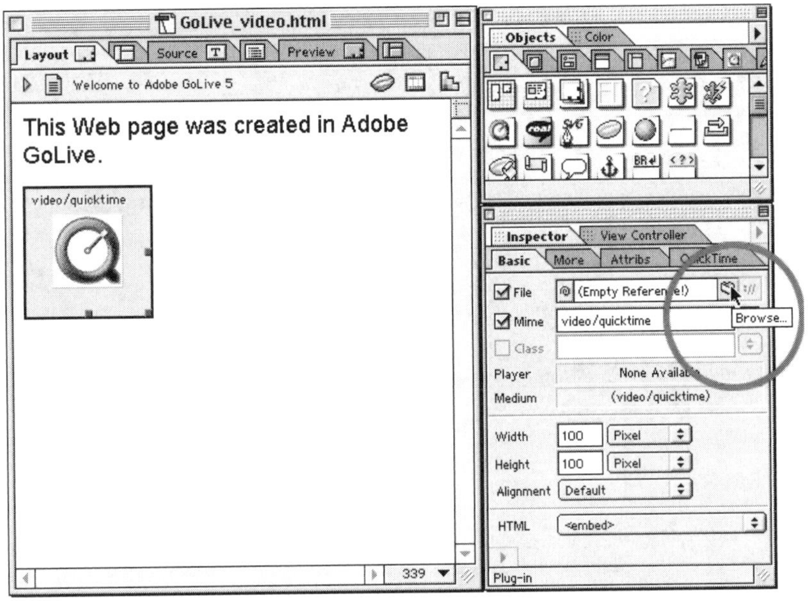

Figure 7.10
Click on the Browse button in the Inspector.

6. Use the resulting dialog box to choose the QuickTime movie that you want to include in your Web page (**Figure 7.11**).

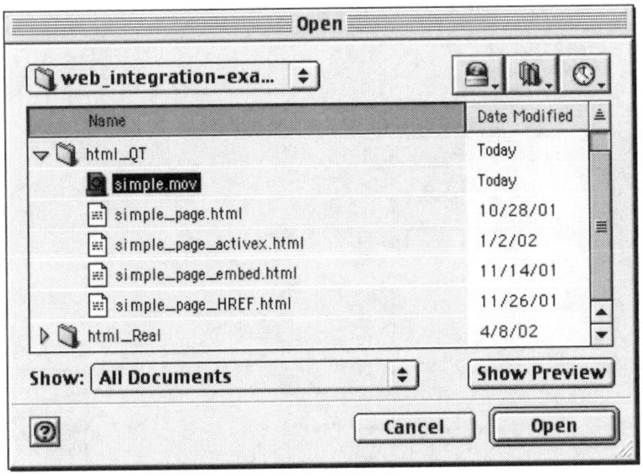

Figure 7.11
Choose the QuickTime movie you want GoLive to include in your Web page.

7. Once you choose a movie, the file expands to its full size and the information about the movie gets filled into the various fields in the Inspector (**Figure 7.12**). To change the size or positioning of the movie, you can either click and drag the movie (or the handles on the corners of the movie) or enter new numbers in the appropriate fields of the Inspector.

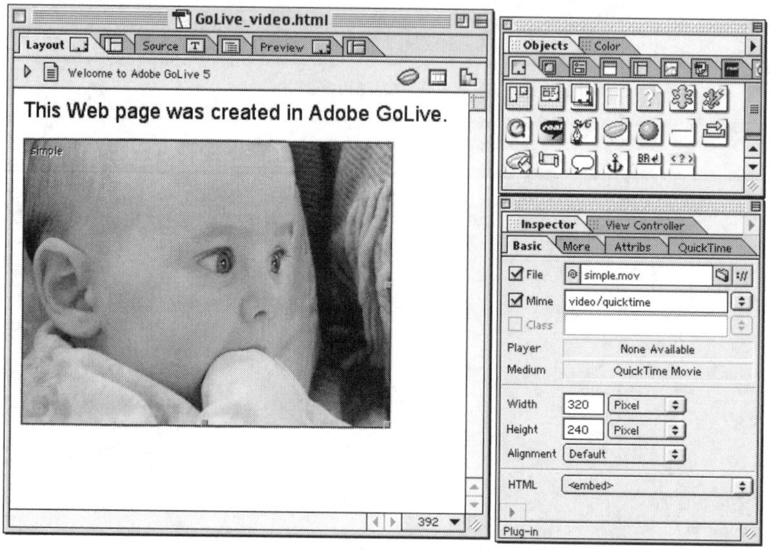

FIGURE 7.12
The movie is displayed at its full size, and info about the movie is filled into the fields in the Inspector tab.

8. Click on the QuickTime tab of the Inspector, and click the check boxes for the various QuickTime attributes to customize the playback of your movie (**Figure 7.13**). (See "QuickTime Attributes," earlier, to learn what they do.) Then click on the Attribs tab to see the resulting list of attributes you've chosen (**Figure 7.14**).

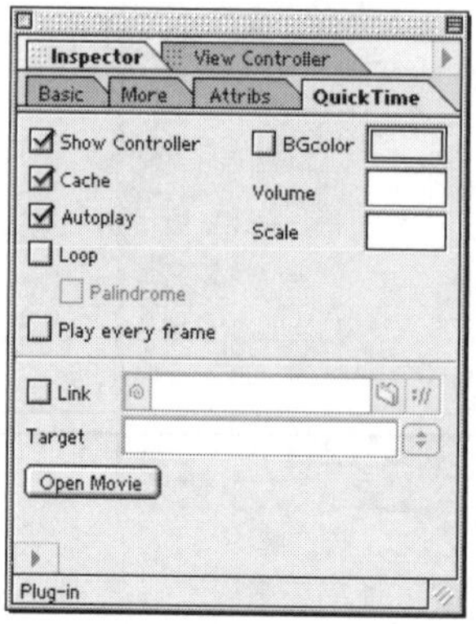

FIGURE 7.13
The QuickTime tab in GoLive's Inspector is where you set various attributes to customize your movie.

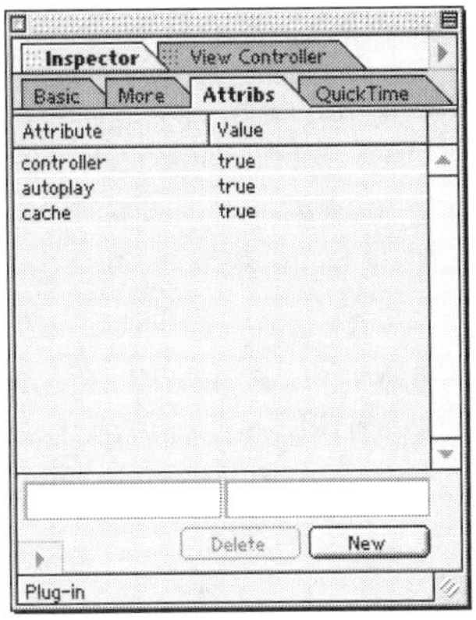

FIGURE 7.14
The Attribs tab in GoLive's Inspector indicates the status of the attributes you set in the QuickTime tab.

9. Save this new HTML document.

10. Open your HTML document in a Web browser.

    (To launch a browser from within Adobe GoLive, click the Browser button on the toolbar or choose Special > Show in Default Browser.)

The resulting Web page should look like **Figure 7.15**.

FIGURE 7.15
A Web page created in GoLive with an embedded QuickTime movie.

The Internet Explorer Problem and Web Authoring Tools

Since the plug-in compatibility problem with later versions of IE is so new, many Web authoring tools haven't yet been updated as of mid-2002. (However, the tryout version of GoLive on the CD-ROM that came with this book is version 6.0. Fortunately, it *has* been updated to automatically put in the complete and correct `<embed>/<object>` tag combination.)

But if you're using Web authoring software that hasn't been updated, then for now you'll need to hand-code these lines of HTML into your Web pages. In other words, you will go back to the HTML version of your Web page to enter the following lines of code (indicated in italic type):

```
<object CLASSID="clsid:02BF25D5-8C17-4B23-BC80-D3488ABDDC6B"
WIDTH="160"HEIGHT="144"
CODEBASE="http://www.apple.com/qtactivex/qtplugin.cab">
<PARAM name="SRC" VALUE="simple.mov">
<PARAM name="AUTOPLAY" VALUE="true">
<embed SRC="simple.mov" WIDTH="320" HEIGHT="256" AUTOPLAY="true">
</embed>
</object>
```

You will include these lines of HTML in each page of your Web site that has an embedded QuickTime movie (unless you've designed your Web site so that visitors must enter through the front door, as described in the tip earlier in the chapter, in which case you may only need to modify that page).

Here's how:

1. Click on the Source tab at the top of the main screen to expose the raw HTML code (**Figure 7.16**), which is usually behind the scenes when you're in Layout mode (**Figure 7.17**).

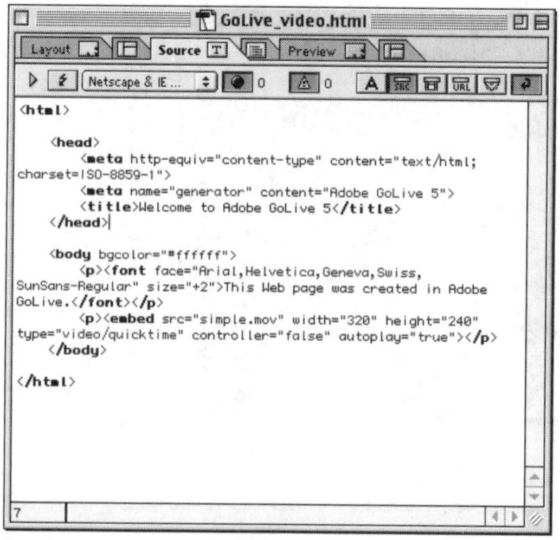
GoLive_video.html
Layout
Source
Preview
Netscape & IE ...
<html>
<head>
<meta http-equiv="content-type" content="text/html; charset=ISO-8859-1">
<meta name="generator" content="Adobe GoLive 5">
<title>Welcome to Adobe GoLive 5</title>
</head>
<body bgcolor="#ffffff">
<p><font face="Arial,Helvetica,Geneva,Swiss,SunSans-Regular" size="+2">This Web page was created in Adobe GoLive.</font></p>
<p><embed src="simple.mov" width="320" height="240" type="video/quicktime" controller="false" autoplay="true"></p>
</body>
</html>

FIGURE 7.16
The GoLive main window in Source mode

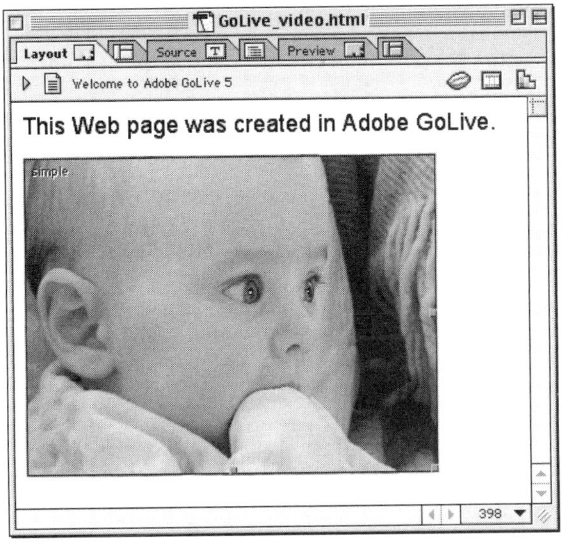
GoLive_video.html
Layout
Source
Preview
Welcome to Adobe GoLive 5
This Web page was created in Adobe GoLive.
simple
398

FIGURE 7.17
The GoLive main window in Layout mode.

2. Select the line or lines of HTML code that include the `<embed>` element for the QuickTime movie (**Figure 7.18**).

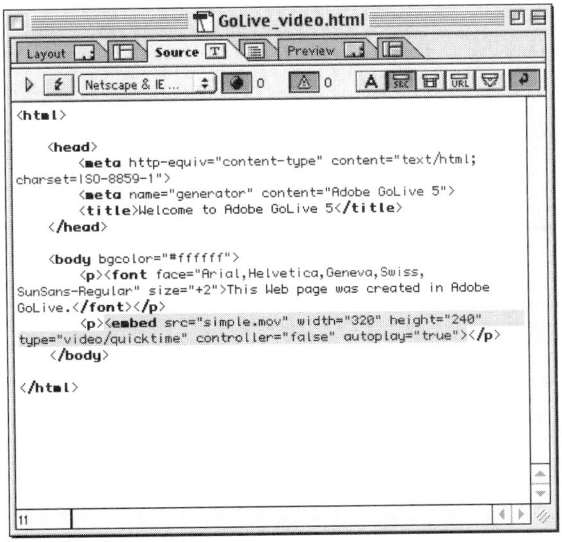
GoLive_video.html
Layout
Source
Preview
Netscape & IE ...
<html>
<head>
<meta http-equiv="content-type" content="text/html;
charset=ISO-8859-1">
<meta name="generator" content="Adobe GoLive 5">
<title>Welcome to Adobe GoLive 5</title>
</head>
<body bgcolor="#ffffff">
<p><font face="Arial,Helvetica,Geneva,Swiss,
SunSans-Regular" size="+2">This Web page was created in Adobe
GoLive.</font></p>
<p><embed src="simple.mov" width="320" height="240"
type="video/quicktime" controller="false" autoplay="true"></p>
</body>
</html>
11

FIGURE 7.18
The selected code here includes the `<embed>` element that invokes the QuickTime movie.

continued ›

3. Do one of two things:

   Delete the selected code and then type in the new lines of HTML code by hand.

   or

   Open the simple_page_activex.html document on the accompanying CD-ROM. Use a text editor to copy the new lines of HTML code from that document. Then switch back to GoLive and paste it in to replace the selected code with the new code. You will need to adjust some of the elements (such as the width and height of the movie) to fit your particular movies and Web pages.

4. Click on the Layout tab at the top of the main screen to see a WYSIWYG view of the movie in the Web page.

5. Once you've pasted in the new code, choose Special › Rewrite Source Code to have GoLive make your changes permanent. The resulting Source view should look like **Figure 7.19.**

You can open the GoLive_video_object.html document on the CD-ROM to use it in GoLive.

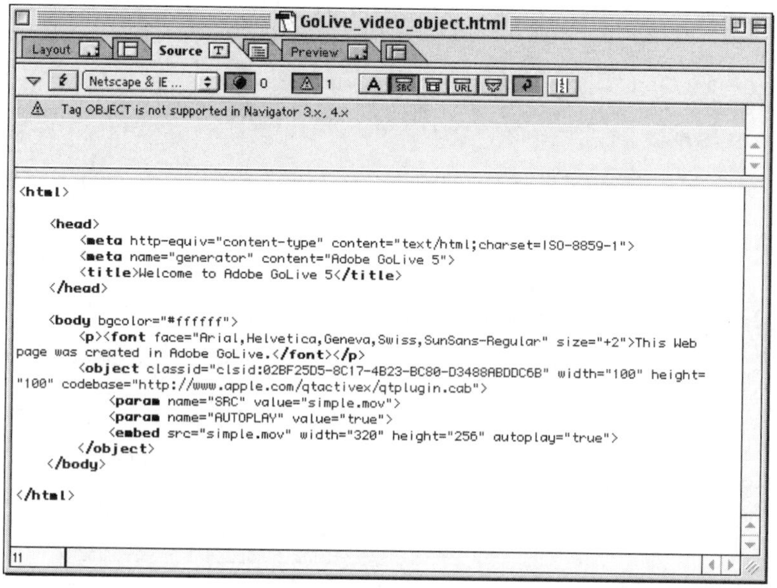

FIGURE 7.19
The new code replaces the old code.

6. Save your changes and test the page in various browser configurations, as described in a tip earlier in the chapter.

Building a Web Site in GoLive

Building a page with an embedded movie is a good first step, but creating an entire Web site, with multiple pages, is a more satisfying enterprise, and one that GoLive and other Web authoring tools make easy to accomplish. Here's how to use GoLive to create a simple Web site with two pages that you could use as a template to create a site that will present your movie as it plays back at different data rates (our task later in this chapter).

In the Chapter7_Web_integration folder on the CD-ROM, you will find a folder called Simple_folder, which contains the completed GoLive site and its component parts.

Creating the First Page

1. Open GoLive and choose File > New Site > Blank.

   You will be prompted for a site name, and a location for that site on your hard disk. A new Site window appears, complete with a blank index.html home page. This window is where you keep track of each of your Web pages.

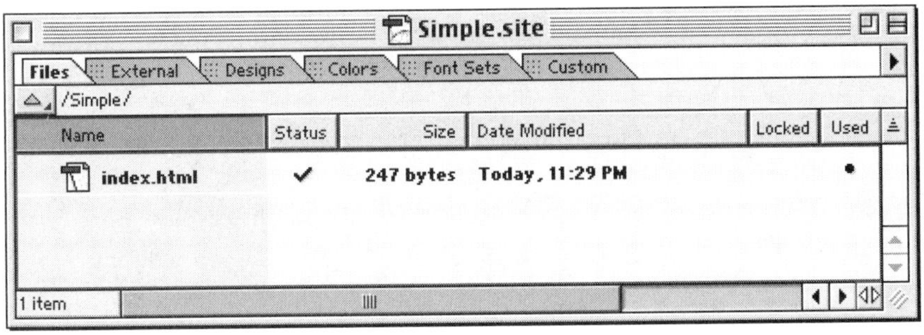

FIGURE 7.20 When you select New Site in GoLive, a new Site window appears, complete with a blank index.html home page.

2. Double-click the index.html page to open it in the Document window. This is where you'll build each page.

3. Click once on the Page icon in the upper-left corner of the Document window (**Figure 7.21**) to open the page settings in the Inspector palette, located at the lower right of your screen. This palette allows you to set attributes for text and objects in the Document window, as well as for files and other elements in the Site window.

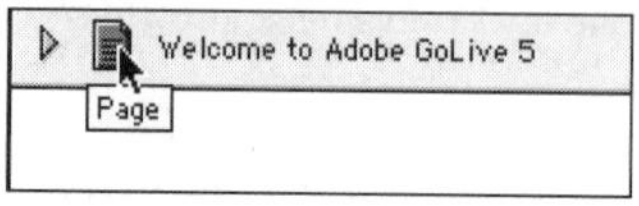

FIGURE 7.21
Clicking the Page icon in the Document window opens up the Inspector palette—command central for Web page construction.

4. Give the page a new name by typing one into the "title" field in the Inspector.

5. Click the blank color field under Background in the Inspector. The Color palette appears and offers you nine ways to select colors for your page. I like to use the color wheel, the fourth icon from the left.

6. Choose a background color by clicking on it in the color palette. (Dark and neutral colors are best for Web video backgrounds.)

7. Click on the Objects tab above the Color palette to open up the Objects palette.

8. Click and drag the leftmost icon (the Layout Grid icon) in the Objects palette onto the Document window. (As you move the cursor across these icons, text appears at the bottom of the palette to identify each of them.) The Layout Grid applies a temporary grid pattern to the Web page that is helpful in laying out text, graphics, movies, and such. (Later, when you open the page in a Web browser, the grid will be invisible.)

9. Click and drag the little blue corners of the grid so that it covers the entire page (**Figure 7.22**).

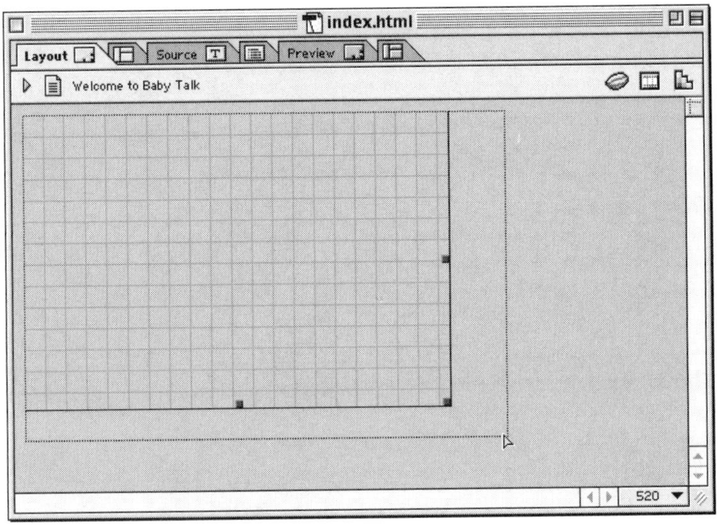

Figure 7.22
Making the layout grid larger makes it easy to properly align the objects on your Web page.

10. Click and drag the Layout Text Box icon (the next icon in the Objects palette) onto the Document window.

11. Resize the box so that you can type a line of text into it.

12. Type a heading into this new box. This becomes the heading that your viewers see on the Web page (**Figure 7.23**).

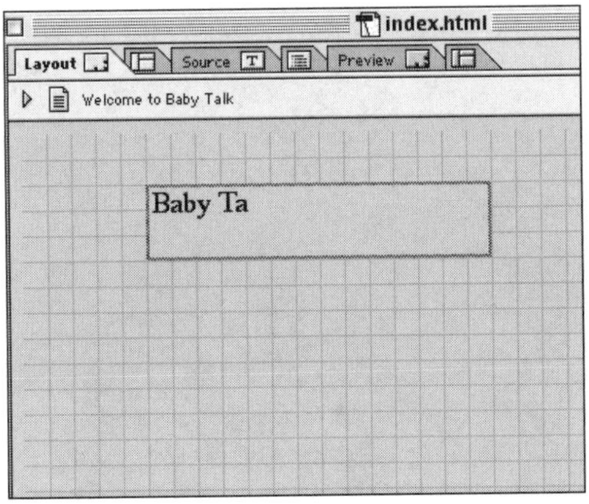

Figure 7.23
Typing a heading into the layout text box creates the heading your viewers will see.

13. Select the text and use the Type > Header pop-out menu to choose a heading size for the text. Experiment until you find the size and style you like.

14. Select the Image icon (the question mark) on the Objects palette, and drag it to the Document window (**Figure 7.24**).

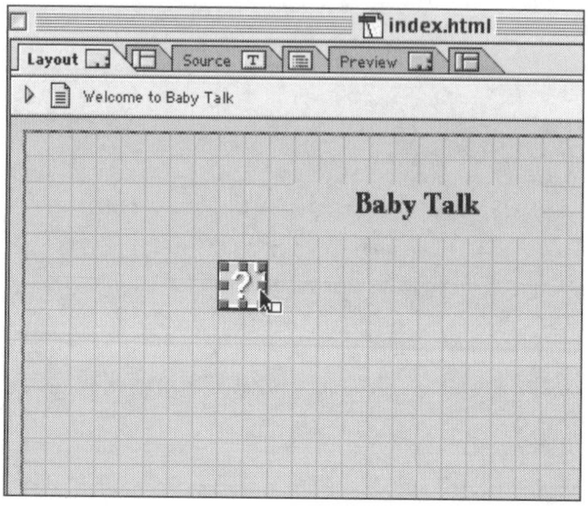

FIGURE 7.24
Dragging the Image icon into the Document window tells GoLive that you want to place an image on that page.

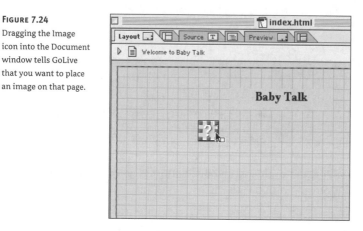

15. Select the Image icon that you just placed in the Document window, and click the Browse button in the Inspector palette to find the graphic image that you want to place on that page. The Browse button looks like a yellow file folder. There's a ready-made image called simple_320.jpg on the CD. The image will fill the icon in the Document window (**Figure 7.25**).

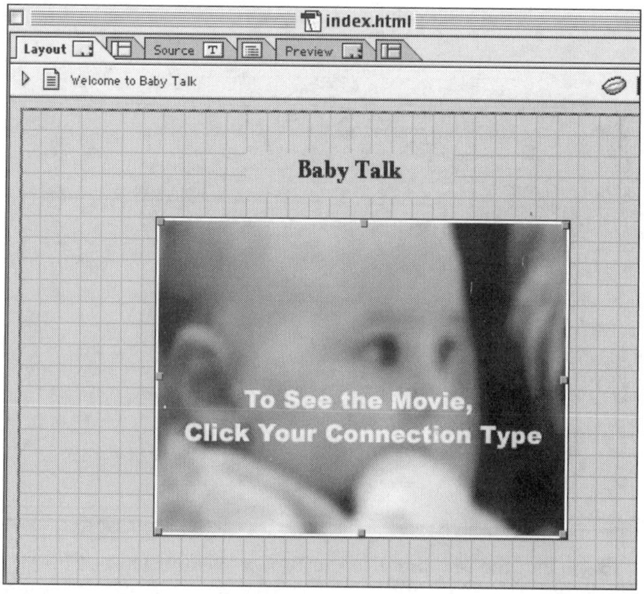

FIGURE 7.25
The selected image fills in the Image icon in the Document window once you've successfully placed it on the page.

16. Drag a second Layout Text Box just to the left of the image, and add the following lines of text to it:

    56K modem
    ISDN
    DSL/Cable

17. Select the new text and adjust it with the Type > Size menu, and with the Align Right button in the toolbar. To adjust the position of items on the screen, just select an item and press the arrow keys on your keyboard to move it.

18. Save your work by selecting File > Save.

Creating a Second Page

1. Select the index.html icon in the Site window.

2. Choose Edit > Duplicate to create a new page, which GoLive will call index1.html.

3. Rename the new page in the Site window to dsl.html by selecting it and then typing in a new name in the Inspector palette (**Figure 7.26**).

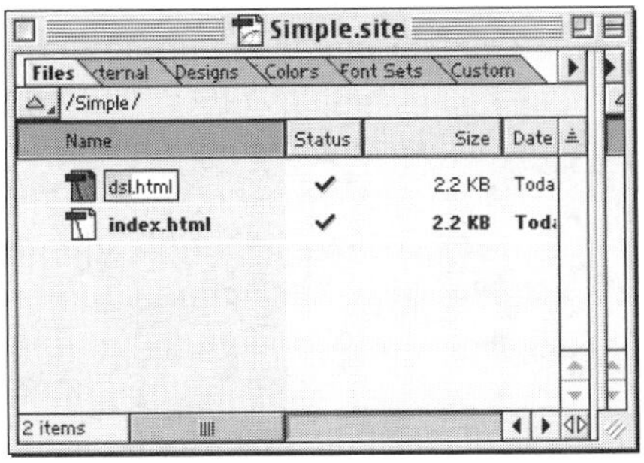

FIGURE 7.26
After you've renamed your new page dsl.html, it appears above the index.html page in the Site window.

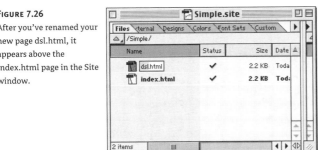

4. Double-click dsl.html to open that page in the Document window.

5. Delete the image that's there. You don't want to use the same image that's on the index page. Instead, you'll place a movie that's optimized for viewers with DSL connections.

6. Click and drag the QuickTime icon from the Objects palette (look for the *Q*) onto the Document window (**Figure 7.27**).

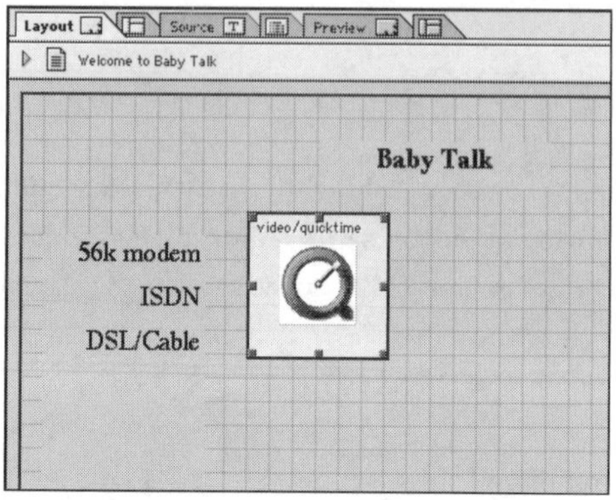

Figure 7.27
The QuickTime icon on the new "DSL" page.

7. With the QuickTime icon selected in the Document window, click the Browse button in the Inspector palette and navigate to a QuickTime movie.

There's one in the Simple_folder on the accompanying CD-ROM.

The movie image will fill the space in the Document window where the still image used to be.

8. Click on the Attribs tab in the Inspector palette, then change the CONTROLLER attribute to "true" to add a controller to the movie on your page (**Figure 7.28**).

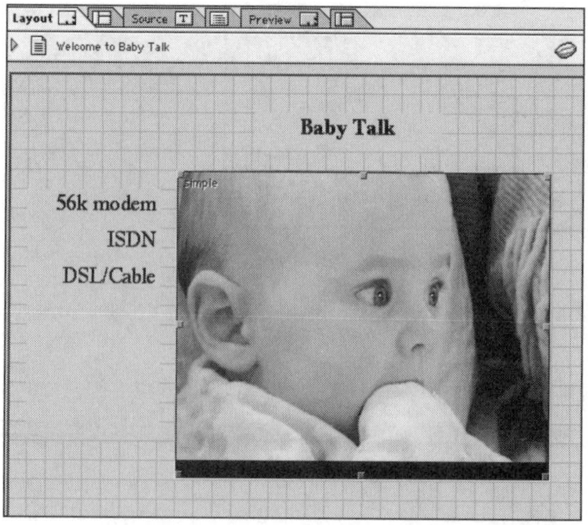

Figure 7.28
The QuickTime movie on the new "DSL" page with an added controller.

Linking the Two Pages

1. Place your cursor in the text box on the left side and type *Home* beneath DSL/Cable.

2. Select the word *Home*. The Inspector changes to Link mode.

3. Click the blue Link button on the Inspector palette (it looks like links in a chain).

4. Click on the small spiral icon that is next to the Link icon. This tool is called the Point and Shoot tool. You can use it to create links between pages in your site.

5. Without letting go of the mouse button, drag this tool over to the index.html page in the Site window (**Figure 7.29**). This creates a link from this dsl.html page to your Web site's home page. When viewers click on the word *Home*, they'll be transferred to the home page.

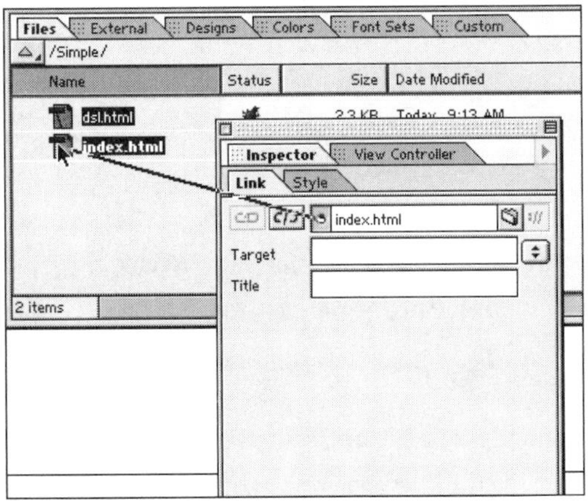

Figure 7.29
Use the spiral-shaped Point and Shoot tool to create a link from the word *Home* to index.html.

6. Select index.html in the Site window and double-click it to open the page in the Document window.

7. Select the words *DSL/Cable* in the text box and click the Link icon.

8. Select the Point and Shoot tool and point it at dsl.html in the Site window. Now you've created a link that will take people from the home page to the DSL page.

9. Save your work. (Each page must be saved separately.)

Putting It All Together

To truly create a Web site that can display your movie at several different data rates, you'll have to perform a few more steps. First, following the same procedure you just used to create the first two pages, you'll need to create two more pages: one for a 56K modem connection and one for viewers with ISDN. Second, you'll need to use what you learned in Chapters 5 and 6 to make versions of your movie (or mine) for each of the three connection speeds featured here and then embed and link each version into the appropriate page. Finally, if you know you want to reach Windows users, you'll need to insert the HTML code discussed in this chapter to make sure that they'll be able to play your movies. Once you're done, you'll have created a Web site that can display a movie that many kinds of viewers will be able to see.

Getting on the Web

Finding Server Space

Once you've compressed your Web movies and created your Web pages, you're ready to place all of these files on a Web (HTTP) server so that your audience can access and view your movies. If you don't already have available server space, you'll need to shop around and find some. Check first with your own Internet Service Provider (ISP); most of the major ISPs include about 10 MB of free server space for your personal use in their standard subscriber package. If you need more space, many Web hosting services will rent you hundreds of megabytes of server space for around $15 a month. (For *streaming server* information, see the next chapter.)

Uploading Movies Using FTP

Now that you've built your site and rented server space to host it, you need to upload your pages to the host Web server before anyone will be able to download them and play your movies. To do that, you'll need either a standalone File Transfer Protocol (FTP) program or a Web publishing tool that includes FTP features. There are many inexpensive FTP software tools for transferring files between your computer and a remote Web server. Two popular ones are WS_FTP Pro (for Windows) and Fetch (for Mac OS).

TIP ▸ *You can download WS_FTP Pro for $40 from* `www.ipswitch.com/`*. You can download Fetch for $25 from* `http://fetchsoftworks.com/`*.*

These programs work much the same way and do one thing really well: They get your files to where they need to be. Both require that you have an ID and password (your Web host will supply it to you) and that you know the location of the server and the directory that you want to transfer files to. Once you log in, you'll have access to the home directory for your Web files. (WS_FTP Pro opens two windows: one for your (local) computer and one for your directory on the remote Web server.) Depending on the program, you use buttons or menus or drag-and-drop to create or change directories and transfer your files (**Figures 7.30** and **7.31**). Once you've transferred the files, make a note of the directory path of your HTML files. This will form the Web address for your Web movie, such as: **`http://members.home.net/thomaslue/simple.html`**.

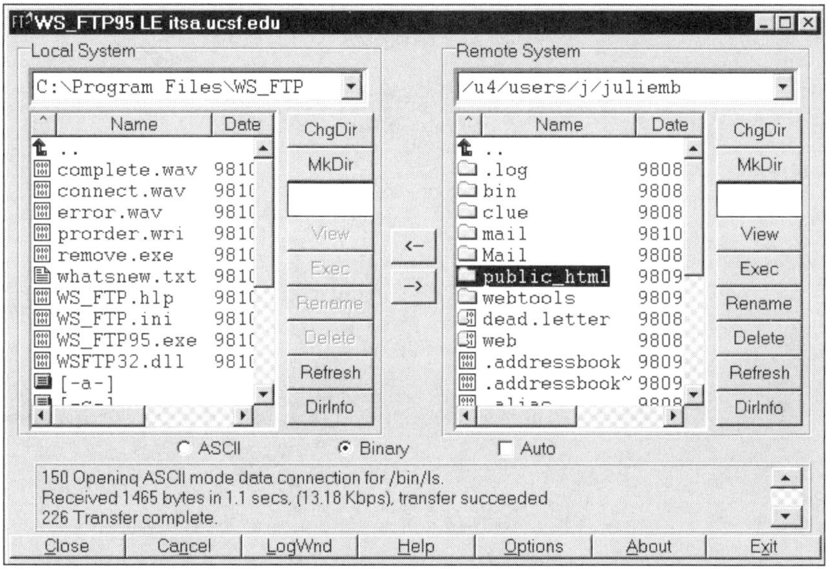

FIGURE 7.30
WS_FTP Pro allows you to select the files on your local computer and then click the arrow buttons to move the files to the remote server.

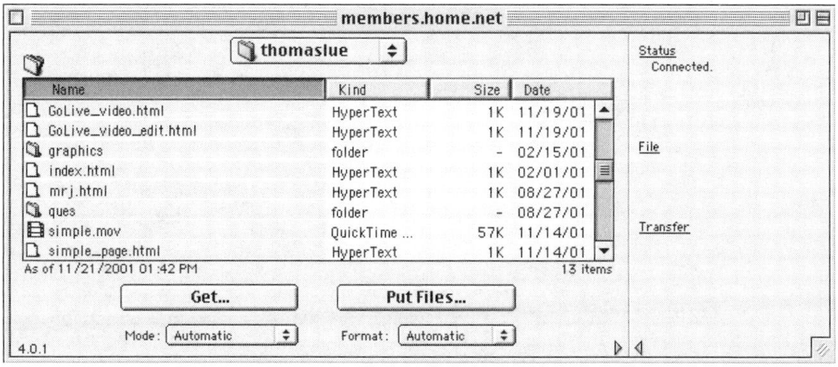

FIGURE 7.31
Fetch allows you to drag and drop files directly into the Fetch window from your Mac desktop, or use the "Get" or "Put Files" button to select files in a dialog box.

TIP ▸ *HTML files should be transferred as ASCII or text files. Movies and image files need to be transferred in binary format. Most FTP software tools have an "automatic transfer mode" option that automatically determines the correct file transfer mode to use when you upload or download files.*

Uploading Movies Using a Web Authoring Tool

If you're using a WYSIWYG authoring tool, you don't need to buy any of the FTP tools out there; you've got FTP built in. Adobe GoLive, for example, has several kinds of FTP file transfer features. One of them works almost exactly the same way standalone FTP software does. Here's how to use it:

1. Choose File > FTP Browser.
2. Fill in the server name, directory name, user ID, and password for the server you want to connect to.
3. Make sure you're connected to the Web.
4. Click Connect to connect to the Web server.
5. Do one of the following:

- To upload a file or folder, drag it from your desktop to the FTP Browser window.

  or

- To download a file or folder, drag it from the FTP Browser to your desktop (**Figure 7.32**).

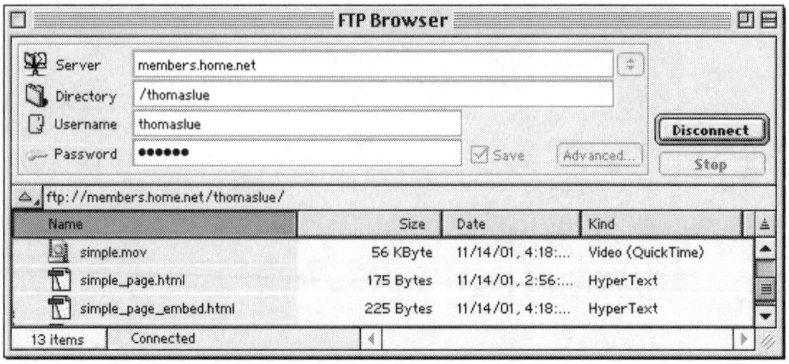

FIGURE 7.32
GoLive's FTP Browser window makes it straightforward to upload or download your files by dragging them between the window and your desktop.

Designing Web Pages for Video

As with most movie-making, there are logistics and then there are aesthetics. I've focused until now on getting your movie to *play* on a Web site, but it's also critical that you think hard about *how* the movie is arranged on the Web page so that you can most effectively present your movie's message or experience to your audience. You wouldn't be satisfied watching a tiny movie on a blank page, and neither will your audience. Here are some tips and techniques you can use to present your movies with maximum impact.

Making the Movie Fit the Frame

You had to determine the dimensions of your movie when you compressed it. But now that you're laying out your Web page, you may find it necessary to adjust the size of the movie to better fit the rest of your design. You can define the display size of the movie by changing the height and width numbers that you use with the HTML `<embed>` element (`<embed src="sample.mov" width="320" height="256">`). Doing so, however, resizes, or *scales*, your movie, which often causes problems. Scaling down movies can waste bandwidth, and scaling up movies can make them look *pixelated*—an effect that makes the individual pixels in the frame large and blocky. If you compressed your movie with QuickTime and selected the Sorenson codec, you can scale up to 200 percent with minimal loss in image quality; but it's generally a better idea to go back and recompress the movie at the correct size (**Figure 7.33**).

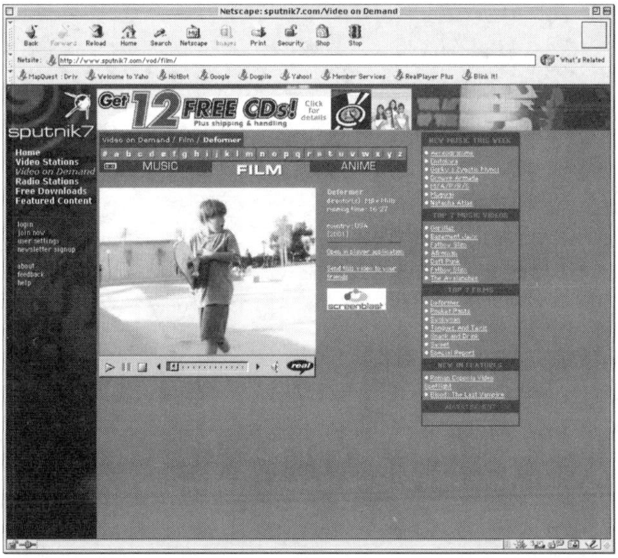

FIGURE 7.33
An example of an appropriately sized movie. Any larger video would have made the page too crowded. Any smaller video would have let the text and interface distract from the movie.

Publishing Multiple Movies

The way to provide the best possible presentation of a movie to the widest possible audience is to do what we started to do when we built the Web site using GoLive: offer multiple versions of the movie, each with its own bandwidth, frame size, frame rate, and compression details. At minimum, this means one low-bandwidth movie (for 56K modems) and one high-bandwidth movie (for DSL, cable modem, and high-speed data lines).

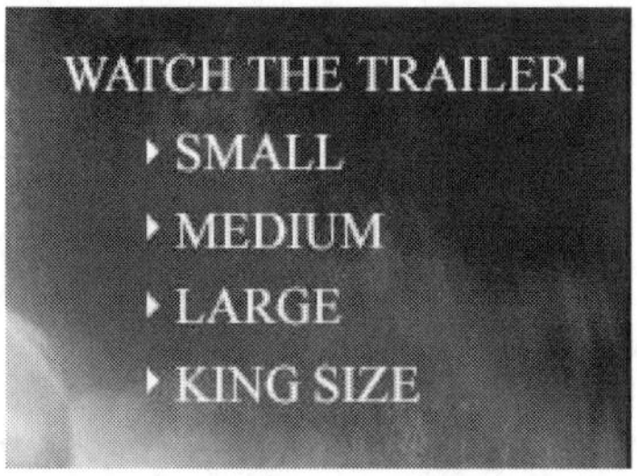

FIGURE 7.34
Sites with movies in multiple bandwidths label the choices in a number of ways. This example mentions the "size" of each option, referring to both the frame size and the file size.

Figures 7.35 to **7.37** show one way to display movies at different sizes and data rates.

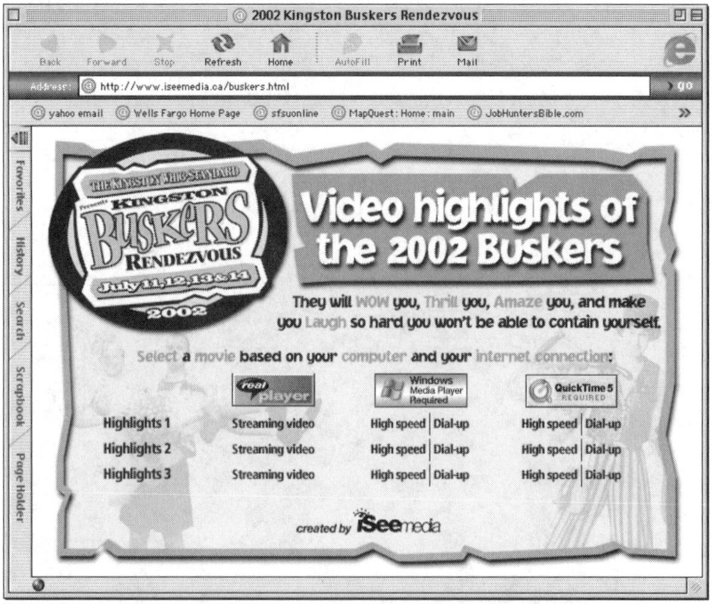

FIGURE 7.35
In this example, viewers can choose from a "High speed" or "Dial-up" version of both Windows Media and QuickTime versions. The RealPlayer option is a SureStream file that adjusts the data rate (but not the frame size) automatically for the viewer's connection speed.

FIGURE 7.36
This is the "High speed" version in Windows Media format.

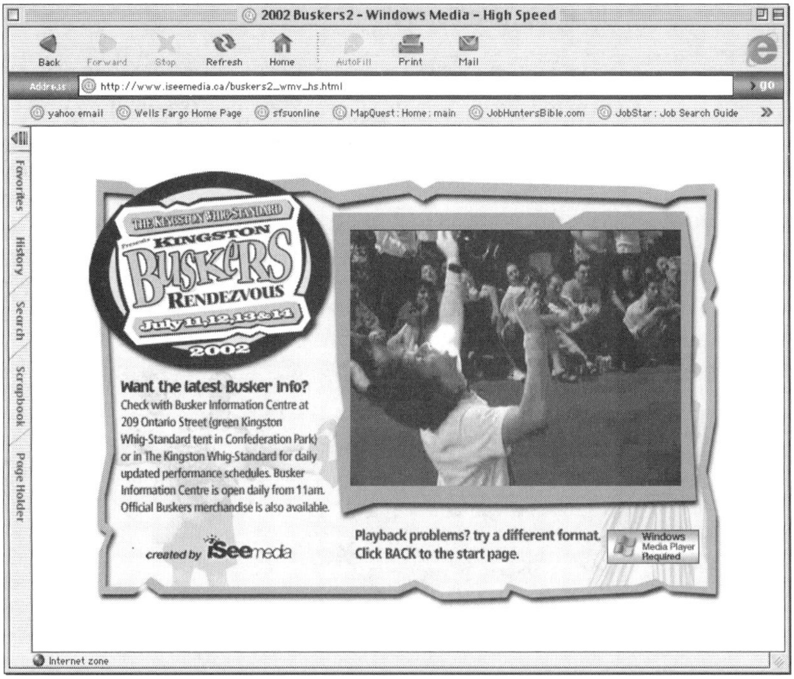

FIGURE 7.37
This is the "Dial-up" version in Windows Media format, with its smaller movie size. The gap around the movie could be avoided by adjusting the size of the "picture frame" graphic to match the movie size.

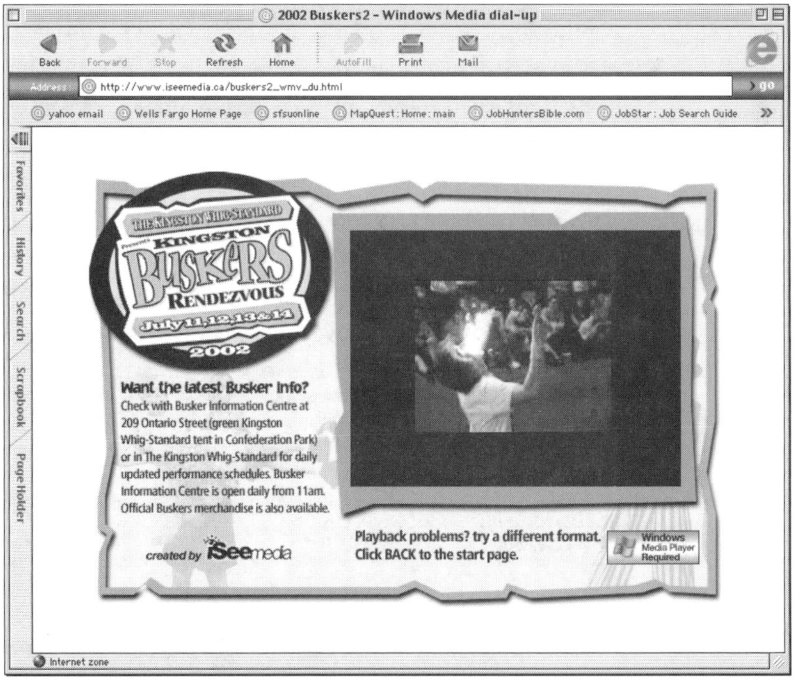

Choosing Your Format

To get your movie seen by as many people as possible, you have to make it *easy* for them to watch. Usually, you can't assume that your viewers have a particular media player installed—people reconfigure their computers all the time. Anticipating the likelihood that the viewer may have just one or two of the Big Three media players installed, many Web sites offer their movies for all three media players (**Figure 7.38**). The more media player formats you offer, the more likely it is that people will actually see your movie. Some corporations, for instance, install just one type of media player and prevent employees from installing any other. Hedge your bets in this game of Web video Russian roulette: Offer your movies in all three formats.

FIGURE 7.38
IFILM.com typically offers its movies in all three players and at different speeds (shown in kilobits per second).

The Missing Media Player Problem

Another good reason to offer your movie in all three formats is that some viewers may have their media player improperly installed. No matter how good your movie looks, if the media player software in your audience's Web browsers isn't working right, they won't be able to see your film. Wise Web moviemakers make it a practice to help their audience find the player that they need and to install it before the show begins. At the very least, they make sure the viewers know where to go to download and install the media player software. One popular way to handle this is to create an explicit link to the appropriate site (and page) for downloading the player software. **Figures 7.39** and **7.40** show two examples of how to do this.

FIGURE 7.39
Clicking on the buttons takes you to the appropriate download sites.

FIGURE 7.40
Additional help in installing media player software is always welcome.

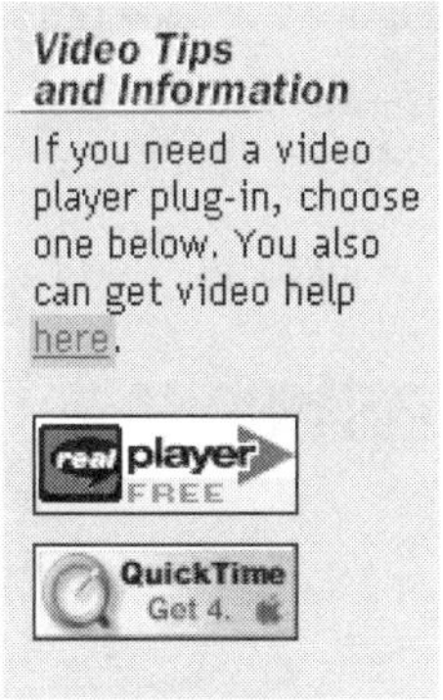

Your Web page's HTML can also provide an automatic link to the appropriate site for downloading the plug-in. One of the parameters available with the HTML **<embed>** element is called **pluginspage**. If a viewer arrives at your Web page and doesn't have the correct browser plug-in, this bit of code automatically tells the browser where to go get it.

Here's the HTML that you need to add these automatic links to the **<embed>** element:

For QuickTime:

```
pluginspage="http://www.apple.com/quicktime/download/"
```

For RealPlayer:

```
pluginspage="http://www.real.com/"
```

For Windows Media Player:

```
pluginspage="http://www.microsoft.com/windows/windowsmedia/download/"
```

The slickest solution to the missing media player software problem is auto-detection, in which your Web site actually reports to the viewer what media player software they have installed. This requires that you add some extra HTML coding and embed samples of each player format on your page. Unfortunately, how to do this is beyond the scope of this book.

Here's how it looks: On the right side of **Figure 7.41**, you can see how sputnik7.com's detection scheme has discovered that the current browser has RealPlayer installed but not Windows Media Player.

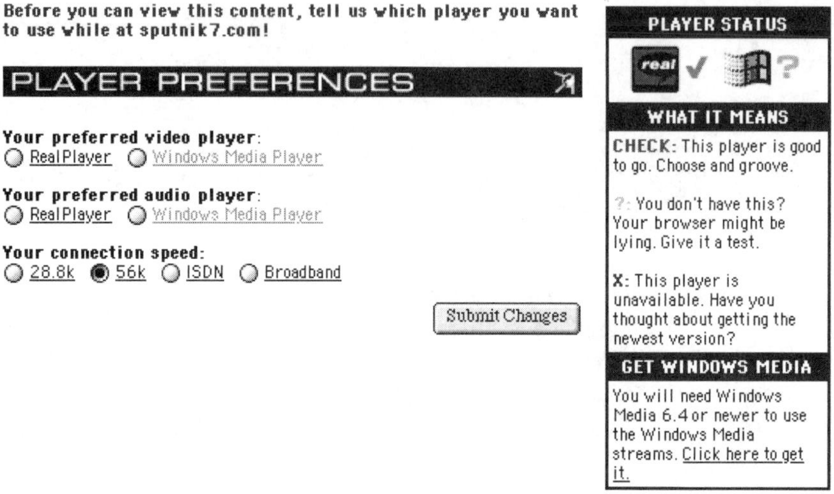
Before you can view this content, tell us which player you want to use while at sputnik7.com!
PLAYER PREFERENCES
Your preferred video player:
RealPlayer
Windows Media Player
Your preferred audio player:
RealPlayer
Windows Media Player
Your connection speed:
28.8k
56k
ISDN
Broadband
Submit Changes
PLAYER STATUS
real
WHAT IT MEANS
CHECK: This player is good to go. Choose and groove.
?: You don't have this? Your browser might be lying. Give it a test.
X: This player is unavailable. Have you thought about getting the newest version?
GET WINDOWS MEDIA
You will need Windows Media 6.4 or newer to use the Windows Media streams. Click here to get it.

FIGURE 7.41
Sputnik7.com's Player Status window reports that RealPlayer is installed but Windows Media Player is not.

Web Video and Flash

Until now, I've focused on the Big Three media players. But they're not the only way to get video on the Web. Lately, many people have built Web sites using Macromedia Flash, a popular authoring tool for creating rich, streaming, vector-based graphics, animation, and interactivity with relatively small file sizes.

Flash can import and export digital video (QuickTime) movies. And now it also can export a Web-optimized Flash file that contains video—you need Flash MX and the Flash 6 Player plug-in to do this (**Figure 7.42**). Flash's Web-optimized file type is known as a "swiff" file. That's Flash slang for "Shockwave Flash," which uses the .swf file extension. Nonvideo SWF files can also be played back with, and imported into, RealPlayer and QuickTime.

Figure 7.42
This Web site (`www.billabongodyssey.com/`) was one of the first sites to use Flash MX's new video capability.

At the moment, Flash video doesn't match the quality of video played in the Big Three media players, but this is a rapidly evolving technology, so stay tuned. For now, though, if video quality is paramount for your Flash site, then you might consider linking out to a separate media player window or HTML window.

Putting Your Movie on Its Own Page

Embedding makes the movie part of your page design, but there are times when you might want to have the movie play separately in the media player or on a separate HTML page.

There are some good reasons for doing this: When the movie plays separately in the media player, viewers can leave the original page to visit other pages in your Web site and still continue to play the movie uninterrupted. Linking out to a media player also prevents the possibility (in the case of longer movies) of using up the browser's RAM. Or maybe your page just doesn't have room for anything else, especially a movie with a large frame size (in this case, another solution would be to link to a new HTML page in a separate, pop-up browser window). And until recently, it was not possible to play video files within the Flash (SWF) player.

That meant that if you wanted to produce your entire Web site using Flash and still integrate Web video into it, you had to link out to a separate (HTML) page that had the video file embedded in it.

The Web site for the band Phish (at `www.phish.com/farmhouse/index_flash.html`) is a good example of this approach. The designers wanted to include video clips, but the site was built in an earlier version of Flash that couldn't embed video. Their solution: link out to a separate HTML (non-Flash) pop-up window to play the movie (**Figures 7.43** and **7.44**).

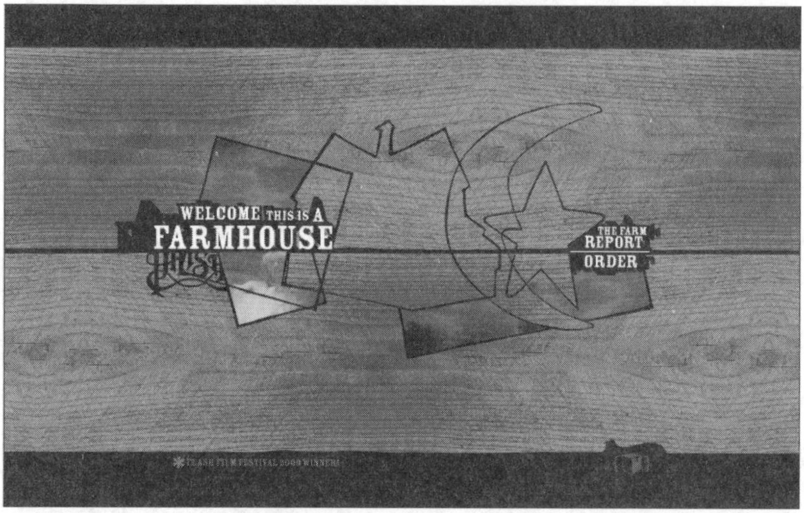

FIGURE 7.43
The Phish site was built in an older version of Flash that couldn't embed video. That's why if you click on the Flash interface...

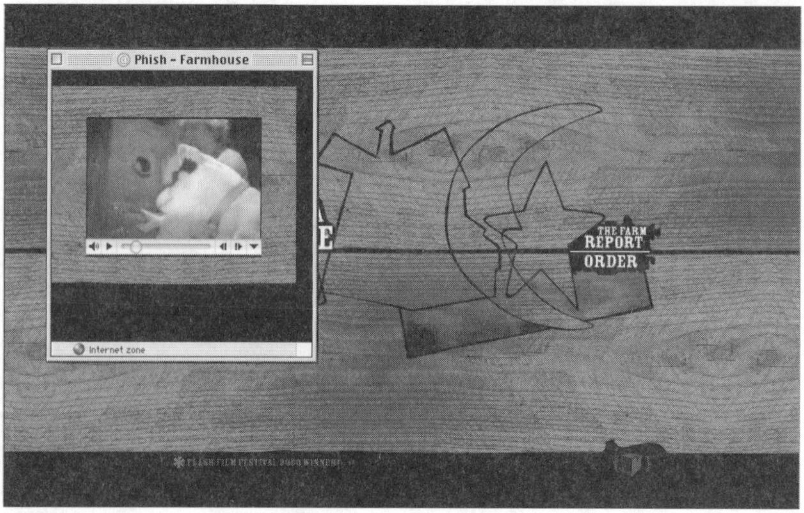

FIGURE 7.44
... a pop-up window appears, complete with movie and matching background.

I find that linking out to a separate window has the added aesthetic bonus of focusing the viewer's attention on the video, rather than on the original page. There's another way to do this: The Web site shown in **Figures 7.45** and **7.46** achieves the same result without actually opening any extra windows. Clicking on the "See the Spot" button opens the movie (surrounded by black) in the same frame.

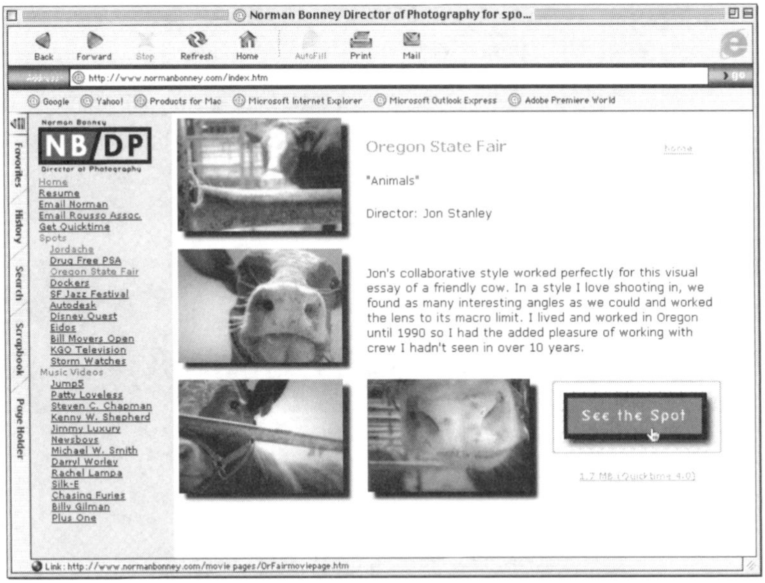

FIGURE 7.45
When you click the "See the Spot" button...

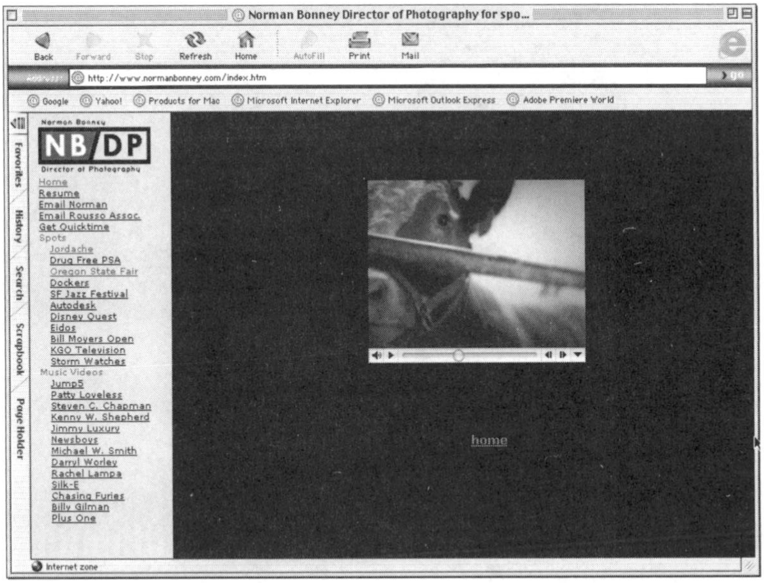

FIGURE 7.46
...it opens the movie (surrounded by black) in the same frame.

Controlling the Controllers

Web video lives in the inherently interactive medium of computing, not the passive, couch potato medium of television. Whenever I produce interactive media, I try to make all of the interactivity available to the viewer, whether they actually use it or not. Unfortunately, this jumble of media player controllers and interfaces can be distracting to the viewer. How much control and how many buttons can we provide before it's too much?

Figure 7.47 shows a movie (encoded in the Real format) at AtomFilms (`http://atomfilms.shockwave.com/`). I find this standard implementation of the RealPlayer controls to be obtrusive: The controls detract from the actual movie because they're so big and bright.

FIGURE 7.47
This Real movie at AtomFilms is presented with the standard display of controls and buttons.

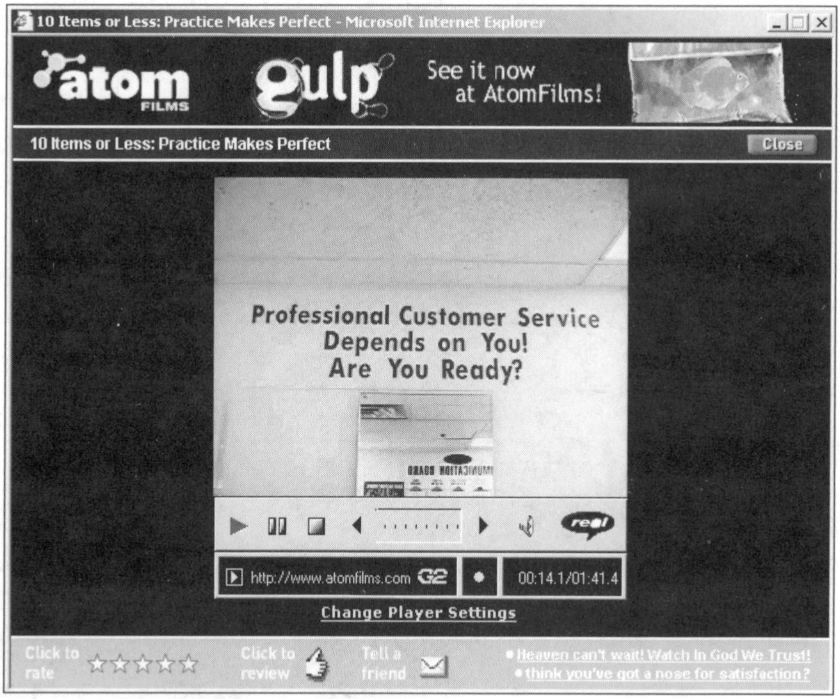

Copyright 2000-2002 AtomShockwave Corp. Content is from the film "10 Items or Less" presented by AtomFilms and produced by Release Entertainment.

Figure 7.48 shows a movie without any controls.

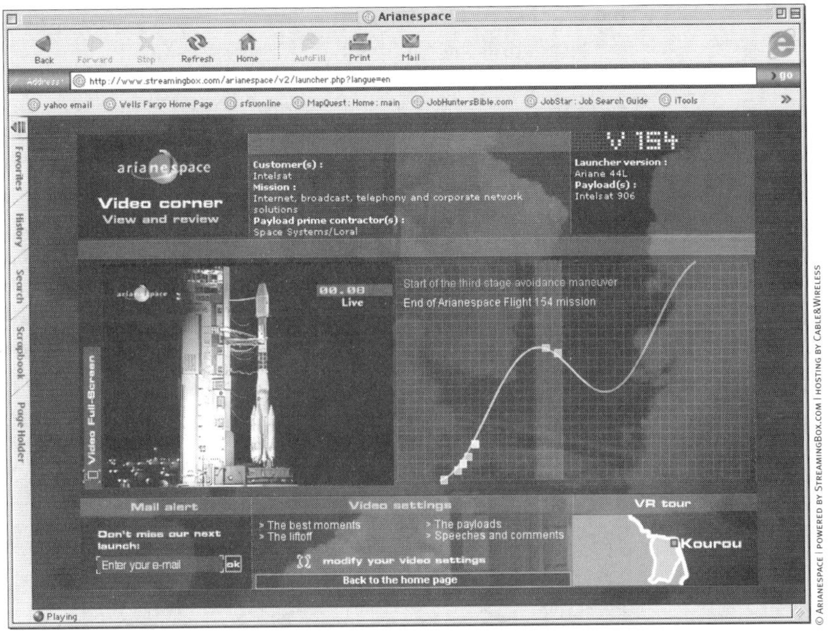

Figure 7.48
This Real movie interface, created for Arianespace by StreamingBox.com, contains no movie controls at all.

Figure 7.49 shows a standard controller bar for embedded QuickTime movies. This is more subtle and less distracting than the standard Real controls in Figure 7.47.

Figure 7.49
The CyberChef section of WRGB Online (`http://www.wrgb.com/`) uses the standard QuickTime controller.

Building Standalone Interfaces for Video

If you want to invest some extra time and effort, you can dispense altogether with the standard-issue controllers that come with the Big Three media players and create your own instead.

A stunning example of this strategy is the series of Web video ads made by famous directors at BMWFilms.com (`www.bmwfilms.com/`). The BMW Film Player is a downloadable, interactive interface created in Macromedia Director that takes over your whole computer screen when you launch it. The movie appears in the center of the black screen (**Figure 7.50**).

FIGURE 7.50 BMWFilms.com's Film Player takes over the entire computer screen when you launch it.

New *media skins* technology offers Web video producers another way to control the look and feel of Web video presentation. You can create a custom interface, or *skin*, complete with custom playback controls for your Web movie. Windows Media Player and QuickTime both use the term *skins* for this technique, although their implementations are slightly different on those platforms. RealMedia uses SMIL technology to accomplish the same thing, and then some (more on that below).

QuickTime Media Skins

In the case of QuickTime Media Skins, you can create this interface (or player window) in any shape or size you like, and in any of the file formats that QuickTime supports. You can create a unique interface for each QuickTime movie; and since the interface is simply a QuickTime movie playing inside the QuickTime player, the viewer can drag it around the screen, independent of the Web browser. A good example of the

QuickTime Media Skins technology is the Dido Sampler (`http://195.92.224.73/dido_hunter/`), which includes a choice of several music clips and one video. The entire presentation appears within an irregularly shaped box that looks nothing like the standard, rectangular QuickTime player window (**Figure 7.51**).

FIGURE 7.51
The Dido Sampler uses QuickTime Media Skins to offer music and video clips, complete with custom playback controls, in a custom-designed box. This interface was designed and created by Graphico New Media Limited for BMG UK & Ireland Ltd.

WINDOWS SKINS

In the Windows world, you customize the graphical interface for entire computer programs rather than for individual movies. You can create a skin for Windows Media Player, your Web browser, or even your entire Windows operating system—but not for an individual movie (**Figure 7.52**).

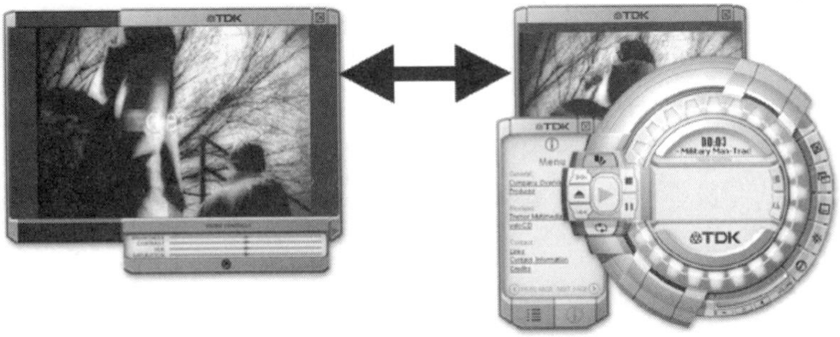

FIGURE 7.52
TDK Digital MixMaster for Windows Media Player created by The Skins Factory (`http://www.theskinsfactory.com`) shows a skin with several movable panes. The round pane contains playback controls such as Play, Pause, and Stop. The movable video pane expands and contracts to fit the dimensions of the particular movie.

continued ›

RealPlayer and SMIL

Synchronous Multimedia Integration Language (SMIL for short) provides another way to build an interface around your video, all within a single streaming file. It allows you to synchronize video, text, animation, graphics, and audio content, and then use script commands embedded in the streaming media to specify exactly when and how those elements are presented (**Figure 7.53**).

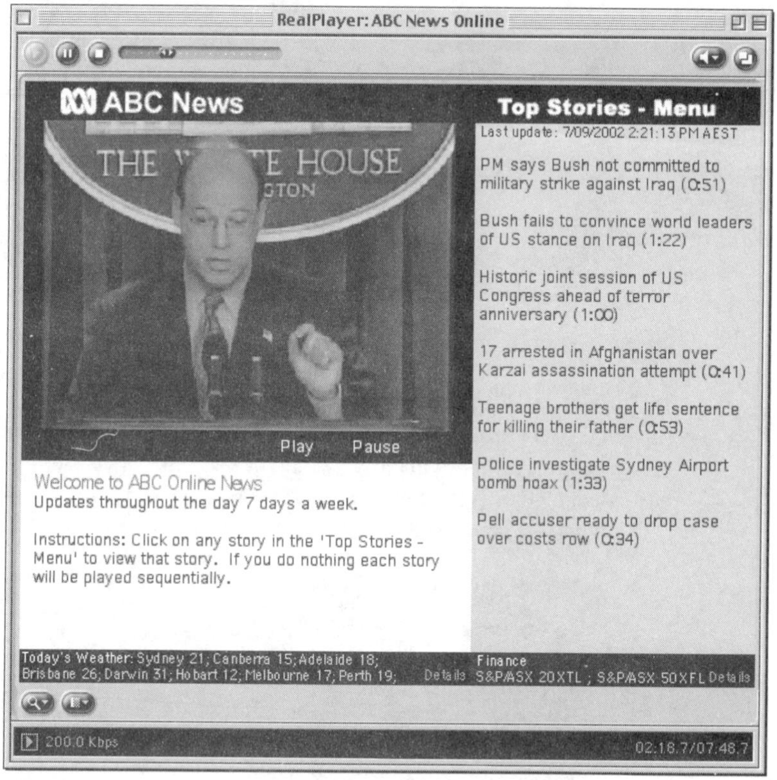

Figure 7.53 The Australian Broadcasting Corporation uses SMIL technology to build an interface for the streaming news site ABC News Online. Viewers can click on the headlines on the right, and the video plays in the window on the left. The entire interface is contained within a streaming RealPlayer movie, with the standard Real playback controls in the upper-left corner and a numeric readout of the current data rate and the elapsed time along the bottom of the frame. See it in action at `http://abc.net.au/broadband/`. But don't confuse this site with ABCNews.com (`http://abcnews.go.com/`), which also happens to use SMIL technology for its streaming news interface.

Congratulations! If you're sure you're never going to make a movie that's delivered via RTSP streaming video, you're done. Go out there and make movies for all the world to see. But if you think that just *maybe* you'd like to take advantage of the ability to dynamically adjust your movie's frame rate to better suit your viewer's optimal connection speed, or if you think you'd like to send out live footage to your audience someday, read on. In the next chapter you'll learn how to set up and deliver streaming video.

WEB VIDEO SPOTLIGHT

Vertical Online

What if you need to produce a clip for the Web *and* for broadcast television?

That's the question Logan Kelsey, principal of San Francisco's Vertical Online, had to ask himself when Earthy Foods approached the company to create a commercial spot simultaneously for online and on-air broadcast. Kelsey has created a number of online projects and a number of broadcast projects, but not many for both at the same time (**Figure 7.54**).

One of the first items of business for Kelsey was to convince the client to shoot in 35mm film (the standard for most broadcast television spots), rather than the video they had budgeted for. Says Kelsey: "The spot was totally visually driven. We wanted it to look sexy, so it would hold up as a broadcast spot, but we also realized there would be constraints for the Web—slow motion, slow edits, locations with simple backgrounds. During preproduction, we sent the client screen tests of the locations (shot on DV) to show a crude approximation of what it would look like, and explained that things would look much better when shot on film."

On this particular shoot, Kelsey's lean crew worked "guerilla-style." It consisted of Kelsey as director, the client from Earthy Foods, a producer, a director of photography, a camera assistant, a grip, and two makeup artists. Kelsey says, "I think it's a great way to work these days. Since the script was voice-over, we shot everything without sound—so we didn't need a sound person on the shoot. We had to beg, borrow, and steal on-camera talent, because that line item in the budget was very limited." Kelsey points out that he had to make clear to the crew that all the shots

FIGURE 7.54
The broadcast TV version and the Web version of this spot launched simultaneously.

needed to be in close-up, since the final Web frame size would be no more than 320 × 240.

"Since we had preplanned our shoot, it all went very smoothly. We brought the film to Monaco Labs for processing, and then to Varitel Modern Videofilm, where a colorist transferred the processed film to Digital Betacam videotape using a million-dollar da Vinci color-correction system."

Kelsey then captured the footage on his Media 100i editing system. He created the titles in Adobe Illustrator and the Web-friendly effects (such as the soft vignettes around the edges) in Adobe After Effects. Compression was done in Cleaner 5. A composer was hired to create the score, and the voice-over narration and final mix were completed at Vertical Online's office. Kelsey says, "We heavily utilized the Web in the approval process; the clients were able to quickly look at different versions of the cut online. From the initial meeting with the client to final delivery, the entire project took three weeks. The final result was a 60-second version for the Web and a 30-second version for television."

To see the Web version, go to **`www.verticalonline.com`** and click the link for the cross-media campaign for Earthy Foods.

CHAPTER EIGHT

Streaming Your Way

The last tool in your Web video bag of tricks is delivering your movie as a streaming video file. A streaming movie is never downloaded to the viewer's hard drive; instead, it plays directly from a streaming server located elsewhere on the Web. So, to be precise, this tool isn't really *in* your bag of tricks.

Setting up a streaming video delivery system is a bit more complex than placing a downloadable movie on a Web page, but it offers some significant advantages that make it worth the extra trouble for certain kinds of video projects. First, most streaming systems have the intelligence to adjust the data rate of the streaming movie to current conditions, such as the viewer's personal connection speed, or Net congestion. That means that the video your audience receives has been adjusted to ensure the best possible viewing experience. Second, if your viewers just want to watch the last five minutes of an hour-long movie, they can skip ahead and watch it without having to wait for the entire file to download. Third, since the video stream goes directly from a remote server to your viewer's screen, it's difficult (if not impossible) for them to make unauthorized copies And finally, live Webcasting *requires* streaming with a streaming server. If you're planning to go live over the Web with as-it-happens video, streaming video is your only option.

Adding Streaming Movies to Your Web Site

All three media players let you add streaming video to your Web site, though each differs somewhat in how it's implemented. But no matter which player you choose to work with, all true streaming video files have three essential elements:

- The actual **compressed media file**, either video or audio. It resides on a special streaming server.
- A small text or placeholder document known as a **pointer file** (also known as a **reference movie**). It contains at least the address of (path to) the actual compressed media file on the streaming server. This pointer file resides on the regular Web (HTTP) server where your HTML files are located.
- A **link** in your HTML document to the pointer file.

As you'll see in the rest of this chapter, each media player makes use of these three elements in a different way. But all of them require a *streaming server*, which is a server with special streaming software installed on it. When a viewer clicks to stream a movie, the streaming server software, the media player, and the video file work in concert to stream the file using the Real Time Streaming Protocol (RTSP) protocol. (Windows Media uses its own protocol.) If you don't want your movie to play back in a separate window when it streams to your viewers, but instead want it to play as an integral part of your Web page, you must take one more step: You have to *embed* your streaming movie in that page.

Unless you plan to do a lot of streaming, find an Internet Service Provider (ISP) that includes video streaming as a part of its services package. Then you can just upload and stream your video without the headache of having to set up a streaming server yourself.

If you can't find an ISP that provides streaming/hosting services, you might want to use a content delivery service to stream your video. Ideally, this would be one that specializes in inexpensive Web video streaming. One such company is PlayStream (`www.playstream.com/`). PlayStream happens to be offering a special 35 percent discount on the first month of service to the readers of this book. Just use the word *Elmwood* in the Offer Code field when you sign up on the Web site. *Disclaimer:* I do get a cut of any services that you buy at PlayStream.

TIP ▸ *The Real Time Streaming Protocol (RTSP) really is* real time, *meaning it's designed to transport packets as soon as possible, as opposed to guaranteeing their delivery. On the other hand, the TCP/IP and HTTP protocols (which progressive downloading uses) are* guarantee-based protocols, *meaning they resend any packets that get lost or mangled in transmission. The former method can cause dropped frames or noise. But when you're playing movies, a dropped packet is preferable to the delay involved in resending it.*

Streaming Servers: If You Must Have One

If you decide you need your own streaming video server, this information will get you started:

Helix Universal Server (formerly known as RealServer) Software

- Helix Universal Server Basic lets you serve up to 10 simultaneous streams. It doesn't support QuickTime or Windows Media, so you'll still need other servers for those formats. It's free for a year, after which RealNetworks would very much like you to pay for the real thing.
- Helix Universal Server supports all major formats (MPEG-4, QuickTime, RealSystem, and Windows Media). It will cost you anywhere from $8400 to stream up to 10 Mbps (plus $2,400 a year for additional years of upgrades and support) to $46,000 (plus $13,120 per year thereafter) for unlimited bandwidth.

At the time this book went to press, RealNetworks changed the name of RealServer to *Helix Universal Server*. Confused? I'll try to keep it simple by referring to this as RealServer (Helix Universal Server) whenever possible. All of the server software and details of the hardware and operating system requirements are available on the RealNetworks Web site (`www.realnetworks.com/products/index.html`).

Windows Media Server Software

Windows Media Services, the server software for Windows Media Player, is free with a Windows 2000 server, which lists for about $1000.

continued ›

Streaming Servers: If You Must Have One › *continued*

Here is a summary of the hardware requirements according to Microsoft; however, I recommend doubling all of these requirements to get a more realistic system, as these system requirements seem awfully low:

A 266-MHz or better Intel Pentium II processor, 128 MB of RAM, 32 MB of RAM for administrator only; 64 MB of RAM for server, and 500 MB of hard disk space.

Windows Media Server for Windows NT Server can be downloaded at:

`www.microsoft.com/windows/windowsmedia/technologies/services.asp`

QuickTime Server Software

QuickTime Streaming Server requires a Power Mac G4 processor, 128 MB of RAM, Mac OS X Server 10 software, and 1GB of hard disk space.

There is also a multiplatform version of QuickTime Streaming Server known as Darwin Streaming Server. It's available for Linux, Solaris 7, Free BSD Unix 3.4, and Windows NT Server 4.0 and Windows 2000 Server.

Both QuickTime Streaming Server 4 and Darwin Streaming Server 4.1 are free, with no per-stream license fees. Both can be downloaded at

`www.apple.com/quicktime/products/qtss`

Streaming with RealSystem

As far as I'm concerned, if you're serious about streaming video, the RealSystem format offers the best system for doing it. The easiest way to make all the components you need for RealSystem streaming is to use Premiere's Save for Web/Cleaner 5 EZ plug-in. Unfortunately, this option is only available in Premiere 6.5 for Macintosh users running System 9, but not Mac OS X. (My advice here: Use Premiere 6.0 if you want to do streaming this way, or buy Discreet Cleaner as a standalone application.)

Creating Streaming Video

Using the Cleaner 5 EZ Plug-In

If you use Premiere's Save for Web feature and choose any kind of RealSystem movie as the intended export file, the plug-in will automatically create all three of the components required for streaming: the compressed movie, the pointer file, and the link. You will be able to cut and paste the link directly into your HTML document. The pointer file will be ready to upload to your Web server, provided that you entered the proper address for the streaming server when you first installed Premiere/Cleaner 5 EZ. (Since the pointer file is a text file, you can easily adjust it at any time using a text editor.) And the compressed movie will be ready and waiting for you to post on your streaming Web server.

TIP ▸ *The full version of Cleaner will even upload the compressed movie to the streaming server automatically at the end of the compression process.*

Creating the Compressed Movie File

If you've compressed your movie as a RealSystem file using any of the techniques described in Chapter 6, and if you've confirmed that it has a .rm extension in its name, your movie should be ready to go. The only thing left to do is to upload it to the proper directory on the streaming server using your FTP software.

TIP ▸ *When you create movies to be streaming video files (as opposed to progressive downloading movies), it's important that the data rate be as low as, or lower than, the slowest connection speed your audience might use to view the movie. Otherwise, the movie will stutter and choke in the limited bandwidth.*

Creating the Pointer File

The RealNetworks term for the pointer file is the *RAM file*. The purpose of this file is to launch RealOne Player and then provide it with the complete name and location of the actual compressed video (.rm) file on the streaming server—in this case, a RealServer (Helix Universal Server). Here is the entire sample text of a typical RAM file:

```
rtsp://myrealserver/folder/simple.rm
```

The *rtsp* part indicates that this is a true streaming server address, and that this is a movie that's supposed to stream using the RTSP protocol. The *myrealserver* portion is just my stand-in name for the actual RealServer (Helix Universal Server) address. And *folder* indicates the directory or subdirectory the video file resides in. Finally, *simple.rm* is the name of the actual compressed video file.

You must save this RAM file (an ordinary text file) and name it with a .ram extension (for example, simple.ram) to work properly. Then you can upload it to the Web server, using FTP software, and place it in the same directory as the HTML document that references it.

You can find the simple.ram file in the Chapter8_Streaming/Real_HTML folder on the accompanying CD-ROM. Because it contains a fictional address, you'll get an error message when you open the file. To make it work, replace the fictional address with your actual streaming server's address.

TIP ▸ *If you would like to have several RealSystem video files play automatically in a sequence, you can just list them in their playback order in the RAM file. For example: rtsp://myrealserver/folder/simple1.rm, rtsp://myrealserver/folder/simple2.rm, rtsp://myrealserver/folder/simple3.rm, rtsp://myrealserver/folder/simple4.rm.*

TIP ▸ *You can save a RAM file from a Web page by right-clicking on the link (Control-clicking on the Mac). Then you can use the RAM file to connect later (by opening it with RealOne Player).*

Creating the Link to the RAM File

To create a link to the RAM file that you just created, you'll combine the HTML tags `<a>` (which stands for *anchor*) and `<href>` (*hyper-reference*). Here's how to add this tag to the sample HTML file that you created in Chapter 7:

1. Open the file called simple_page.html in your text-editing application.

You can open the simple_page.html file you created in Chapter 7, or just open the file with the same name in the Chapter8_Streaming/Real_HTML folder on the accompanying CD-ROM.

2. Replace the line of HTML that contained the `<embed>` tag with the following:

```
<A HREF="simple.ram">Click to view the RealPlayer movie.</A>
```

The resulting HTML document should look like this (**Figure 8.1**):

simple_page_HREF.html
<html>
<head>
<title>A Simple Web Page</title>
</head>
<body>
<p>This is a very simple, text-only, Web page.</p>
<p>This is about as simple as it gets.</p>
<A HREF="simple.ram">Click to view the RealPlayer movie.</A>
</body>
</html>

FIGURE 8.1
A new **<href>** tag after it's added to simple_page.html.

3. Save the file as real_simple_href.html.

4. Open this HTML document in a Web browser (**Figure 8.2**). The new line of text appears in blue (the default hyperlink color) to indicate that it is a hypertext link.

If you like, you can just use the simple_page_href.html file in the Chapter8_Streaming/Real_HTML folder on the CD-ROM that came with this book. (Remember: This HTML file is for demonstration purposes only. It won't actually link to a streaming server.)

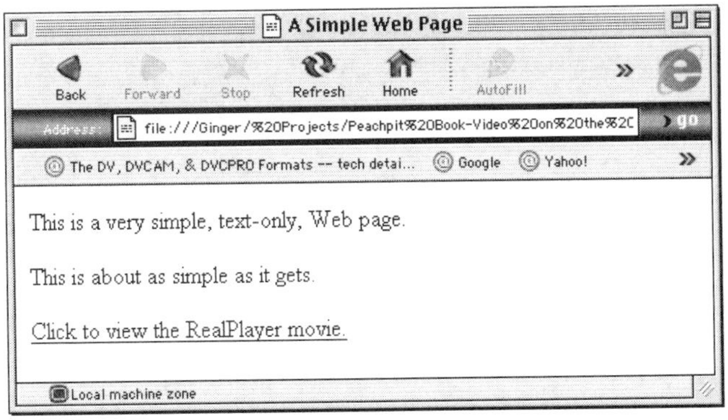
A Simple Web Page
Back
Forward
Stop
Refresh
Home
AutoFill
Address:
file:///Ginger/%20Projects/Peachpit%20Book-Video%20on%20the%2C
go
The DV, DVCAM, & DVCPRO Formats -- tech detai...
Google
Yahoo!
This is a very simple, text-only, Web page.
This is about as simple as it gets.
Click to view the RealPlayer movie.
Local machine zone

FIGURE 8.2
Here is the file simple_page_href.html as it would appear in a Web browser.

Putting It All Together

With the HTML link and the RAM file (the pointer file) on the Web server, and the video (.rm) file on the streaming RealServer (Helix Universal Server), your streaming video setup is complete. Viewers can just click on the link in the Web page, and (if RealOne Player has been properly installed on their computer) RealOne Player will open and stream the movie on their screen in a separate window (**Figure 8.3**).

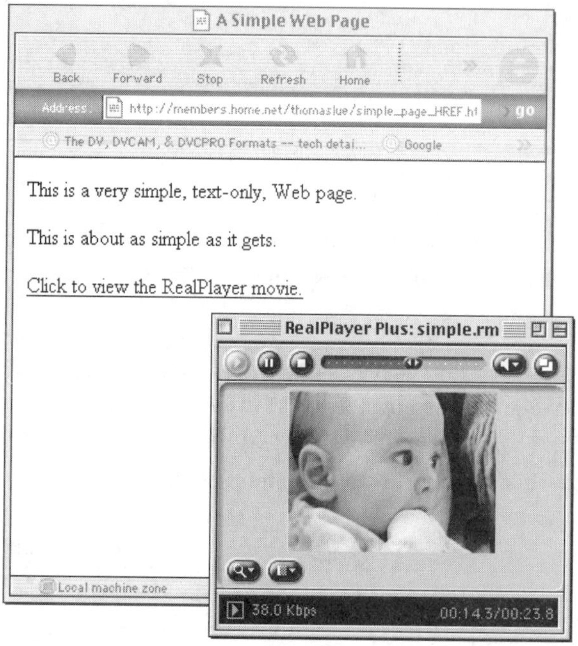

FIGURE 8.3
Click on the link, and RealOne Player streams the movie in a separate window.

TIP ▸ *The RealMedia system can deliver video or audio from both RealSystem (Helix) streaming servers and regular Web (HTTP) servers. If you would like to have your Real movie play from a regular Web server as a progressive downloading movie, simply store the movie (naming it, for example,* moviename.*rm) on the Web server. Then change the contents of the RAM file so that it reflects the new server name and the movie's new HTTP status. For example:* **`http://domain/folderonyourwebserver/simple.rm`.**

Embedding RealSystem Movies with GoLive

If you don't want your movie to play back in a separate window, though, you'll have to embed it. You've got two choices here: doing it by hand and using a Web authoring tool like Adobe GoLive. As you might have guessed, using an authoring tool is easier.

Using GoLive makes embedding a streaming RealSystem movie a snap, because you don't have to write the HTML yourself. Other Web authoring tools will also take the pain out of coding, but you've got GoLive on the accompanying CD, so let's use it. Because I want you to be able to see the results of your work without actually having to set up a streaming server or buy space on one first, the following procedure shows you how to embed a downloading RealSystem movie. Then I'll *tell* you what to do differently to embed a streaming video file.

IMPORTANT ▸ Use GoLive 6 for this task. GoLive's support for RealSystem media has been significantly enhanced in this version.

Embedding a Downloading Movie

1. Open a new or existing Web page with GoLive.

2. Drag a Layout Grid icon into the Document window and stretch it to cover the full window area.

3. Add a RealSystem movie by dragging the RealSystem plug-in icon from the Objects palette (it uses the "Real" logo as an icon) to your Web page in the Document window (**Figure 8.4**).

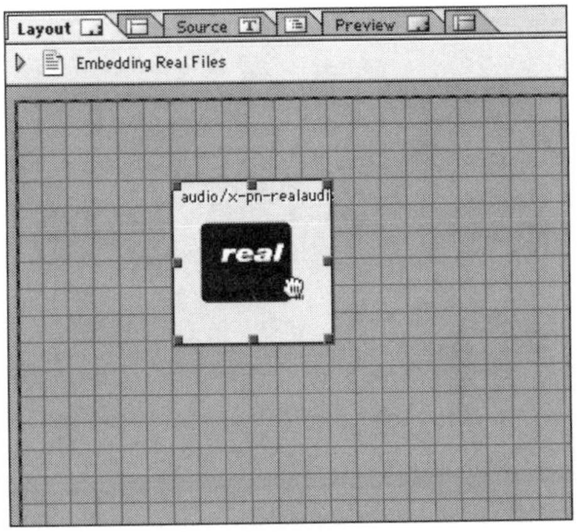

FIGURE 8.4 Dragging the RealSystem plug-in icon to GoLive's Document window places a RealSystem movie on your Web page.

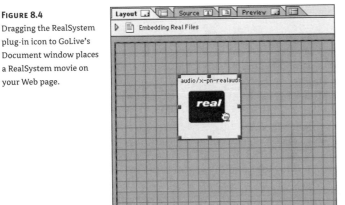

4. If the Inspector palette isn't open, choose Window > Inspector to open it.

5. With the RealSystem placeholder icon still selected in the new Web page, do one of the following:

   Click the Browse button of the Inspector palette and use the resulting dialog box to choose the RealSystem movie that you want to include in your Web page.

   Choose the simple.rm file located on the accompanying CD in the Chapter8_Streaming/Real_Embed_GoLive folder.

   or

   If the desired RealSystem file is already in the Site window, link to it by clicking on the Inspector's Point and Shoot tool (the small spiral icon that's next to the word *File*). Without letting go of the mouse button, drag this tool over to the simple.rm movie on the page in the Site window.

   Whichever option you choose, the name of the RealSystem file ("simple") should now appear in the upper-left corner of the RealSystem icon.

6. Type "320" in the Width field and "240" into the Height field in the Inspector palette (**Figure 8.5**).

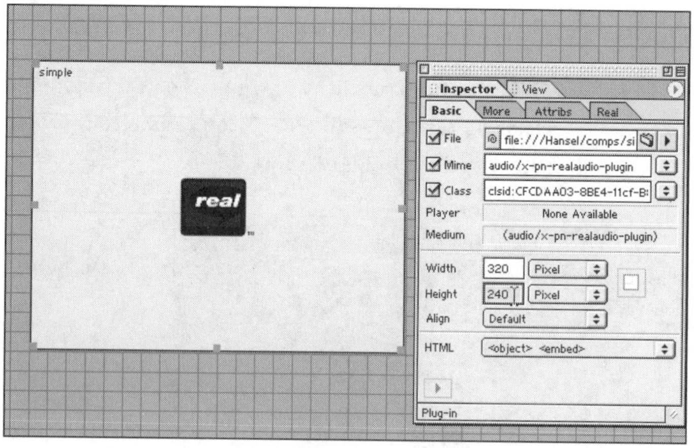

FIGURE 8.5
Adjust the movie's width and height info in GoLive's Inspector palette.

7. To test the page at this point, click the Preview tab at the top of the Site window or choose Special > Show in Default Browser. (If this is the first time you've selected this option, you'll need to tell GoLive what your default browser is.) When you open the page in the browser, the movie should play (**Figure 8.6**).

If the movie doesn't play in the browser, make sure that RealOne Player is properly installed. Note that the movie has no controller. We'll add that next.

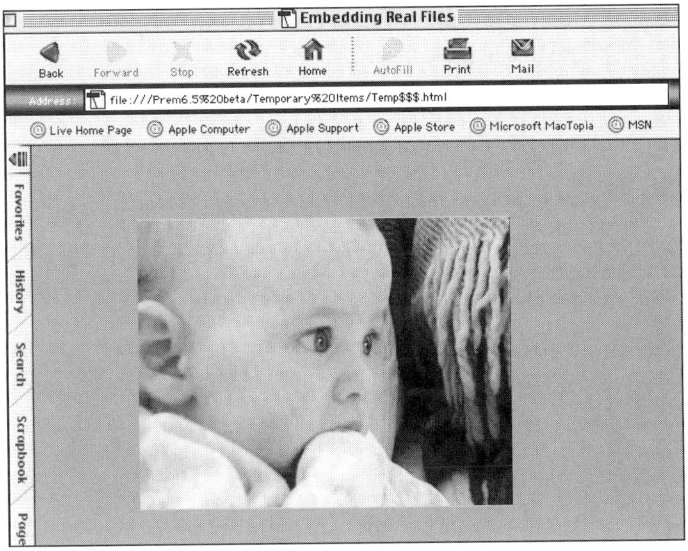

FIGURE 8.6
Here's what your page should look like when you run a preliminary test of the movie in the browser.

Adding a Controller

1. With the movie still selected in the Document window, click the Real tab in the Inspector.

2. Click the pop-up menu next to the Console field, and choose "_master." This will link this icon to the set of controls you are about to create (**Figure 8.7**).

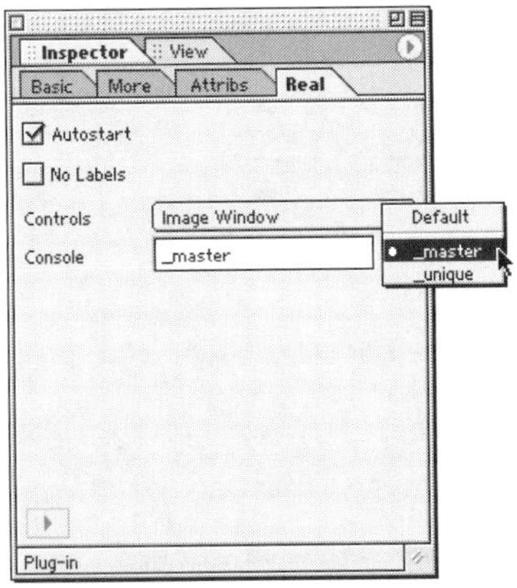

FIGURE 8.7
Setting the Console master links an icon to the set of controls you're creating.

3. Drag a second RealSystem plug-in icon from the Objects palette to your Web page in the Document window.

4. With the RealSystem placeholder icon still selected in the Document window, do one of the following:

   Click the Browse button of the Inspector palette, and use the resulting dialog box to choose the *same* RealSystem movie that you chose for the first icon.

   or

   If the desired RealSystem movie is already in the Site window, use the Inspector's Point and Shoot tool to link to the *same* RealSystem movie.

   Whichever way you select the movie, the name of the RealSystem file ("simple") should now appear in the upper-left corner of the RealSystem icon.

5. Position this second icon underneath the original icon. Make it about two grid squares high and as wide as the original movie icon (**Figure 8.8**). This second icon will soon become the controller bar for the embedded RealSystem movie.

FIGURE 8.8
Make sure to leave room for the controls as you add the second icon to the Document Window.

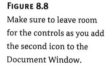

6. Select this second icon in the Document window.

7. In the Real tab of the Inspector palette, click the Controls pop-up menu and choose Control Panel (**Figure 8.9**). This defines this *instance* (copy) of the movie as the controller bar.

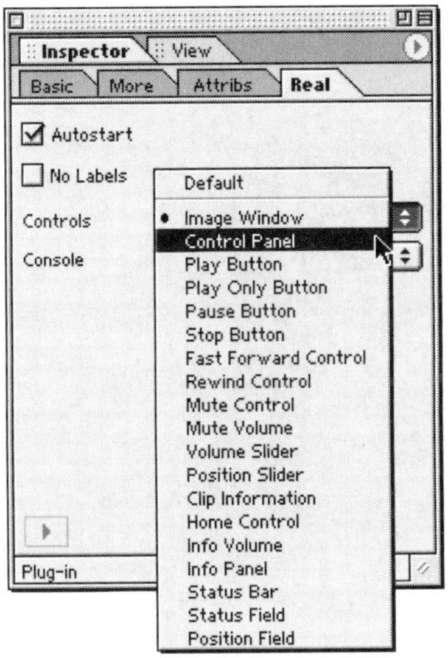

FIGURE 8.9
Choosing Control Panel in the Controls pop-up menu creates the movie's controller bar.

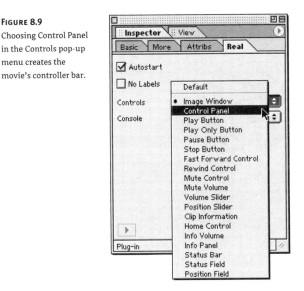

This Controls menu contains many other elements as well: All of them are RealSystem interface and control elements that you can add to your Web page. In this example, we are going to keep things simple by just using a complete control panel. You could, however, construct a more customized interface by arranging individual Play, Stop, Rewind, and other such buttons.

WARNING ▸ You must have one RealSystem icon for each control. For example, if you want to provide both Play and Pause buttons for your movie, you first add one RealSystem icon and assign a Play button to it from the Controls pop-up menu, then add a second RealSystem icon and assign a Pause button to it from the same menu.

8. Save this HTML file.

9. To test this page, click the Browser button on the toolbar or choose Special> Show in Default Browser (**Figure 8.10**).

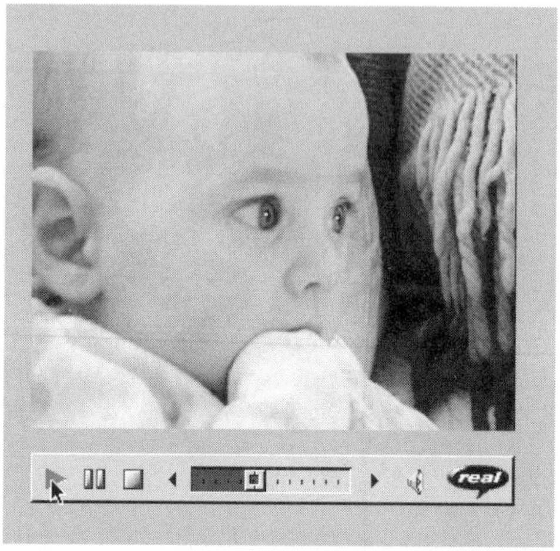

FIGURE 8.10 Here's what the final, embedded movie—complete with controller bar—should look like.

You can find this file (simple_page_embed_rm.html) and its RealSystem movie (simple.rm) in the Chapter8_Streaming/Real_HTML folder on the accompanying CD-ROM.

Embedding Streaming RealSystem Movies with GoLive

To embed a streaming version of the same movie, do the following:

1. Upload the .rm movie to a RealServer (Helix Universal Server) streaming server.
2. Create a .rpm link that points to the .rm movie on the server by changing the extension of the RAM movie from .ram to .rpm. This extension tells the browser to start up its RealOne Player browser plug-in and play the file in the browser window rather than in the standalone RealOne Player window.
3. Follow all the same steps in "Embedding RealSystem Movies with GoLive," but instead of linking to the .rm movie directly (Step 5 in "Embedding a Downloading Movie" and Step 4 in "Adding a Controller"), link to the .rpm file instead.

Using Ramgen

Some versions of RealServer (Helix Universal Server) allow you to make the viewer's browser launch RealOne Player without having to manually create a RAM file. In other words, rather than pointing to a RAM file which then points to the .rm video file, you can point directly to the .rm video file through the special "ramgen" virtual directory. Check with your streaming server provider to find out if they support this feature.

The link will look like this in your HTML:

```
<a href="http://realserver.yourdomain.com:8080/ramgen/media/
simple.rm"</a>
```

The following table explains each component in this string of code:

http://	This causes the browser to contact RealServer (Helix Universal Server) through HTTP (as opposed to the RTSP protocol, which Web browsers don't use).
realserver.yourdomain.com	This is the Internet address for the RealServer. (Obviously, "yourdomain" is a placeholder; you replace it with your actual address.) The address usually uses an identifier such as "realserver" instead of "www." It may also use a numeric TCP/IP address, such as 287.17.415.5.
:8080	This is the port RealServer uses for HTTP connections. Port 8080 is the default for RealServer, but check with your RealServer administrator for the correct port number to use.
/ramgen/	This parameter launches RealOne Player without the use of a separate RAM file.
/media/	Following /ramgen, this is the directory where the clip resides on the RealServer. (Your name for the directory may differ. You can add subdirectories as well.)
simple.rm	This is the RealSystem movie that you want to stream.

Embedding RealSystem Movies by Hand

As with all things HTML, you don't *have* to use an authoring tool to create your Web pages or embed movies. (You don't have to have a car mechanic or an accountant, either, but that's another story.) The point is, you can create the HTML code necessary to embed either downloading or streaming Web video files in a Web page by hand; it just makes things a bit more complex.

1. Change the RAM file's extension from .ram to .rpm. This .rpm extension tells the browser to start up its RealOne Player plug-in and play the file in the browser window rather than in the standalone RealOne Player window.

2. In the HTML file, you're going to use the same combination of `<embed>` and `<object>` tags that I described in Chapter 7 (see "Fixing the Internet Explorer Problem"), and then reference the .rpm file inside the `<embed>` tag.

   If the contents of your .rpm file look like this:

   ```
   rtsp://myrealserver/folder/simple.rm
   ```

   then your `<embed>` tag should look like this:

   ```
   <EMBED SRC="simple.rpm" CONTROLS=ImageWindow WIDTH="320"
   HEIGHT="240" CONSOLE="simple">

   </EMBED>
   ```

   Figure 8.11 shows what the HTML version of the simple Web page should look like. (For simplicity's sake, this example shows only the `<embed>` tag.)

FIGURE 8.11
The HTML code for an embedded Real movie.

simple_page_embed_rm.html

```
<html>
<head>
<title>A Simple Web Page</title>
</head>
<body>
<p>This is a very simple Web page with an embedded Real movie.</p>
<p>This is about as simple as it gets.</p>
<EMBED SRC="http://www.example.com/media/simple.rpm"
WIDTH=320 HEIGHT=240
CONTROLS=ImageWindow CONSOLE=one NOJAVA=true>
</body>
</html>
```

You can find the file simple_page_embed_rm.html in the Chapter8_Streaming/ Real_HTML folder on the accompanying CD-ROM.

Figure 8.12 shows what the resulting Web page would look like in a browser.

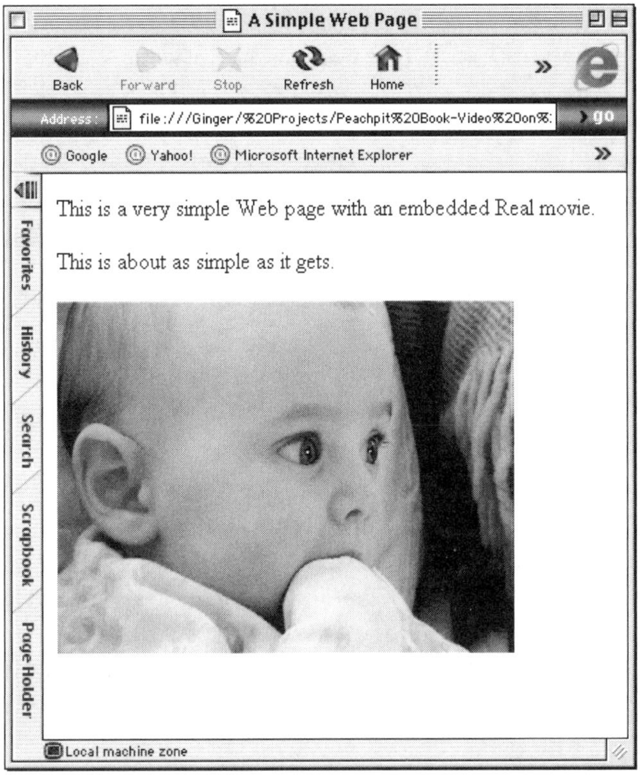

FIGURE 8.12
The very simple Web page with an embedded Real movie.

3. This is obviously a very basic presentation. It doesn't even include any playback controls. You can use the various attributes of the `<embed>` tag to customize the presentation of the movie and its playback controls. And you would also have to combine the `<embed>` tag with the `<object>` tag to make the page compatible with the various versions of Internet Explorer. As a result, the HTML for a Web page ready for the real world would look more like this:

```
<html>
<head>
<title>A Simple Web Page</title>
</head>
<body>
<p>This is a very simple Web page with an embedded Real
movie.</p>
<p>This is about as simple as it gets.</p>
<OBJECT ID=RealMedia CLASSID="clsid:CFCDAA03-8BE4-11cf-
B84B-0020AFBBCCFA"
WIDTH=320 HEIGHT=240>
<PARAM NAME="Name" VALUE="simple.rpm">
<PARAM NAME="AutoStart" Value="true">
<PARAM NAME="Controls" VALUE="ControlPanel">
<EMBED width="320" height="240" src="simple.rpm"
controls="ImageWindow" nojava="true" console="_master">
<EMBED SRC="simple.rpm" WIDTH=320 HEIGHT=240 NOJAVA=true
CONTROLS=All CONSOLE=one>
</EMBED>
</OBJECT>
</body>
</html>
```

The ID tag in the first line of the `<object>` tag names the RealSystem ActiveX control as the target player. The long number is the unique identifier for the RealSystem ActiveX control.

The resulting Web page would look like **Figure 8.13** in a browser.

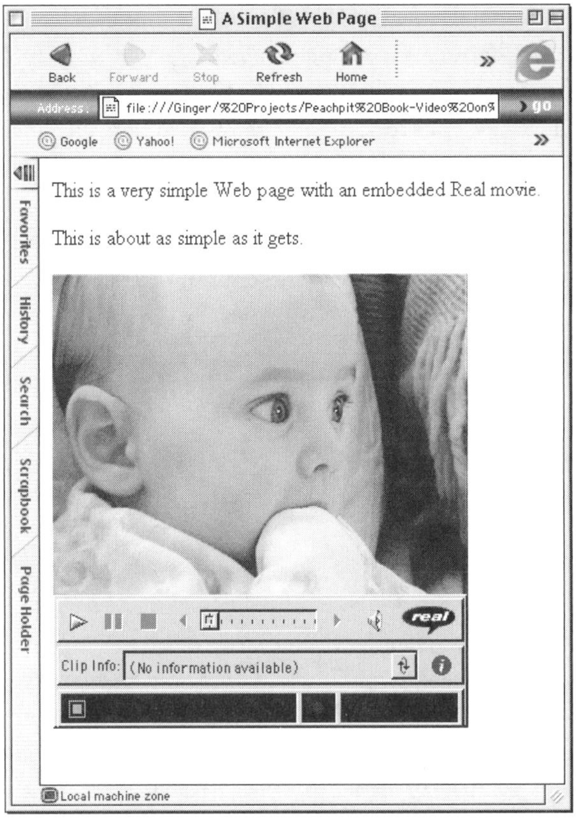

FIGURE 8.13
The same page but with attributes for a control bar.

Streaming with Windows Media

Setting up a Web site for streaming Windows Media movies is a lot like what you just did for RealOne Player. And because Windows Media has a large installed base, streaming your movie via Windows Media will make it viewable by more of the Web users out there. As with RealSystem, the HTML document links to the pointer file, and the pointer file then opens the media player and points it to the video file on the streaming server. And just like with streaming RealSystem movies, either you can link out to play the streaming file in the standalone Windows Media Player window or you can create a Web page with an embedded player.

One significant difference between creating streaming video files for RealSystem and creating them for Windows Media is the terminology that each uses for the pointer file and the media file itself (the compressed video and audio). The link is in an HTML document, so that doesn't change much. I guess they just *have* to use different words, otherwise it would be too easy for all of us out here in Web land, trying to use systems from different providers. Here's a phrasebook to help you bridge the gap.

	POINTER FILE (REFERENCE MOVIE)	MEDIA FILE (MOVIE)
RealOne Player	.ram (stand-alone player)	.rm (RealVideo)
	.rpm (embedded)	.ra (RealAudio)
Windows Media Player	.wvx	.wmv (Windows Media Video + Audio)
	.wax	.wma (Windows Media Audio only)
	.asx	.asf (Advanced Streaming Format, for non–Windows Media codecs)

TIP ▸ *In the Windows operating system, the suffix (called an "extension") at the end of the file name determines what player is used to open the file. Originally, there were only. asx and .asf. for Windows Media Player files. This combination was the general-purpose format for all video and audio data, and it still works. However, Microsoft now recommends the .wax pointer file and the .wma filename suffix for audio-only files made with the wma codec. This indicates that they're playable on new types of wireless devices and audio player software that can't play video. In this new naming system, that leaves the .wvx/.wmv combination for video-plus-audio files or video-only files made with the wmv codec.*

Creating the Compressed Movie

When you compressed your movie for the Windows Media Player using Advanced Windows Media Export in Chapter 6, and selected the multi-bit-rate streaming option, you created a multi-bit-rate (MBR) movie with an .asf extension. (Similar to Real SureStream movies, Windows Media MBR files contain two different streams inside a single movie.) When these MBR files play from a streaming server, the server will first detect the viewer's connection speed and then adjust the stream accordingly. These MBR files are what you want to post on the streaming server.

Creating the Pointer File

The pointer file that you need to create in this case is called an .asx file in the Windows Media Player world. It does the same thing that the .ram file does in the Real system. It provides the complete name and location of the actual compressed video (in this case, the .asf file on the Windows Media Server), which launches the media player (in this case, Windows Media Player). The .asx file can also do one extra thing (that RealSystem's .ram can do too): It includes author and copyright information about the movie in the pointer file.

TIP ▸ *With RealSystem files, you can add this* meta-information *(information about the file, such as author or copyright) through the CONTROLS parameter. With QuickTime you add this information to the movie as you compress the file; with QuickTime Pro you add it afterwards.*

Here is a typical .asx file:

```
<ASX version = "3.0">
<TITLE>simple.asx</TITLE>
<ENTRY>
<TITLE>A Simple ASX</TITLE>
<AUTHOR>Thomas Luehrsen</AUTHOR>
<COPYRIGHT>(c)2001 Elmwood Studios</COPYRIGHT>
<REF HREF = "mms://win.elmwoodstudios.com/folder/simple.asf"/>
</ENTRY>
</ASX>
```

You can find this file, simple.asx, in the Chapter8_Streaming/WindowsMedia_HTML folder on the accompanying CD-ROM. (This file is for demonstration purposes only. It won't actually link to a streaming server.)

Creating the Link

Here's how to link the Web page, player, and movie together:

1. Write `<a href="simple.asx">Click to view the Windows Media movie.</a>`

   This creates a link to the pointer (meta) file named simple.asx.

The resulting HTML document should look like this:

```
<html>
<head>
<title>A Simple Web Page</title>
</head>
<body>
<p>This is a very simple, text-only, Web page.</p>
<p>This is about as simple as it gets.</p>
<A HREF="simple.asx">Click to view the Windows Media movie.</A>
</body>
</html>
```

2. Save the file as wmp_simple_href.html.

3. Open this HTML document in a Web browser. The new line of text appears in blue (the default hyperlink color) to indicate that it is a hypertext link (**Figure 8.14**).

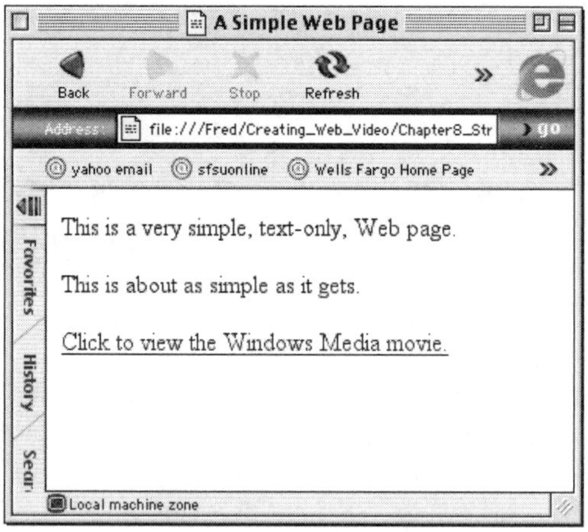

FIGURE 8.14
The HTML file viewed in the browser, with a link to the. asx file.

See the resulting wmp_simple_href.html file in the Chapter8_Streaming/WindowsMedia_HTML folder on the book's CD. (Remember, this HTML file is for demonstration purposes only. It won't actually link to a streaming server.)

Embedding Streaming Windows Media Movies

As with RealSystem, if you don't want your streaming movie to play back in a separate window in Windows Media Player, you'll have to embed it in your Web page. Unfortunately, GoLive doesn't offer integrated support for Windows Media in its Objects palette the way it does for RealSystem and QuickTime. So for our purposes, I'll just show you how to do it by hand. You can use another Web authoring tool, such as FrontPage, if you want to avoid hand-coding.

Here's how to write the HTML code for embedding a streaming Windows Media Player movie in a Web page:

As you did before when embedding a RealSystem movie, in the HTML file you're going to use the same combination of `<embed>` and `<object>` tags that I described in Chapter 7 and then reference the .asx file inside the `<embed>` tag. Here's what it should look like:

```
<html>
<head>
<title>A Simple Web Page</title>
</head>
<body>
<p>This is an embedded Windows Media movie.</p>
<p>This is about as simple as it gets.</p>
<OBJECT
ID="WinMedia" classid="CLSID:22d6f312-b0f6-11d0-94ab-
0080c74c7e95"
CODEBASE= "http://activex.microsoft.com/activex/controls/
mplayer/en/nsmp2inf.cab#Version=5,1,52,701" width=320
height=240 standby="Loading Microsoft Windows Media Player
components…" type="application/x-oleobject">
<PARAM NAME="FileName" VALUE="simple.asx">
<PARAM NAME="AutoStart" Value="true">
<PARAM NAME="ShowControls" Value="true">
<Embed type="application/x-mplayer2"
pluginspage=
"http://www.microsoft.com/Windows/MediaPlayer/"
```

(continues on next page)

```
src="simple.asx"
Name=MediaPlayer
AutoStart=0
Width=320
Height=240
autostart=1
ShowControls=1
</embed>
</OBJECT>
</body>
</html>
```

You can find this file, wmp_simple_embed.html, in the Chapter8_Streaming/WindowsMedia_HTML folder on the CD.

The ID tag in the first line names the Windows Media Player as the target player. The long number is the ActiveX control for Windows Media Player. The only part you'll need to customize for your own Web page is the width and height of the video and the "<param> names"—or `<object>` tag parameters. (Those are IE-speak for *attributes*.)

Here are some short explanations of a few of the more commonly used parameters. For a comprehensive list, go to:

http://microsoft.com/windows/windowsmedia/default.asp

Parameter	Explanation
<PARAM NAME="AutoStart" Value="true">	"True" means the video will play automatically when the page loads. "False" means you have to click the Play button to start the movie.
<PARAM NAME="ShowControls" Value="true">	This adds the basic control panel, including Play, Stop, Fast Forward, Pause, and so on.
<PARAM NAME="ShowDisplay" VALUE="1">	"1" (true) means that clip, author, and copyright information will be displayed.
<PARAM NAME="Volume" VALUE="-150">	Sets the audio level.
<PARAM NAME="AutoRewind" VALUE="1">	"1" (true) means that the movie will play back continuously in a loop.

Streaming with QuickTime

While RealSystem and Windows Media tend to dominate the true streaming realm, QuickTime also offers an RTSP streaming system. Streaming QuickTime movies work a lot like streaming RealSystem and Windows Media movies except that they require a few adjustments both to the movie files themselves and in the way they're integrated into a Web site. QuickTime streaming also uses a unique "alternate movies" model instead of the on-the-fly adjustability of the other two streaming formats.

In addition, progressive downloading QuickTime movies and RTSP streaming QuickTime movies have a couple of small, but significant, differences:

- Streaming QuickTime movies must be *hinted*.

  Hint tracks contain information about the server, the transmission packet size, and the protocol to be used, and they are stored in the movie. Hinted movies have a hint track for each one of their video and audio tracks.

- Streaming files must not exceed the target connection speed.

  Whereas progressive downloading files can have data rates higher than the viewer's connection speed, streaming files' data rates must match (or be less than) the target connection speed. If the data rate is higher than the connection speed, playback results will be poor. (This is true for all media players.)

TIP ▸ *When you are compressing your QuickTime movie using the techniques described in Chapter 6, and you choose any compression or export method explicitly labeled "streaming," then your movie will automatically be hinted. For example, when you choose any of the Streaming presets in Premiere's Save for Web feature, the movies will automatically be hinted.*

Creating the Compressed Movie File

If you already have a low-data-rate QuickTime movie that's been compressed for the Web and you would like to stream it, here's what you need to do.

1. Open the movie in QuickTime Player Pro. (You won't have this handy pro version of QuickTime Player unless you bought it expressly from Apple. You can buy it for $30 at `www.apple.com/quicktime/buy`.)

2. Determine whether the movie has already been hinted by choosing Edit > Extract Tracks from the File Menu (**Figure 8.15**). This will open a complete list of tracks in the movie (**Figure 8.16**).

- If you see a hinted track for every sound or video track, the movie is already hinted and you don't need to do anything further. Click Cancel without extracting any tracks.

- If you don't see any hinted tracks, you must now add them. Click Cancel without extracting any tracks and proceed to Step 3.

Figure 8.15
In QuickTime Player Pro, choose Edit > Extract Tracks to see if a movie's already been hinted.

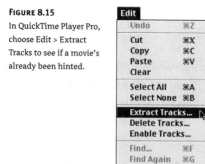

Figure 8.16
The complete list of tracks in a movie that's already been hinted.

3. Choose File > Export.

4. In the Export pop-up menu, choose Movie to Hinted Movie.

5. Enter a name for the new movie, click Save, and add .mov as a file extension.

Creating the Pointer File

To set up the pointer file necessary for streaming, you have two choices that are similar to RealOne Player's RAM file and "ramgen" methods. You can either embed a pointer *reference* movie that links to the streaming movie, or you can add an `<embed>` tag attribute that points to the streaming movie. The former method creates a movie similar to a RAM, or pointer, file that opens the QuickTime plug-in and points it to the location of the actual movie on the streaming server. The latter method does the same thing, but all from within the HTML code on your Web page.

The first of these two methods can use either a text file or a QuickTime movie as the pointing file.

Using an Embedded Movie to Point to the Streaming Movie

1. Upload your streaming movie to a QuickTime Streaming Server.

2. Open the QuickTime Player.

3. Within QuickTime Player, choose File > Open URL in New Player (**Figure 8.17**).

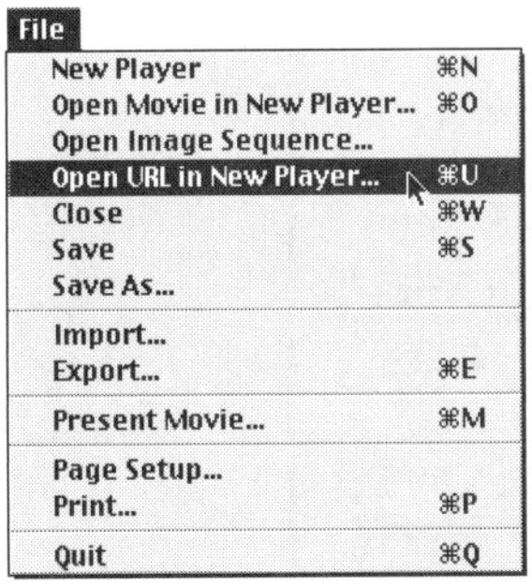

FIGURE 8.17 Choose File > Open URL in New Player to create a link to your streaming movie.

4. Enter the address (URL) of the movie you just uploaded—for example, `rtsp://streaming.elmwoodstudios.com/simple_hint.mov`— then click OK (**Figure 8.18**).

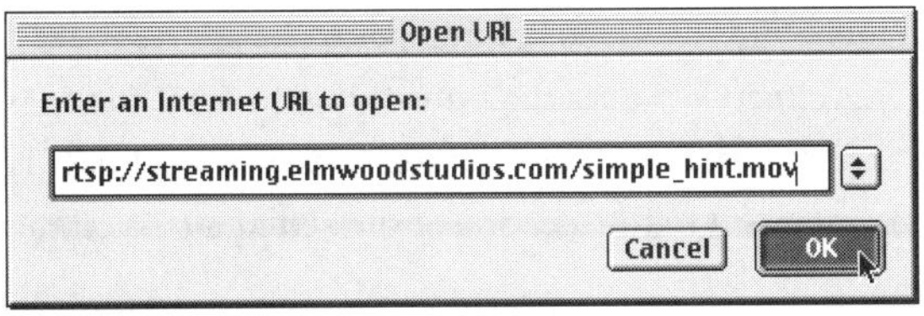

FIGURE 8.18 Enter the Web address of the movie you just uploaded to the streaming server, and click OK.

5. Choose File > Save As (**Figure 8.19**).

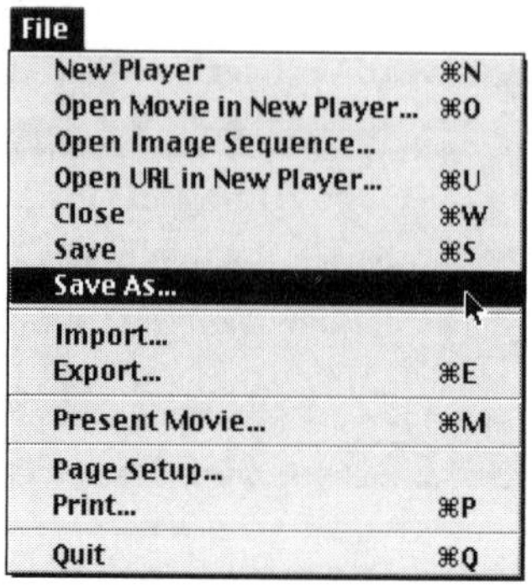

FIGURE 8.19
Choose Save As to save your movie.

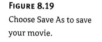

6. Enter a name for this new reference movie: for example, simple_hint.mov. (While it's permissible to give it the same name as the movie you uploaded to the QuickTime Streaming Server, it will be less confusing if you give it a different name.)

7. Select the "Make movie self-contained" radio button and click Save (**Figure 8.20**).

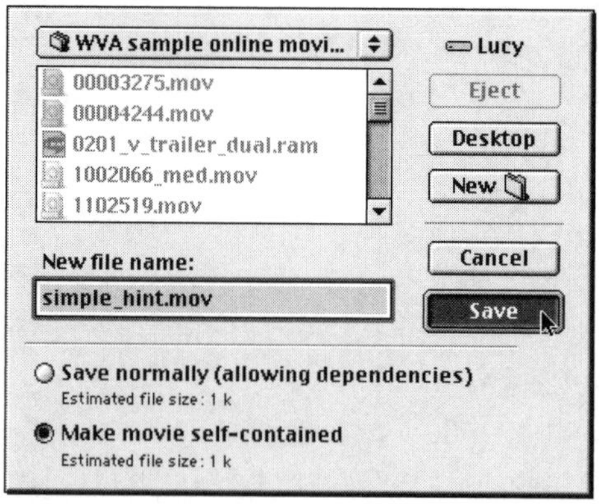

FIGURE 8.20
Give your reference movie a new name to avoid confusion, then click Save.

Note that the resulting reference movie will be only 1 kilobyte in size. This is because it contains no video or audio, only the address (URL) of the streaming movie. This effectively does the same thing the RAM file does for RealSystem movies and the. asx file does for Windows Media movies: This file opens QuickTime Player and points it to the location of the actual movie on the streaming server.

8. Now you embed this new reference movie in your Web page by adding the following code to the HTML page:

```
<embed src="simple_hint.mov" width="320" height="256">
```

What you see here is just the plain `<embed>` tag. Inside the Chapter8_Streaming/QuickTime/Embedded_Pointer folder on the CD-ROM, you'll find a file called simple_embed_pointer.html, which includes the ActiveX `<object>` tags for compatibility with the various versions of Internet Explorer. I've also included simple_pointer.mov in the same folder. Remember: The streaming movie used in this example is a fictitious one, so these files won't actually link to anything.

9. Upload the modified HTML file and the pointer movie to your regular Web server. When someone clicks on the embedded pointer movie, it will activate the streaming movie.

Using an <Embed> Tag Attribute to Point to a Streaming Movie

1. Upload your streaming movie to a QuickTime Streaming Server.

2. Upload a placeholder movie to a Web server. (This movie won't actually be opened, so it can be a very small, single-frame movie.) Name it placeholder.mov.

3. In your HTML page, include the following tag:

   ```
   <embed src="placeholder.mov">
   ```

   (In your version, you will have to include the full address, or URL, of the movie that resides on your QuickTime Streaming Server.)

4. In the next line of HTML, include the following attribute:

   ```
   QTSRC="rtsp://streaming.elmwoodstudios.com/simple_hint.mov"
   ```

   (This fictitious movie is just for demonstration purposes. In your version, you will put the actual URL of your own movie on your streaming server.)

5. In the next line of HTML, include the following:

```
width="320" height="256"
```

(Adjust these dimensions to fit your own streaming movie.)

6. The complete code should look like this:

```
<embed src="placeholder.mov"
QTSRC="rtsp://streaming.elmwoodstudios.com/simple_hint.mov"
width="320" height="256">
```

Although the standard SRC attribute says placeholder.mov, the QTSRC attribute will override this and open the movie on the streaming server.

What you see here is just the plain `<embed>` tag. Inside Chapter8_Streaming/QuickTime/Placeholder folder on the CD-ROM, you'll find a file called simple_placeholder_activex.html, which includes the ActiveX `<object>` tags for compatibility with the various versions of Internet Explorer. I've also included a tiny placeholder.mov file in the same folder so you don't have to make one yourself. Remember: The streaming movie used in this example is a fictitious one, so these files won't actually link to anything.

QuickTime Alternates

One of the main benefits of streaming servers is their scalability. That is, they have the intelligence to adjust the data rate of a streaming movie to conditions such as the viewer's connection speed.

The "intelligent" part of QuickTime streaming uses a different model than the other two player formats (see "Comparing Scalability" below). Rather than creating one big movie that contains several different streaming files within it, you use the QuickTime system to create several different *alternate* movies (each with its own data rate) and a single master *reference* movie. You then embed the reference movie in your Web page, and it points to the appropriate alternate movie at playback time. This means viewers with high-speed connections will see the high-quality versions of the movie, while viewers with slower connections will see more compressed versions (preferable to watching a high-data-rate movie stutter and stick over a low-bandwidth connection).

Comparing Scalability

Each of the three media player formats handles the issue of scalability (adjusting the data rate of the streaming movie) slightly differently. RealSystem (RealOne Player/RealServer, now known as Helix Universal Server) and Windows Media (Windows Media Player/Windows Media Services) work in the same way: You create multi-bit-rate video files that contain several different streaming files within them. The streaming server then uses the different streaming files to create a custom data rate for each viewer based on their viewing conditions. During playback of the streaming movie, the server and the media player constantly communicate with one another and repeatedly "switch gears" between different streams to deliver the highest-quality stream that the viewer's connection can support at that moment. A RealSystem SureStream file can contain up to eight audio and video tracks, each with its own data rate. Windows Media files can handle only one audio track at a time.

Apple's QuickTime Alternates method "thinks different." It uses the following criteria in deciding which movie to stream from the QuickTime Streaming Server: the viewer's connection speed, the version of QuickTime, the preferred language, the processor type, and the processor speed of the viewer's computer. QuickTime determines the connection speed by relying on the information the viewer enters in the QuickTime Settings control panel, rather than by detecting it on the fly. I see the latter point as a weak link in the QuickTime streaming system—it can't adjust the data rate of a movie in midstream, the way the other two formats can. It can only make a single decision about which movie to deliver, rather than the more flexible, dynamic method of the other two systems, in which they constantly switch between streams to deliver the optimum data rate at any given moment.

Still, you *can* do some other interesting things with QuickTime Alternates (see "Cool QuickTime Features" below).

Creating QuickTime Alternates with Premiere's Save for Web Feature

The easiest way to create all the elements you need for QuickTime Alternates (the alternate movies, the master reference file, and the HTML `<embed>` tag) is to use either Premiere's Save for Web feature (Cleaner 5 EZ) or the full version of Cleaner. When the program asks you to select a delivery method, you'll have to select QuickTime Streaming, and you'll need to know the address of the directory where you'll store your movies on the QuickTime Streaming Server (in this example, the address is `rtsp://stream.elmwoodstudios.com/media`). When you're done, Cleaner EZ will create each of the alternate movies, and several other related files.

Here's how to get the system working:

1. Open the folder where you saved the files. That folder will contain a Read Me text file, a folder called Upload to HTTP Server and a folder called Upload to Streaming Server (**Figure 8.21**). The Read Me text file contains useful information and instructions for adding these QuickTime Alternate movies to your Web page.

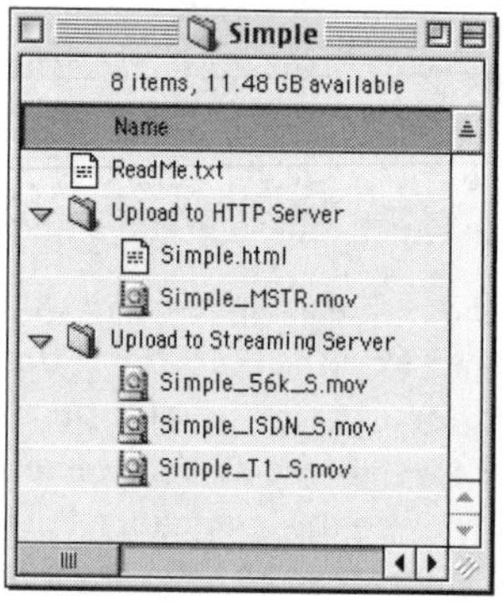

FIGURE 8.21
When you use Premiere's Save for Web/Cleaner 5 EZ feature to make QuickTime Alternates, it will create a folder of files and subfolders.

2. Open the folder called Upload to HTTP Server. It will contain a master reference movie and a text file containing the simple `<embed>` tag for the master movie.

   Here is the text of simple.html file in my example:

```
<EMBED SRC="Simple_MSTR.mov" WIDTH=640 HEIGHT=496
AUTOPLAY=true CONTROLLER=true LOOP=false
PLUGINSPAGE="http://www.apple.com/quicktime/">
```

In the Upload to HTTP Server folder inside the Chapter8_Streaming/Quicktime/Simple_Alternates folder, I have left the simple.html file untouched so you can see just how it comes out of Premiere's Save for Web feature. I have also included a customized version this HTML file (complete with the ActiveX `<object>` tags) for compatibility with the various versions of Internet Explorer. It's called simple_alternates_activex.html, and you can find it in the Chapter8_Streaming/QuickTime folder on the CD.

IMPORTANT ▸ Embed the master movie (simple_mstr.mov in my example) into the HTML of your Web page, and *then* upload both the HTML document and the master movie to your regular Web server (*not* to the QuickTime Streaming Server).

3. Upload the movies in the Upload to Streaming Server folder to the appropriate location on your QuickTime Streaming Server.

Now, when the viewer clicks on the embedded master movie, QuickTime will deliver the most appropriate alternate movie.

For more advanced control of QuickTime Alternates, including the use of *fallback* movies discussed below, use the full version of Discreet Cleaner 5.

TIP ▸ *There's another way to make a master (reference) movie. If you have QuickTime movies that are already compressed, you can use Apple's MakeRefMovie utility. It's available as a free download at* `http://developer.apple.com/quicktime/quicktimeintro/tools/index.html`.

Cool QuickTime Features

You can do lots of other things with QuickTime Web video. These are some more advanced uses of QuickTime Alternates:

- The QuickTime plug-in can detect the processor type of the viewer's computer—so it knows whether the viewer uses a Mac or a PC. Since images look darker on PC monitors and lighter on Mac monitors, you can create alternate movies with the gamma (brightness) setting adjusted for each and then let QuickTime automatically play the appropriate movie.
- The QuickTime plug-in can detect the viewer's preferred language, so you can create alternate-language versions of your movie (Latvian, Korean, Urdu) and then let QuickTime automatically play the appropriate movie.

For more details about creating QuickTime Alternates from scratch using QuickTime Player Pro and MakeRefMovie (the free tool from Apple Computer) and the many other wonders of QuickTime, see Peachpit's *QuickTime 6 for Macintosh and Windows: Visual QuickStart Guide*, by Judith Stern and Robert A. Lettieri.

TIP ▸ *The QuickTime Alternates system also works for progressive downloading movies: QuickTime selects the version that the author indicates is best for the user's connection speed.*

Creating Fallback Movies for Backwards Compatibility

Remember, no one can watch your movies unless they have the right media player—and the right version of that player. With all of the Big Three media players, a movie may not play if it was made with a newer version than the viewer has installed. For example, if the viewer tries to play a RealVideo 9 movie with RealOne Player 5, it won't work. However, if the viewer is using a relatively recent version (such as RealOne Player 8), all three media players can automatically update themselves to play the new version. Here's how to adjust your movies for viewers who use a very old version of the media player that can't update itself.

QuickTime Backwards Compatibility

Streaming QuickTime movies can be seen only by viewers who have QuickTime 4 or a later version. To handle viewers running versions that don't support streaming video, you can create a *fallback* movie: a single-frame movie that tells viewers they must install a recent version of QuickTime to view your movie (**Figure 8.22**).

FIGURE 8.22
A single-frame fallback movie, compatible with QuickTime 2, tells the viewers that they need to upgrade their version of QuickTime to see streaming video.

Whenever you use Cleaner EZ to make QuickTime Alternates, the master movie will automatically contain a fallback movie for any viewer who can open a QuickTime 2 movie. If you're not using Cleaner 5 EZ, you can use the **<embed>** tag's QTSRC attribute to trigger a fallback movie.

Here's how to make and embed a QuickTime fallback movie:

1. Open an image that you would like to use as the fallback movie with PictureViewer (which comes as a part of the QuickTime installation).

2. Choose File > Export.

3. Choose QuickTime Image from the pop-up menu (**Figure 8.23**). This file type ensures that the fallback image will not be opened by Windows Media Player or RealOne Player.

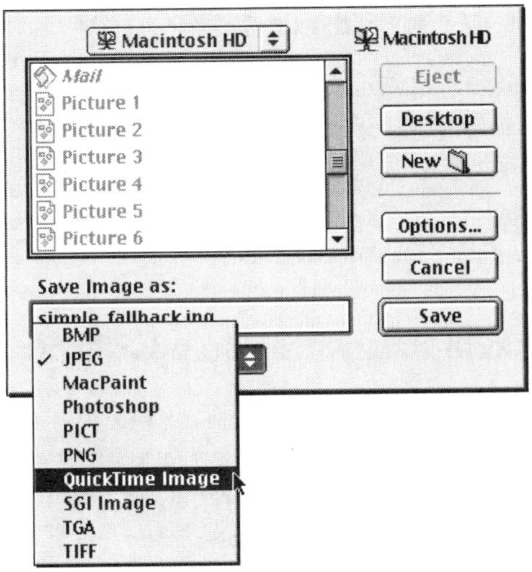

FIGURE 8.23
Choose QuickTime Image from the file type pop-up menu to create an image for your fallback movie.

4. Add a .qti suffix at the end of the filename.

   (Make sure your Web server has a listing for "image/x-quicktime" with the .qti extension.)

5. Change the **<embed>** tag to read as follows:

```
<EMBED SRC="simple_fallback.qti" QTSRC="Simple_MSTR.mov">
```

   (Replace my example names with your own filenames.)

Here's what you've just done: The required SRC attribute is pointing to a default QuickTime 2–compatible image file called simple_fallback.qti. The QTSRC attribute points to the QuickTime 4–compatible master movie. The QTSRC attribute will always override the SRC attribute if it can. In other words, if the viewer has QuickTime 4 or later, the plug-in will play simple_mstr.mov. If the viewer doesn't have QuickTime 4 or later, it will play simple_fallback.qti.

You can find this file, simple_page_fallback.html (complete with the ActiveX `<object>` tags for browser compatibility) in the Chapter8_Streaming/QuickTime/Fallback folder on the book's CD-ROM.

RealSystem Backwards Compatibility

Premiere's Advanced RealMedia Export plug-in and RealSystem (now Helix) Producer both have a Preferences button on the main window. When you click this, click the SureStream tab; and in the Player Compatibility section, choose either RealOne Player G2 or RealOne Player 5.0. The slowest stream in the SureStream file will be backwards compatible.

Windows Media Backwards Compatibility

The trick to creating backwards compatibility with Windows Media Player is selecting the right video codec. You do this when you're creating a custom profile using the Advanced Windows Media Export plug-in (see "Using Advanced Windows Media Export" in Chapter 6 for all the details). If you click and hold on the "Video: Codec" pop-up menu there, you'll get a list of five available video codecs. Microsoft currently recommends using Windows Media Video 8 as an all-purpose codec. However, Windows MS MPEG-4 v3 and Windows Media Video 7 are older codecs that allow compatibility with older versions of Windows Media Player, so use them if you need backwards compatibility.

Compressing Streaming Movies

There are some things to keep in mind when you're compressing streaming movies as opposed to downloading movies. The biggest issue is the data rate. You never want the data rate of a streaming movie to exceed the connection speed of your intended audience. If it does, the movie will play in stops and starts, and the video and audio tracks will be broken up. (As a default, the formats sacrifice the video before the audio.) Stick with the default settings in Premiere's various export plug-ins to help prevent this; they are programmed with relatively conservative data rates.

Multi-Bit-Rate Movies

Self-adjusting multi-bit-rate file types like RealSystem SureStream and Windows Media Intelligent Streaming can certainly help prevent the data rate problem. But monster multi-bit-rate movies that contain every possible data rate from 14.4K modems up to T3 connections can do more harm than good. This strategy creates unwieldy files that require frequent "stream hopping" like shifting gears in a car with manual transmission too often. Besides, even in the best-case scenario (SureStream), you're limited to eight streams in one movie. A better solution is to create two or more multi-bit-rate movies: a low-speed version (containing streams from 30 to 80 Kbps) and a high-speed version (containing streams from 80 to 150 Kbps) for example. Just remember to be conservative and make sure the minimum data rate is below the target connection speed. Otherwise, even self-adjusting multi-bit-rate movies won't play properly.

Codec Control

Almost all of the Web video codecs for the Big Three media players offer Variable Bit Rate Encoding (VBR). (In the case of the QuickTime Sorenson Video codec, it's in the professional edition only.) With this feature turned on, the codec allocates more data to the sections of the movie that need it the most. This is not a good idea in the case of streaming movies where the data rate may not fluctuate above the current connection speed. So turn off VBR for streaming movies, especially for QuickTime.

Streaming Features

Codecs have other advanced streaming features that are generally not accessible through Premiere and its plug-ins (you'll need a more advanced tool like Cleaner for that), but I will briefly mention some anyway, in case you encounter them. Besides control over the VBR feature, the professional edition of the Sorenson Video 3 codec offers Bidirectional Prediction and Temporal Scalability for adjustable frame rates; and Force Block Refresh, which refreshes parts of the video that haven't been updated in a specified time period—which helps in cases where the user experienced packet loss during the transition of a keyframe. These quality-enhancing features were created specifically for streaming files. RealVideo's system has a feature called "Loss Protection" that adds error correction data to the stream.

The Force Block Refresh and Loss Protection features should be turned off for downloading files, because they waste bandwidth.

Minimizing RealOne Player's Buffering Message

Sometimes when you watch a streaming RealSystem movie, the video stops and an annoying little buffering message appears while you wait for the connection to return. What's that message about, and how can you avoid it?

For each streaming clip, RealOne Player (and the other streaming formats) keeps a *buffer* (a sort of holding area) in RAM that acts as a data reservoir. Data enters the buffer as it streams to the media player and leaves the buffer as the media player plays the clip. The buffer helps ensure that interruptions in the available bandwidth don't stop the show. If network congestion stops the stream for a moment, for example, the media player can keep the clip playing with the buffered data. RealOne Player buffers a few seconds of data before every clip it plays. (This technique is also known as *preroll.*)

The best way to minimize initial buffering and eliminate rebuffering is to choose the right data rate for the target connection speed. Remember, there's no margin for error with RTSP streaming movies. They must be delivered through the available connection speed and in the time available. In addition, with QuickTime streaming, the buffers can get huge; so if the connection speed is higher than a clip's data rate, the Skip Protection feature in the QuickTime Streaming Server will buffer as much of the file as possible—and the viewer will have to wait for the whole file to download before it plays.

The Future

The beauty of Web video is that you don't have to be a Hollywood movie producer to get your films, shorts, or presentations shown to a potentially vast audience. Armed with little more than a camcorder, microphone, and some video-editing software, anyone can create a movie and broadcast it to anyone connected to the Internet.

While you now have a good grasp on the basics of creating video for the Web, keep in mind that this is only the beginning. Web video is a *constantly* changing technology (heck, it changed several times while I wrote this book), with the price of camcorders, computers, and software dropping in price. And as broadband makes its way into more households, the painful experience of watching jerky, pixelated video will soon become the exception, not the norm. With these changes come new opportunities for media creators around the world, whether you're a documentarian, filmmaker, Web developer, or corporate video producer. Get out there and show off your movies!

Index

B

C

D

E

F

N

O

P

Q

R

S

T

U

V

W

Z

SAVE 90%

10 full-motion video clips for the price of 1

Unlock the 10 clips included with this book's CD-ROM and use them forever for just:

$ 50.00

Plus: Your purchase will grant you a special offer from Cinenet for other great images.

- Professionally-created images as seen in this book and previewed on the companion CD.
- Originally created on 35mm film.
- A $ 500.00 value offered exclusively for the readers of this book.

Contact us today to unlock your clips and receive a special gift!

Cinenet®
CINEMA NETWORK

footage@cinenet.com

www.cinenet.com/bookspecial

Limited time offer. All images are Copyrighted. Signed agreement and payment required before clips can be used.
© 1988-2002 Cinema Network, Inc. All Rights Reserved Worldwide.